EMBRACING
LIFE

Frank and Carla,

Frank, you inspired
me. Now enjoy my
twists and turns in life.

Dick

EMBRACING LIFE

with Twists and Turns

Richard Stuckey

To order additional copies of this book, contact:
Xlibris
844-714-8691
www.Xlibris.com
Orders@Xlibris.com
831301

CONTENTS

FOREWORD AND ACKNOWLEDGMENTS

Procrastination ruled from the initial suggestion from family and friends "you should write a book of the stories you have experienced in your life." Fifteen years ago I thought of doing this, by taking a summer or at least several months off to travel to the mountains of Colorado to reflect and write a book. My late brother-in-law, Ron Birkey, was going to accompany me as he worked on architectural drawings. Unfortunately, that never happened. Fourteen years later the subject came up again, and this time I decided to tackle the project. The process has been mostly enjoyable and has had the wonderful benefits of recalling memories and history of my life, well lived. My brother, Larry Stuckey, first cousins and friends are a part of many stories throughout this book.

What I have learned from my parents and grandparents from the time I was a kid, and the changes that have occurred in my lifetime are truly staggering. This book is written to give incite to my grandchildren, Jacob, Casey, Logan, and Emily, and to their future children. By the time their children become adults it is unfathomable to imagine what life will entail.

Each chapter consists of a narrative and stories of that time. Some stories are humorous, some frightening, some entertaining, and some enlightening. Photos at beginning of each chapter are author residences for the chapter time frame.

This book is dedicated to my wife, Judy, of 55 years, who has been encouraging, supportive, working with me, and spending many hours in first edits, organizing, and processing photo materials. Thanks beyond words go to her. Sons, J.J. and Jon, have assisted in the photo search and their families also have been encouraging and patiently waiting to read the final copy.

Finally, Faye Peters, Joy Daniels, Mary Cambridge, Kaye Parsons and the staff at Xlibris have expertly advised me along the way and provided valuable suggestions and edits.

My only regret is that my book was not written sooner. Unfortunately, my late brother, parents, in-laws, and brother-in-law were deprived the opportunity to read this book. The moral of the story is...... "Don't wait" ...... "Just do it"! Start yours today!

TESTIMONIALS

Dick Stuckey provides an honest, real-world and engaging account of the prototypical "road warrior" extension specialist who brings science in the service of agriculture to farmers and growers near and far. One feels the energy and sense of purpose so vital to this under-appreciated endeavor.

> – Dr. David Smith, Former Dept. of Plant Pathology Chair, University of Kentucky

I like the way you described your hiring for the U.K. Extension position. In addition, you accurately depicted the kinds of programs and work that Extension Plant Pathologists might need to do on the job. Newly graduating University Plant Pathology students could learn from your efforts. It is good to see a process so well described.

> – Dr. John Hartman, Extension Professor Emeritus at the University of Kentucky

"The chapter on the CAST years brought to life some of the challenges of managing a national organization and helped me to appreciate even more Dr. Stuckey's pivotal role in the success of the organization. The energy and management skills he brought to CAST as Executive Vice President were key to bringing the organization to national prominence as the go-to voice for agricultural science. Sometimes these historical memoirs are a difficult read, but this one had me wishing for more. I look forward to reading the entire volume."

— Harold Coble, CAST President 2000-2001

It is a pleasure to endorse the author's assessment of his involvement and contributions to the success of an organization in which he served as CEO. The Council for Agricultural Science and Technology (CAST), by its very nature, presents a challenge for any leader. Comprised of a number of highly independent, unique organizations along with a broad-based mission and often addressing highly controversial issues contributes to the challenges for a leader. That the author navigated quite successfully over an extended period (10 years) and provided leadership for this diverse organization is a reflection on his ability and use of a multitude of leadership skills to achieve success. Consequently, it is my pleasure to offer a full endorsement of this chapter and this book.

The reader will be rewarded by learning about an important agricultural-related organization, but more importantly will be an enhanced appreciation of the employment of many skill sets used by a leader to achieve success.

– Gale A. Buchanan, Former USDA Chief
Scientist and Under Secretary of Agriculture
for Research, Education & Economics
Dean and Director Emeritus, University of Georgia
College of Agricultural and Environmental Sciences

"Facilitating/leading CAST to its position as a source of highly needed credible science-based information about food and agriculture to a wide domestic and international audience is not without challenges as clearly indicated. This is characteristic of Dr. Stuckey's career. "

– Dr. David Lineback, Former Director,
Joint Institute for Food Safety and Applied
Nutrition and CAST President

"Four generations later I am in the same position that the author served for nine years. Many of the challenges he faced continue to be challenges. An interesting read for those who had connections to CAST during that time."

– Kent Schescke, CAST Executive
Vice President, 2015-present

Dick Stuckey is all about collaboration and bringing the right people to the table to get things done for the community. He is passionate about making others' lives better while showing his grandchildren how to be servant leaders, his legacy will live on for many generations.

– Joanne Thomson President/CEO Benevilla

PhD Richard (Dick) Stuckey is a highly intelligence, servant leader who shares his life successes and challenges through this easy-to-read book. It was my privilege to work and associate with Dick during his years in Surprise, Arizona. His leadership of Benevilla, a church-based entity that provides social and community services for in-need seniors adults, reflected his beliefs and desire to help those in need. He was a highly effective President of the Sun City West Rotary Club, serves on the District Finance Committee, and was the principal recruiter for the second Rotary club in Surprise. Dick has been blessed in life and he shares those blessing with those in-need.

– George Wheeler Past Governor, Rotary
District 5490 Governor-line Mentor
"Service Above Self" and
"Distinguished Service" Awardee

I have always admired my older brother growing up. I have watched with respect the positions he has held and his increasing circle of influence. His integrity, tenacity and staying true to himself has been a constant and a huge factor in his success. His commitment to his friends, colleagues and family has been unparalleled. My parents were so proud of their son and all his achievements. I am honored to be his brother, and glad to be part of his incredible journey through life.

— Larry Stuckey, Brother

CHAPTER 1

Life before I Was Born

What was it like back in the late nineteenth century and the early twentieth century? I had the good fortune of having two parents and knowing all four of my grandparents. Their stories of life shared with me as a small child gave me an insight into what life was like before I was born. There were no automobiles, planes, or trains. Travel was largely by horse, by boat, or by foot.

Where they lived in rural America, there were a few stores, only those that carried very necessary supplies. For example, one did not go to the store to buy clothes; all clothes were made at home, including shoes. Thus, it was very common to have hand-me-downs among siblings. It was not important to have clothes that were in fashion; it was important to have clothes for warmth and protection, and that was all that mattered.

The industrialized society that we know today had not begun. It was a largely agrarian society, and all family members were involved in that activity. Well over half of the population was engaged in some form of agriculture, where feed and produce were grown for the livestock and family needs. One could say these families were very self-sufficient and did not rely on the many other services that we do today. The horse and the one share plow were the mainstays of farm equipment.

Farms were very diversified with crops grown and livestock produced. Large fruit and vegetable gardens were common for fresh consumption, and the canning of both fruits and vegetable for preservation to consume later was very common. The major crops grown in the region where my grandparents had settled were corn, alfalfa, oats, and wheat. Livestock consisted of mainly chickens, cows, swine, and beef. Sheep, goats, turkeys, and rabbits could be additional sources of meat nutrition. Some of the popular sayings of today like "Eat fresh, buy local" were actually practiced in those days and the only choice for my parents and grandparents.

Families settled in close proximity to one another, where aunts and uncles and their families lived on the farm next door.

It was a tight cluster, and many families had frequent gatherings because of the geographical closeness. It was just a short walk away to the neighbors for a visit and sharing of a meal. If you could imagine life without congestion and pollution and crowding, this was it. As one of my sons would say in his early years, "What about kids' rights?" There were no kids' rights. It was not debatable, end of subject—but I've jumped ahead of my story.

Family values and church were very strong for many families, including our own. However, occasionally, with some searching and prying, one could turn up or uncover an embarrassing family secret. This knowledge often came as a big surprise, and while there were none that I had discovered of our immediate family, there were some of extended family that are not repeated here because I cannot verify them. Suffice it to say that all was not perfect back then. Humans had shortcomings then as they do today.

As time passed, the nearly total self-sufficiency that the family farm had became a bit more specialized; where one family member had a special talent, they utilized that talent to provide services to other families in the area. A good example would be the making of shoes. Thus, the barter system came into play, where no money was exchanged but one service was provided in return for another service. This is a small glimpse of the world that I was born into.

Stories:

1. Perhaps one of my favorite stories told to me by my father was when he was a teenager and walked out on a

dock while at the lake and looked down into the water, which appeared to him to be about three feet deep. He jumped in and discovered it was nine feet deep; he did not swim but learned to swim in a hurry. He went down two times, and prior to going down for the third and final time, when he surfaced, he learned to swim. How frightening that must've been! Water depth can be deceiving based on the clarity of the water.

2. I found stories of dating, marriage, and honeymoons to be fascinating. Going to pick up your date in a horse and buggy sounds romantic today. This happened before my time. My parents shared with me that my father was late to his wedding because he had to finish sowing oats in the field prior to getting to the wedding.

They did have car transportation at that time, if you wanted to call them cars, and his bride lived fifty miles away from where he lived, so it was a couple hours' commute. Where did they spend their honeymoon? At my mother's parents, of course! That is something that few kids would consider these days, and I was not into that when I got married, that is for sure. So the honeymoon was usually for two or three days, and then it was time to get back to work and the chores that waited. Following the honeymoon, my parents moved from my mom's parents' house to my dad's parents' house, where they lived for a couple of years with his parents. This was not uncommon in those days. Today the norm seems like honeymoons are spent on international travel for many young couples, and perhaps the future will include extraterrestrial/planetary travel. My, how times have changed!

3. It was truly a man's world; women were to be supportive of the men they married regardless of the women's talents. My grandpa expected his wife and daughters to prepare and serve the food. Later in life, this expectation continued. I recall my elderly grandfather. His daughter, my aunt, put the food on his plate, but considering his age, it was not uncommon to assist your elders. With age, he became a man of fewer words, and his method of getting more food or seconds was to take his fork and bang it on his plate. Of course, with his sense of humor and if he were here today, he would likely say he wanted to be polite and not interrupt the ongoing conversation.

4. I had several uncles who had some neat sayings that I always liked to hear. For example, when my uncle was asked what he would like to drink, he often commented, "I will just have water. I don't always have to have the best." Today many consider water to be the best. How ironic! Another saying was that it would not take too many that size to make a dozen. When I asked if he would like more food, he would respond, "No, I'll just take a toothpick, and I think I'll be full after I use a toothpick." When he was asked if he would sing a song, he would ask us if we had ever heard of "Lost Sheep on the Mountain." Our response was no, and he would respond with a "baa-baa!" Ha ha! Another uncle had a saying that did not make me feel good whenever I lost a competition. He would state that for every winner, there has to be a loser.

5. I'll close with this story. My perception was that parents in those days, like today's parents, took great pride in the accomplishments of their children. While I did not feel the pressure then, I do believe that some kids today feel their parents' pressure to accomplish scholastic and especially athletic success that they did not achieve. I observed this while refereeing soccer and basketball games.

Chapter 2

Preschool Years, 1944-1950

Here are some basic facts:

- I lived in three houses in three locations, all within one and a half miles of each other: first with my parents, living with grandparents; second, at a rental property owned by my father's uncle; and third, at a purchased farm and farmhouse.

- We were a close family, with frequent get-togethers with grandparents, aunts and uncles, and cousins. These often included Sunday and holiday dinners, social gatherings, and birthday parties.
- There was no preschool and no regular play dates with other kids, only unscheduled get-togethers with cousins and the neighbors' kids.

- Very, very infrequent babysitters just got dragged along with parents when they went out in the evening to visit friends. We often fell asleep before they were ready to come home. No problem.
- We went to bed at reasonable hours, but there was no curfew; generally, just when one got tired, one went to bed and slept.
- We had a big garden and wonderful food from the garden when in season. We canned a lot of vegetables for eating in the off-season. Chicken and pork were the most prominent meat dishes served. Lots of salads and lots of desserts were offered with pies, and homemade bread was very common.
- No seatbelts were used in cars or while riding in trucks, either on the seats or in the open bed of the pickup truck in the back. There was generally one visit, possibly two visits, to the lake for swimming and a picnic during the summer.
- I loved animals.

- During the last two years of this age span, I went along to help and learn how to do chores as well as to feed and take care of the animals.

It was a comfortable life, not luxurious but simple and happy.

Stories:

1. The most famous and retold story during this period was the time I followed the dog and got lost. I was two years old, going on three, and the neighbor across the street had a dog. I followed the dog out of their backyard and down the lane into the woods about a quarter of a mile away. I did not return and was not worried, but my parents became extremely worried when I turned up missing. A search party was sent out for me. My parents and many of my uncles and aunts searched high and low—but no Richard. Nighttime approached, and the worries deepened. Did I meet with some ill fate? Kidnappings were rare in those days. More likely, I fell and injured myself, or some other health hazard happened to me. Concern was that at nighttime, there were animals in the woods and surrounding areas, and without food and water, harm could come to me. To make what could be a much longer story short, my uncle Otto found me in the woods and immediately became the hero in our family. For many years, he delighted in retelling the story and how he had found me and

perhaps saved my life. It was only the first of many times that my life could have ended.

2. Another story that has had some traction is my helping my father milk the cows for his uncle at the neighboring farm. The traditional way to do that was to hand-milk the cow or to put a milking machine on the cow's udder to gather the milk. Then with either a pail or a bucket, you would take the milk to the milk can, where a large funnel was placed above the can with a cloth strainer put in so that when the milk was poured in, it would go through the strainer and into the large milk can, ten gallons at the minimum. The milk cans were then put into a large chest-like cooler with ice water in it, awaiting pickup by the milk truck the following day or two. On with the story. Around the farm, there were often many cats and a dog or two. We did not go to the store and buy dog food or cat food; they mostly ate table scraps and other trash that they could encounter. Cats hanging around the barn were commonplace, and especially during milking time, they would look for any spilled milk. I remember my dad milked a cow when a cat would come around, and he would take one of the cow's teats, squeeze it, and squirt a stream into the cat's mouth. About 25 percent would hit its target, the mouth, and the rest would be dripping around the area, which the cat would come back to later to lap it up. Being an observant youngster, I soon recognized that cats love milk. So one evening, while doing the chores and milking the cows, I decided to do the cat a favor.

My dad had just dumped two to three gallons into the big funnel container with a strainer and gone back to continue milking and get another bucket when I snatched up one of the cats and threw the cat into the funnel. Well, cats don't like water or being wet, so the cat did not take his time and lap up the milk but went splashing around, trying to get out of the funnel. About that time, my father came back with another bucket of milk and saw the cat and was not amused. He quickly removed the cat and admonished me with a pat on the backside, saying I was never to do that again. There was a real health risk with cats in the milk, and we could get banned from selling our milk if cat hairs or other materials were found in the milk. That was the first time I recall my dad being upset with me but not the last.

3. My Ohio cousins, I saw on a regular basis. My mother was from Indiana, about fifty miles away. So when her sister or brothers, with their families, came out to visit, it was a big deal because we only saw them once a month or less. As kids, "kick the can," "hide and seek," "Annie I over," and "Red Rover, let one of the kids come over" were some of the more popular games, and just chasing one another around the yard was fun. That leads to my final story in this section. I was five, and my elder cousin, who was six, was chasing me. As it was getting to dusk, I cut across the driveway next to where a windmill had stood but had been cut down a year earlier. The four remaining angle irons remained in the ground and were about eight inches tall. I fell across one of those angle irons, and the iron penetrated my leg, above my right knee. To this day, some seventy years later, I bear the scar. I recall the blood gushing from my leg such that I thought I was going to lose all my blood. My parents quickly wrapped up my leg and put it on ice to try to reduce the bleeding. This must've worked since I did survive. Seldom did we go to the emergency room for treatment. They tried to do that treatment at home. Today I am sure there would've been many stitches that would've been applied to that wound.

CHAPTER 3

The Grade School Years, 1950–1956

Half-day kindergarten was common in those days, so half of the kids went to morning kindergarten and the other half to afternoon kindergarten. In the small town of Archbold, there were a total of fifty to sixty kids that age. Lunch buckets were not a prerequisite since lunch would be obtained at home after morning kindergarten or before afternoon kindergarten; however, a rug was a necessity. We took the rug from home and used it a couple of times during the morning or afternoon session to have quiet time at school. The kids would roll out their rugs, lie on them, and pretend to sleep. After twenty to thirty minutes of rest time, we were allowed to roll up our nap rugs, and we were back to interactive class instruction. I always thought quiet time was the time to give the teacher a break more so than the students.

Reading and listening to stories was a big part of that year. Just like today, a child felt like they were moving to the big time when they went to first grade and a full day of school. Parents were apprehensive to see their kids go off to school after having been homeschooled the first five years of their life. What a relief that must've been for parents (with the exception that there was an 80 percent chance there remained siblings at home, so the parents were not really free)!

One of my favorite teachers was my first-grade teacher, Ms. Aschliman. She was young, she was cool, and she cared for all the kids. She was soft-spoken, and, well, I just liked her. To this day, as I write, she is still living in her nineties and has never been married. We still stay in touch on occasion as for many years, she did the college preschool class where I went to college in Goshen, Indiana, but that's another chapter.

The subject matter in grade school was the traditional three Rs: writing, reading, and arithmetic. Interestingly, only one of those really starts with an R, but Rs are prominent in all three words, which is where I guess it got its name. I can still recall all of my teachers' names throughout my grade school. We had just one homeroom teacher for each grade. Other favorite teachers besides Ms. Aschliman were my second-grade teacher, Ms. Rupp, and my third-grade teacher, Mrs. Zimmerman. Ms. Rupp—what a lovely young lady! How I physically fell in love with her and asked her after class one day whether I could give her a kiss! She was just so hip and cool and nice. If I had stayed more than one year in her class, I probably would've proposed to her. Mrs. Zimmerman, on the other hand, was a kindly older teacher who would remind one of their grandmother— very nice, motherly, not a lot to look at but made class fun for the students.

I could easily pass by my fourth- and fifth- and sixth-grade teachers, but they should at least be mentioned. Mrs. Spangler, the fourth-grade teacher, would move to junior high, where I would have more interactions with her. Her husband was superintendent of the schools. The fifth-grade teacher was Mrs. Burkholder, a very strict, autocratic teacher who was married to the high school principal. Many more interactions with her husband were awaiting me in high school. The sixth-grade teacher was Mrs. Slaughter, and she had a daughter in our class who was disgustingly intelligent. For the first five grades, we kept mostly the same class; approximately thirty students and the other thirty students in our school had a different teacher for each of the classes. For some reason, in the sixth grade, a decision was made to mix and match the classes, so we lost friends in our class and were introduced to new students to become friends. I soon learned that math was one of my favorite subjects in school.

Apart from school, there was home life, which consisted of many chores, from feeding the animals and driving the tractor to helping with the farming operation. It was fun to go with my dad and his pickup into town and other places. My father's brothers and sisters all lived close by in the community, and we saw them frequently, many of them daily, so I had a nice set of cousins about my age and wanted to play with them during free days or evenings. My mother came from a town fifty miles away, quite a distance in those days, yet we maintained close contact with her family and my cousins on her side, getting together, on average, once a month on holidays, birthdays, anniversaries, and special occasions.

Like many kids, we looked forward to those special occasions, especially Christmas, when we would get gifts. Unlike recent years, there were not a lot of gifts, precious few, some that you would need to share with your siblings. As I was growing up, one thing I was assured of was getting three solid meals a day, unfortunately something I still subscribe to today. Travel was limited, vacations were scarce, and we were lucky to get to a lake for a swim and picnic once or twice a year. Living in the country, well about five miles from town, had its advantages and its disadvantages, most of which I saw in those days as disadvantages, but as I became an adult, I realized there really were advantages to living in the country. Hopefully, this gives you a glimpse of the life that I had during my grade school years, back in the early 1950s.

Now we move to the stories. There will be more stories during my high school years and later on in life because during those times, I had transportation, which would get me into trouble.

Stories:

1. Teachers can have a big impact on kids. I felt loved by my first three grade teachers, tolerated by my fourth-grade teacher, despised by my fifth-grade teacher, and detached from my sixth-grade teacher. Perhaps I was the problem rather than the teacher. I leave that open for discussion. One of the most hurtful experiences was when my fifth-grade teacher, Mrs. Burkholder, told my

best friend that he should not hang around with me because I was a bad influence. Despite her advice, we remained the best of friends until he was killed in an auto accident at the age of sixteen. David had just received his driving license, and following a school play, on his way home, on a slippery country road, he lost control, was thrown out of the car, hit his head on a large object, and was killed. The car continued to a stopping point in an orchard and was in excellent running condition. At that time, he was president of our sophomore class, and I was the vice president. David had a great future ahead of him but never got to realize adulthood. He was a scholar, not an athlete.

2. I also lost a friend when I was in the second grade because of a horse accident, where he fell off the horse and was dragged and killed. Doug was an athlete, even in those early years, and I often thought about what it would have been like playing with him on our athletic teams.

3. During recess at school, we would go outside, rain or shine, heat or snow. One very embarrassing incident was when it was winter and there was snow on the ground; we got into a snowball fight with the girls in our class. I'll never forget meeting more than my match when I tussled with Connie and she promptly threw me to the ground and washed my face in the snow. How humiliating!

4. The farm can be a dangerous place to live. We had all sorts of animals, including cows, steers, pigs, chickens, turkeys, sheep, and yes, even a goat. The last two mentioned animals were mostly housed outside and kept in a confined area by an electric fence. Electric fences were something commonly used, especially in wooden areas, and even animals soon learned the potential danger of crossing their paths—not so for some little boys. My father and my uncle were laying blocks next to our wooded area for a six-sow farrowing building.

The buildings were quite unique in that they were fenced off inside with a door to the outside, with additional fences outside so that a sow who gave birth to a litter of pigs would have a warm place to stay and nurse the pigs; as they grew a bit older, the pigs would have some fun roaming outside in their fenced-in areas. It was always best to keep a sow and her particular litter separate from other sows and their litters. The building had a slanted roof and was about seven feet tall so that adults could walk inside the building to care for and feed the sows and their piglets. I was too young to be of much help but watching the men work, being a bit bored, and I guess looking for adventure, I encountered this rooster who had free rein strutting around nearby. He seemed rather cocky to me, so I thought I would teach him a lesson. I was barefoot at the time, as we frequently were on the farm, and I grabbed the rooster, held him by his feet and his wing, and proceeded to go to the electric fence to teach the rooster a lesson. I placed the rooster on the fence wire; he squawked, obviously surprised, but the barefoot boy holding him got the larger charge and immediately dropped the rooster as he flew away, and both creatures squeaked in terror.

A valuable science lesson was learned; don't mess with electric fences and don't be the grounding source (plus, wear shoes). My dad and uncle thought it was funny and continued to remind me of that during later years.

5. One of my biggest surprises was when I was eight years old and it was my second birthday. Can you figure that out? I was in the second grade, and my mother created the biggest surprise for me by inviting my entire class out to the farm for a special birthday. I was totally surprised and impressed to see many of my town friends come out to our farm. My dad had put up a basketball hoop on the side of the barn, and even though it was February, several of my friends and I went out to play basketball. Also on my eight-year-old "second birthday," our associate pastor gave me his 1944 silver dollar. I was impressed. I never had a more special birthday than that.

6. It was very common when I was growing up, as I believe it is today, for kids to love to chase one another. This is certainly true between my brothers and myself. When I was about ten years old, my brother Larry, who is three years my junior, and I went with our father to the feed mill. Here, we would take corn, soy beans, and/ or wheat to the feed mill to have it ground and mixed together and then add some supplements to it so that it would make a complete meal for the animals that we raised. My brother was chasing me around a stacked-up pile of roof tins that had been removed from roofs and

placed on some railroad ties for potential future use. As we ran around, I looked back to see where he was, and in so doing, I ran into one of the metal tin sheets that was head high, and it cut into my upper gums above my teeth and almost cut my teeth off. I bled profusely and had to be rushed to the nearest doctor's office to get the bleeding stopped and the repair to the mouth necessary. To this day, nearly seventy years later, I am still missing some gum tissue.

CHAPTER 4

The Wonderful Developmental Years of Junior High and High School, 1956–1962

Moving from grade school into the big school building was a big event. Our particular educational system had a six-two-four format—that is, six years in elementary school, two years in junior high, and four years in high school. Junior high was in the same building as high school; thus, we were in with the big folks. In those days, there were many` forms of grade school, junior high, and high school: five-three-four, six-three-three, and, in a few cases, four-four-four. Six-two-four and six-three-three were the most common. Oftentimes the junior high students were separated from the high school students, especially where there were schools of size that necessitated two buildings.

Junior high was a neat experience because we did not have the same homeroom teacher; we would be moved around from class to class and with different teachers for different subjects. So the bell would ring, indicating the end of one class and time to move out in the hallway and move on to the next class. We generally had five minutes between classes to make a quick stop in the restroom if need be and scuttle on to our next class.

This was an opportunity to be exposed to new opportunities and to make some decisions in life regarding the directions one wished to pursue. The junior high years were more about adjustment and preparation to enter high school. Yes, there were extracurricular activities that one could participate in, the beginning arena of sports, band, 4H, dance parties, etc. Here is a brief comment about each.

Being on the farm, I was allowed to participate in basketball as a seventh-grader because it occurred during the winter season, when there was less farm work. Band? Yes, I did take up band and worked my way to second chair in the trombone section (a story later about this). As for 4H, I thought it was just for girls—yes, mostly, but also for an inspiring farm boy who could not wait to get into Future Farmers of America (FFA) and one who wanted to show a steer at the famed Lugbill livestock auction.

I enrolled for several years in 4H and each year had a pet steer to show at the Lugbill fair. My two brothers followed me in showing steers at the auction for many years to come.

I was the eldest of three boys in the family, with a younger brother three years younger than me, and our youngest brother was nine years younger than me. When my mother was questioned about the spacing of the boys, I learned that she had had a miscarriage between sons two and three. So with a mathematical mind, I figured they were on a three-year timing basis.

Regarding dance parties, although I was frequently invited by the girls in my class (they must've been desperate for boy partners), I was never allowed to go because of our religious faith. Dancing can lead to further problems, if you know what I mean. To this day, my wife will attest that I am not a good dancer because of the lack of lessons at an early age and perhaps a lack of coordination.

Twelve to eighteen years old—do you remember those years, if you have already achieved them? At first, I was somewhat timid, but as I aged and progressed, I became a quite confident and successful young man. Many achievements came my way through some talent and hard work but certainly more than the average student. I became viewed as a leader among my peers. There are many stories to tell during this time, but those will have to wait.

I continued to receive love and support from my home life throughout the years, and this helped me in my sense of achievement. An additional activity that I took advantage of was singing in the junior high choir, at a time when my voice was transitioning from a child's to a young adult's.

One of the decisions one had to make when entering ninth grade was what career path one desired to take because this had a bearing on the choices of the courses that would be taken. There was college preparation for those who planned to go on to college after high school. There was industrial arts for those who wanted to pursue a trade profession. There was FFA for those who planned to become farmers or work in an agricultural field. Home economics was primarily for girls who planned to learn the skills of their mothers and be homemakers plus the many services that women provided in our community during these years. Language arts was another. My dilemma was selecting between FFA and a pre-college course curriculum. I tried to do both and followed the FFA curriculum plus took as many pre-college courses as I could. The FFA classes were double periods, so this made it even more difficult. Both choices were excellent for me.

About fifteen of the seventy high school students in my class were enrolled in FFA. As a sophomore, I was honored to be elected sentinel of the four-year group of fifty-five or so high school students from grades nine to twelve. In addition to two hours each day in FFA class, we had one evening meeting a month for a couple of hours to conduct business across all classes. Each officer had to learn and memorize their role. For example, during the meeting, the president would ask for reports from each of the officers. As the sentinel, my memorized response would be "The sentinel is stationed by the door. Through this door pass many friends of FFA. It is my duty to welcome the friends and visitors who pass by this door, assist in the conduction of the meetings, and report back to the president." As a junior, I was elected secretary of FFA and, as a senior, served as president. Each of these positions required memorized learning as well. In fact, by the time I became president, I had learned the responses of not only the offices I held but also the offices of the treasurer, vice president, and advisor. We conducted our meetings using Robert's Rules of Order, which became invaluable to me in future years in running business meetings over which I presided.

FFA classes provided valuable training in shop work, which was not my strong point. This included building shoeboxes, lawn chairs, and lawn tables, doing mechanical reparations such as packing wheel bearings, taking motors apart and putting back together, etc. Shop time was fun because we could get up move around and, in some cases, horse around a bit, if you know what I mean. There were also field trips that were taken and enjoyed.

Two of the extracurricular activities that I well remember were our livestock judging and parliamentary procedure contest. For livestock judging, we had a team of five. I was selected to be on that team during my junior and senior years. As the name denotes, the livestock that were judged ranged from cows to steers, hogs, and sheep, which were the ones I remembered. While I do not recall exactly where we placed each year in the various categories, I know that overall, we did very well and frequently got our names in the local newspaper as well as regional papers.

In parliamentary procedure, competition with each of the FFA chapters in other schools was very keen in the district. There were perhaps twenty or so teams in competition, and as I recall, we won either first or second place each time that I was on the parliamentary procedure team, which would've been three years. This exercise was more valuable than much of the other coursework that I took in preparation for later years.

In FFA, we also had to have projects and keep record books and accounting procedures. Generally, one started out with a single project, and as we moved up, it was common to have three or four projects by the time we completed the twelfth grade. My projects included a crop aspect and several livestock projects. The objective was to increase the size of the project from year to year and to increase the income, along with coming up with an accurate cost of inputs and charges for rental facilities where needed to validate the net profit after the sale of the crop or livestock. I often thought about how valuable this training was later in life, especially when friends and acquaintances of mine did not seem to have the good business sense to make sure that their endeavors were truly profitable.

FFA was a wonderful experience, and I was honored with my vocational agricultural teacher coming to my parents' home to celebrate my wife and me returning home from a two-year overseas assignment. I would consider my years in FFA as a total success as my two brothers followed in my identical footsteps, serving as sentinel, secretary, and president of our local chapter. Awards as state FFA farmer, received by only 2 percent of the students in FFA,

ARCHBOLD, FULTON COUNTY, OHIO; WEDNESDAY, APRIL 25, 1962

Archbold F.F.A. Youth Gets Farmer Degree

Richard Stuckey, son of Mr. and Mrs. Chauncey Stuckey, Archbold, Rt. 3 will receive the State Farmer Degree at the Ohio F.F.A. convention, Saturday evening, April 28, in Columbus.

Only two percent of the boys studying Vocational Agriculture are eligible to win this award. In order to receive the award, a boy must be outstanding in scholarship, leadership, have an outstanding farming program and achieve in F.F.A. work.

Richard has been secretary and president of the Archbold F.F.A. Chapter as well as president of the High School Student Council. He has participated in class plays and has been a member of the varsity basketball and base ball team for two years.

(Continued on page fourteen)

Richard Stuckey

State Farmer

(Continued from first page.)

Richard had had swine, beef cattle, corn, wheat and tomatoes for his farming program. His parents plan to accompany him to Columbus, Saturday, to see him receive the award.

Also attending the annual convention, Friday and Saturday from the Archbold Chapter will be Ross Wyse, son of Mr. and Mrs. Don Wyse, newly elected president of the local chapter; Marvin Miller, son of Mr. and Mrs. Carl Miller, newly elected vice president. They will be accompanied by their advisor, Glenn Gallaway.

Other young men from Archbold who have received the State Farmer award in the past are: Charles Gautsche, 1949; Howard Rupp, 1949; Larry Bourquin, 1951; Virgil Schroeder, 1951; Elmer Oyer, Jr., 1951; Don Rufenacht, 1952; Ralph Burkholder, 1952; Robert Rufenacht, 1955; William Crossgrove, 1955; Rex Short, 1957; Merle Short, 1958; Dale Leininger, 1958; Roger Miller, 1959; Allen Stuckey, 1960; Sam Roth, 1961 and Richard Stuck...

district star beef producer, and other awards came my way as well as to my two brothers. In fact, my youngest brother also had the distinction of being the first FFA student to receive the star state beef and star state swine award in his senior year. All this is to say that the farming operation that my father had was highly respectable in the community and was well communicated to his sons, and each, in turn, became a leader in their high school and the agricultural community.

While I was in high school, next to FFA, math was my favorite subject. I was able to take algebra, plain geometry, and advanced algebra for my math courses. I was not able to take all the math courses that some of my fellow colleagues in pre-college curriculum had taken, such as pre-calculus, but did have the background to pursue math in college.

How times have changed! Today I hear my grandsons saying they are getting all these math courses in late grade school and early high school. It would be a real challenge, even with a college math minor degree, for me to compete with them in math coursework today.

A few other honors that were achieved in high school were sophomore vice president of my class, president of the student council in my senior year, editor-in-chief of the class yearbook, FFA king at the county fair, and escort for the queen at the homecoming of the high school football game See more for this in the stories section.

We also had the famous senior trip, and in our case, this was the six-hundred-mile trip to the great cities of Washington, D.C., and New York City via train and via bus. Also see more in the stories section.

Some milestones in terms of transportation were obtaining a motor scooter, a used Cushman, at the age of fourteen. It was legal to drive a scooter at that age. Also, my first car was a used 1956 Ford that my dad had purchased for me when I was a junior in high school. I think he did that for several reasons: to reward my achievements but perhaps, more importantly, to cut down on the number of trips he and my mother would need to make to transport me to the many activities I had become involved in. These two vehicles lend to more stories.

In high school, I was known as an athlete, not the star athlete but one of several who participated on teams that had unusual success. Basketball was my first love, and I was a starting guard in my senior year, even though I was six feet tall. That was tall in those days. Our team returned only one starting player from the previous season, yet we had a nineteen-to-three season that included a disappointing loss in a tournament game. I was known as the defensive player on the team and the third leading scorer where we had a balanced team scoring with four starters averaging over ten points a game. We were ranked in the state and lost the game before we were to meet the reigning champions, and I was to guard their star player. What a disappointment!

Year End Individual Performances

	FG	FA	FM	FAVG.	Tot. Pts.	Gm. Av.
G. Bridges	135	143	103	72%	373	17.0
D. Miller	136	60	53	80%	325	14.8
D. Stuckey	98	119	88	74%	284	12.9
L. Holland	90	123	69	56%	249	11.3
L. Becker, 17 gms.	34	27	16	59%	84	5.0
D. Hayes, 18 gms.	27	30	17	57%	77	4.3
R. Lovejoy, 15 g.	17	21	12	57%	46	3.0
J. Rupp, 14 gms.	11	12	9	75%	31	2.2

Additional Statistics

Head coach: William Arthur. Reserve coach: Carl Snyder.

Last year's record, 14-6 this year's record, 19-3.

Archbold offensive average per game—62.9; total points scored 1385. Archbold defensive average per game—52.8; oppoents scored 1161.

Archbold highest game (scoring) —83 Fayette; 77 Bryan; Archbold lowest game (scoring)—59 Wauseon; 54 Napoleon; 54 Pettisville; 54 Liberty Center.

Opponent's highest game (scor-ing)—69 Hamler; 64 Wauseon; 63 Napoleon. Opponent's lowest game (scoring) — 35 Montpelier; 37 Lyons; 38 Delta; 38 Wauseon.

Best individual Archbold (scor-ing) — 29 Bridges (Swanton); 25 Bridges (Lyons); 24 Stuckey (Stry-ker); 23 Bridges (Swanton); 22 Stuckey (Bryan); 21 Bridges (Bryan); 20 Miller (Pettisville); 20 Bridges (Pettisville); 20 Stuckey (Wauseon).

Best individual opponent (scor-ing) — 26 Becker (Chesterfield); 24, 23, 21, Rychener (Pettisville); 23 Van Poppel (Hamler); 22 Bos-erman (Delta); 22 Grove (Swan-ton); 22 Volk (Wauseon).

I was allowed to go out for baseball in my junior and senior years as I was rapidly expanding my activities. I played left field for both my two final years of high school. The last year, we lost in the tournament to the eventual champions, who stated that we were the toughest team they faced. It was a tough loss as we were leading the game, two to one, all the way until the final inning and ended up losing four to two.

My arts and drama career began and ended with participation in the junior class play.

My dad had the foresight to enter into a contract with the Campbell Soup Company and grow tomatoes for them. He did this to raise some extra cash so my parents could afford to send their children, including myself, to college. Providing shelter and health standards for migrant tomato pickers provided an extra farm education. Consideration on where to go to college was an important decision to make in my senior year, but I will save that for the college years.

Stories:

1. I recall my fourth-grade teacher, Mrs. Spangler. She must've liked me a lot because she moved from grade school to teach junior high English. Our class was the first class after lunch, and it was about that age where guys love to tell jokes—some clean, some risqué, and some not so funny. We would gather fifteen to twenty minutes before class and sit in a circle and share jokes with one another. On this particular day, Mrs. Spangler came in early and began writing assignments on the chalkboard at the front of the class. One of my best buddies and fellow basketball player Dean Miller, who would be the other starting guard on our varsity basketball team in our senior year, made a bet with me that he could come closer to throwing an eraser in the wastebasket up at the front of the room, which was near the door. He went first and threw an eraser, and it hit the blackboard about six to eight feet from the teacher, who had her back to us. She immediately turned around and asked, "Who did that?" Dean confessed, and she immediately sent him to the study hall to write on a paper five hundred times, "I will not do that again." That was a common form of punishment that she used, removing students from the classroom and having them write over and over a phrase on paper. So off Dean went, and I was left there with the other fellows, having made a promise that I would compete with him on the eraser toss. I felt that I had to go fulfill my commitment, even though I knew it would get me in trouble, but I did not know

how much trouble it would get me into. I wound up throwing the eraser at the wastebasket in the corner by the door and nearly made it, but unfortunately, another teacher who was a bit wobbly, older in age, somewhat nearsighted, and a few other ailments that limited her sense of balance walked through the door to be greeted by an eraser that buzzed just passed her nose. She turned and went screaming down the hall. The other fellows and I thought that was rather humorous, but she and our English teacher, Mrs. Spangler, did not think that was the case. Infuriated, Mrs. Spangler turned around and asked, "Who did that?" I confessed. She told me to go down to the superintendent's office—the big cheese at the school, who was her husband—and wait for him there and then bring him with me to the classroom. It was now about five to ten minutes before the class was to start. I went down to the superintendent's office as instructed. Mr. Spangler, the superintendent, was not in, but the office girls were. They asked me what I wanted, and I said I was there to see Mr. Spangler and that Mrs. Spangler wanted to see him. I waited for fifteen to twenty minutes, and he did not show up yet, so I decided to take my chances and go down to see Mrs. Spangler and tell her that he was not in yet, hoping she may have cooled down—good thought but not the case. She had to leave her class, step into the hall to address me, and make it clear, in no uncertain terms, that I was to remain there until he came and then bring him down to her class. Off I went, and about ten minutes later, he did arrive back at his office. He asked what I wanted, and I told him that Mrs. Spangler wanted to see him. He asked why, and I told him I didn't know and that she had sent me down there to get him. When we arrived back at the class, Mrs. Spangler once again stepped out of the classroom into the hall, explained to her husband what had happened and that my friend Dean Miller was up in the study hall writing "I will not do that again" five hundred times, and recommended that he go and get him and that the both of us get a paddling. So up the stairs we went to the study hall, and he pulled Dean out of the study hall and informed him that the two of us were going down to his office. I will never forget the look on Dean's face when he was pulled from the study hall and realized he was in for some more punishment. Mr. Spangler closed the door behind us and asked which one of us wanted to go first. I was hoping that we could talk him out of it, but once a wife commands, a smart husband knows he needs to follow through. Dean volunteered, bent over the end of the table, and was a recipient of three cracks across his bottom with a door molding frame, a piece of wood about two by one inches used to frame doors and houses. He took his three hits, and then it was my turn. While it hurt, I endured the first two smacks, and the third one came with extra emphasis; the stick broke, and the one end went flying across the room. I believe it surprised Mr. Spangler, and he was a bit embarrassed that he may have overreacted. My dad always said that if I ever got a spanking at school, I would get a harder one at home. However, that day and the next day or two passed, and he saw the black-and-blue bottom that I had; I think his compassion for me overtook his earlier statement, for which I am thankful. This was one of several stories that I never lived down throughout my years in school. Can you imagine this type of physical punishment taking place today without a witness?

2. Another similar story of erasers took place while I was in the eighth grade. We had study hall the period immediately before lunch. It was during study hall that a student could go across the street to the library and do some library reading or check out books and spend time there.

We had to sign in when we went to the library so that a list of students who were at the library could be sent over to the study hall monitor for accountability. This was done, and it was not too unusual for some of us to get on the nerves of the librarian by talking a little louder than we were supposed to or knocking a few books off the shelves or some other mischievous things. This one day, after being in the library for about fifteen minutes, three of us were kicked out of the library, and when that happened, we were expected to go back to the study hall. Seventh-graders got dismissed for lunch period fifteen minutes before the eighth-graders and later grades to create less of a jam down in the cafeteria. So we devised a plan where when we went back to our lockers in the hallway and spent a little time there, cleaning out our lockers, we could leave when the seventh-graders were dismissed for lunch. We were planning to go down and have lunch at the local Dairy Queen, about six blocks from the school. This, we did, but little did we know of the surprise that would await us when we returned from lunch. The librarian had not yet sent over the list of those signed in at the library. She erased our names from the list after we had been kicked out; thus, we were not listed when that list went back to the study hall monitor. We showed up as missing for the entire session. We were met by the study hall teacher upon our return from lunch and immediately ushered into the superintendent's office, where we were informed that we were suspended from school. Befuddled, we thought this was an overexertion of power for missing fifteen minutes of class, but what we thought did not matter; remember, kids did not have "rights" in those days. When we asked how we could become reinstated in class, we were told that we would need to have our parents come into the superintendent's office and discuss this issue. Oh, what a dreadful experience, to call our parents and tell them that we were kicked out of school and that they needed to call the superintendent's office!

Fortunately, they made a call, and we were back in class yet that afternoon—but not necessarily in good standing. In fact, I remember one of my favorite teachers, Mr. Parker, commenting to me that if it were easier for the three of us to stand rather than sit, we would be permitted to do so because he thought our bottoms should be very sore after being kicked out of school. Mr. Parker is the same teacher I recall having study hall and punishing a disobedient student by pushing him up against the wall, one hand on his throat, the other slapping his face, back and forth, military style, all in front of other students in school. Yet one more example: the football and wrestling coach who held study hall walked out the front door, entered the back door silently, caught my friend and me talking, and cracked our heads together! Kids did not have rights and were abused.

3. A couple of other shorter stories during this two-year period include the time when one of our teachers was kind enough to let us chew gum in class—if we chewed politely and if it was not grape gum. Can you guess what we did? We did so politely, but we chewed grape gum. We would take turns being the first to chew that flavor, and sure enough, each time, she was able to pick out that there was grape gum being chewed in her class. After a while, we felt a bit sorry for her since she was trying to be nice to us, so we limited the amount of grape gum that was brought into her classroom.

4. In those days, like I suspect is true today, we liked to get and order different objects from joke shops. What I recall is a nose blower. We would put hankies up to our mouths but have little hollow wooden pieces with rubber extending from them so that when one blew into the wooden tube, the air went through the rubber with exasperatingly loud noises. While walking in the halls between classes we would also carry devices that would mimic the sounds of farm animals or birds chirping. Other students would get a big chuckle out of that like there were animals or birds in the halls between classes or think that someone had a really horrendous nose

blow. Finally, a trap was set for us, and we got caught. I think the principal, Mr. Burkholder—who is the husband of my fifth-grade teacher, Mrs. Burkholder—praised him for finally catching the culprits. It is clear that he would've loved to wring our necks. From that point on, he never really seemed to like me until I got to my late junior year in high school. Of course, I always thought that Mrs. Burkholder had predisposed him to not liking me.

5. A couple of farm stories . . . I remember during that age that an important businessman from town came out to visit my dad, and during his stay there, we threw a stone, and it hit his car and did some damage. Neither my dad nor the businessman was pleased. A similar story involved a new tractor equipped with a brand-new windshield for cold protection. While we were farming during the cold weather, a snowball was thrown by either my brother or me, and it cracked the windshield. I recall my father saying, "By grabs, you can't keep nothing new around here." Let's say it was my brother because, as you can see, I was in enough trouble as it was during these somewhat troubling years.

6. As a youngster, I went to Little Eden Camp for four successive years during the summers of the sixth through the ninth grade. The three hotspots where kids came from were the Goshen, Indiana, area, the Archbold, Ohio, area, and Eastern Ohio. There were generally 150 kids who spent a full week together in camp. There were

cabins at the camp, and eight to twelve kids would be assigned to reside in one of the cabins with a counselor who was a young college or post–high school student. There was a nice cool creek running through the camp, and we used that to cool a watermelon for later eating in our cabin. We also put soda pop in the cool creek to cool, and as a bad joke, we picked on one guy by filling a bottle with human urine, placed it in the creek to cool, and used a Mountain Dew bottle so that the contents looked like Mountain Dew pop. We kindly offered this to the young guy, and he took one or two sips, but that was all, and of course, we all laughed. We also had the first sign of elitism and partisanship at camp by the Archbold, Ohio, camp, who challenged the world to a softball game. It was Archbold versus the world. Of course, it rankled the other kids there to think that Archbold kids thought they were the best and could beat the entire world. I remember the taunting from the Archbold kids, who said you could get anyone you wanted on your team, knowing that it was restricted to people at the camp. As a side note, in later years, my sweetheart and later wife, Judy, was at the camp for at least one or two years while I was there, but we did not know or recognize each other then.

7. The purchase of a used Cushman motor scooter gave me the wheels I needed to get around when I was fourteen. We picked up a close friend, Dean, and my father and I, with him, went to Defiance, Ohio, to check on a scooter listed for sale. It was five or six years old, yellow

in color, but it ran and had a price of $125 on it. My dad agreed to buy it, and I was elated. Weeks later, my friend brought a brand-new Cushman scooter, the modern type, and I was a bit jealous, but nonetheless, I did have a scooter and was happy for that. My friend and I traveled around on our scooters, and eventually, a few more people got them, and especially on Sunday afternoons, we would go out for a ride. It's amazing how many miles a person can cover with a machine that goes forty to fifty miles per hour.

8. Freshman and sophomore years at high school were transition years for growing up and developing self-confidence. In those years, there were many older students at school, and we were one of the younger group. As the older classes graduated, we transitioned to the older group, and along with that, our confidence and self-esteem improved. Being successful in FFA and in sports added to my self-esteem. It was also during those early years that I became a sucker for gimmicks. I wanted my body to grow big and strong and take on the Charles Atlas appearance. I bought some pills through the mail that were supposed to enhance the body. An older student discovered that I had ordered those and teased me relentlessly, asking how they were working, saying that he didn't notice much change yet and that perhaps I should take stronger doses. So I learned also how it feels to be picked on.

9. It was around sophomore year that I felt a little bit left out in that many of my town friends were developing relationships with the opposite sex. While I increasingly appreciated cute-looking girls, I was a farm boy and did not have as many opportunities to participate in town activities such as school dances etc. You might even say I was a bit shy, but that was only a temporary time in my life. At church, we had the Mennonite Youth Fellowship (**MYF**) youth group, which met once a month, but there were few girls in that group whom I was attracted to. You see, they were at the awkward stage as well and in the process of developing. I was comfortable with being friends with older boys as well as with younger boys. The older boys had vehicles for transportation before I got my driver's license and my car.

10. Roller-skating was a big event when many kids went to meet other kids and have a good time. There was a large skating rink in Swanton, Ohio, a town about twenty-five to thirty miles from where we lived. Well, the skating rink operated as a skating rink during the week; on Saturday evenings, it became a dance hall. This, my parents did not know, and so when I went out on Saturday night and they asked where I went, I told them the Swanton skating rink, which was the truth, but it was being held as a dance hall on those evenings. It was there that another friend and I met some gals and had some interesting experiences. On one evening, we took two gals out on a sort of pickup double date in my friend's new Chevy car. We ventured into the outskirts

of Toledo, Ohio, where a group of guys began chasing us with their car. I mistakenly flipped them off, and this truly irritated them. We had several close calls that evening as we did not know the streets and territory very well. Trying to evade them, we went into a dead-end street, and I feared that we would be dead as a result, but my friend miraculously did a quick U-turn and got out of there before they were able to totally close in on us. Still, they tracked us down and tailed us, and so we started driving up Interstate 75 to Detroit, thinking this may be the safest place we could be. They kept pulling up beside us, trying to push us over and off the road, and told the driver, my friend, that he would be fine; they just wanted the guy in the back seat. Our gas was getting very low in the car, and we figured we would run out of gas, but at that time, there was some intervention that happened where they backed off and decided they did not want to go all the way into Detroit, and so we were safe and breathed out a sigh of relief. It took me a while to get to sleep that night, thinking of what might have happened. It was one of many close encounters to follow.

11. There are several other car stories, mostly embarrassing. One evening, with permission, I borrowed my dad's car, and my friend Ross, who was a year my junior, and I double-dated to a semi-pro hockey game—the Fort Wayne Comets, in Fort Wayne, Indiana, sixty miles away. My mother's family lived in a suburb of Fort Wayne—Leo, Indiana—and she had brothers and

sisters there and one in Hicksville, Ohio, which was between Archbold and Fort Wayne. Returning home from the hockey game, around 11:00 p.m. to 11:30 p.m., I developed car trouble near Hicksville, Ohio. Not knowing what to do with two dates en route, I decided to call my uncle who lived in Hicksville. He was gracious to come out to pick me up and take us to Archbold so that we could get home and come back the next day to get the car fixed. He was a bit surprised to see two younger (underage) gals with us. He frequently teased me at future get-togethers, wondering if I had more car trouble. I think he sensed that the looks on our faces were telling that we had been enjoying our time with our dates prior to the car breakdown.

12. Here's another car story. As a junior in high school, I drove to our home basketball game, and as tradition, many of us went out to a hangout place for pinball and burgers, Coke, shakes, you name it. It was a restaurant about seven miles out of town and had a nice open stretch of a two-lane paved highway. A buddy of mine was also going, and we decided to open up the cars a bit en route, and I pushed my dad's car up to ninety-plus miles per hour. The next morning, my dad came out, looked at the car, examined the front tire, and said, "Wow! We've got to change this tire. It's very worn in tread, and I would hate to be driving sixty miles an hour on that when it blew out." I felt like I had just dodged another bullet.

13. When we were seniors in school, there would be many times when a group of us would drive to school and then do some extracurricular activity, driving around a bit after school before going home. One day there were three cars—one was mine, and two were my friends'— and we loaded up friends in our three cars and headed off to Bryan, Ohio, doing some zigzagging on the way. There was an altercation between the other two cars, which did some minor damage to the cars by tying them up a bit. The car I was driving escaped unharmed. I went home and said nothing. About three days later, my parents approached me and asked me what had happened on that afternoon and why I had not told them. I responded that it did not involve me; yes, I was with them, but there was no damage to my car. They did not view this as a good excuse for not sharing with them that two of my friends had their cars damaged and that my friends' parents were knowledgeable of the accident but they were not. Being a parent later and now a grandparent, I can understand their point of view better.

14. Here's yet another car story. It was football homecoming night; I was a senior and the president of the student council and given the distinction of driving the homecoming queen during halftime at the football game. To do this in style, we recruited four convertible cars from townspeople to borrow for that evening. My car was a Cadillac convertible owned by a prominent doctor in town, Dr. Neal. I picked up the car early

before noon so that I could go and get it washed and, of course, drive it around a bit, especially around the country, to show off to my friends that here I was in a brand-new Cadillac convertible. The whole event was quite an ordeal where we drove very slowly past the grandstands with the queen of each grade and other cars in the homecoming queen procession to parade past the stands. Then the football king for each grade came to get the queen and escort her to the stands. The cars would come back near the end of the game to pick them up and parade on out. Well, a couple of the other drivers of the cars and I decided, after we dropped the queens off, to take a little spin around a few blocks in town. I should've known that Dr. Neal would be at the game, and he obviously saw that his car was being taken out for a spin and was not happy. When I came back to park the car, he approached me and asked me for the keys. I told him that I needed to pick up the queen at the end of the game to take her back to the school. He said, "Not with my car. I saw you driving around out on the streets, and that was not my intent in loaning you the car." That began my early negotiating skills when I explained how embarrassing that would be to the queen as well as myself and that it was really important for us to complete this homecoming event. After some more talking and pleading, he finally agreed but made it certain that I was to take the car, pick up the queen, take her to the school, and directly bring the car back to his residence. I was more than happy to do so.

15. One story that should be included in the "high school years" chapter was on October or Halloween time. In the country neighborhood in which we lived, there were still a number of outhouses, which is what was used before indoor toilets. Most farmers had pickup trucks. Our town had only one or two cops on duty at a time. We organized a plan to attract cops to one end of town while others delivered outhouses into town and parked them on the main street and in the parking spaces in front of stores. I recall one year when we were successful in transporting six or more outhouses to the main drag of our small town. Imagine the townsfolk waking up the next morning and finding the outhouses lining their downtown streets! Where did the outhouses come from? Where should they be returned? Who put them there? It was difficult to place the blame on any one person or small group since there were so many who could've been involved, but it certainly was more fun than going trick-or-treating.

16. Here is one more car story. I was not involved, but a person who was close and personal verified the story in the summer of 2021. There were three couples in the car—one in the front seat, two couples squeezed in the back seat. We all loved fireworks in those days and frequently had them on hand. The driver of the car noted a person raking stones out by his mailbox and told the others in the car, "Watch this guy jump." He lit an M80 (a powerful firecracker) and threw it out the window while driving thirty-five to forty miles

per hour. The problem is the M80 did not make it all the way out and came back into the back seat, where it landed between the legs of my friend. It went off with a loud noise, ripping the seat and my friend's pants and flesh. The incident, along with the smoke, so spooked the girlfriend of the other couple in the back seat that she threw herself forward, opened the passenger-side car door of the two-door sedan, and rolled herself out of the car while the car was traveling thirty-five miles per hour. She had major bruises and some injuries. The driver escaped personal injury, but the two outside passengers had significant injuries. His car was not so lucky as the back seat had to be replaced. My friend told me that others in the car were relieved several years later when he became a father because they feared his surgery might have prevented him from becoming a father. As a side note, the gal who rolled herself out of the car was a girl whom I had several dates with previously. Fireworks can be dangerous.

17. An entire chapter could be written in this section. There was bribery even in those days by some unethical teachers. A young new teacher who was the track coach bribed me with a promise of a B grade or better in his class if I came out for track. My plate was quite full; thus, I did not submit to this bribe.

18. The two major sports I played were basketball and baseball. A couple of basketball stories follow. My talent while first string in the eighth and ninth grades did

not really blossom until my junior year. During my sophomore year, I did make the junior varsity roster but did not play a lot because of a very strong, totally dominant senior varsity squad that had all juniors in high school playing on the junior varsity team. As the next year progressed, those juniors moved to the varsity team, and I became a starting guard on the junior varsity team, dressed for the varsity games, and did get to play in some varsity games. Then as a senior, I became one of three of the leading players on our team. We lost an early game by one point on the road, sixty to fifty-nine, and then went on a winning streak until we lost another road game in a small gym to a much larger school, sixty-three to fifty-four, and took our two losses and a state ranking into the tournament. Our loss to Hamler that year was devastating. We were leading twenty-eight to twenty-one when our star player picked up his third foul and was benched. The substitute who came in threw the ball away several times, and the other team started hitting unbelievable shots, such that we held a thirty-one-to-thirty lead at halftime, but the momentum was all on their side. We ended up losing sixty-four to fifty-five, and I did foul out of the game and sit helplessly on the bench, watching us go down to defeat. The next anticipated game against the reigning state champs and my assignment to guard the star player never materialized—heartbreak number one.

19. One of the games where I was not a star was a game where the refs had it in for me and loaded me with fouls.

I had four fouls on me and was guarding a person under the bucket who came up with elbows flying and the ball to shoot a shot. I was called for my fifth and final file. On the play, he cut my lip but good, and it required my immediate departure to the doctor's office for stitches while the game proceeded. We were behind at that time, but perhaps that incident sparked the rest of my team members to perform at a higher level and come back and win that game.

20. Another example I remember quite well (and so will my brother) is that ankle sprains were common for many people, in particular for myself. I had my ankles wrapped frequently and, after a sprain, would go home and soak my ankle in hot water in a bucket. I'm trying to think of where the icing came in, but in this case, I remember the heat. I was sitting in my parents' living room with my leg in a bucket of warm water; the water would cool, and I would need to add some warmer water to the bucket. Getting out of the bucket and drying my foot to go get my warmer water was a chore, and so I asked my brother to bring me some hot water. He did; he brought nearly boiling water and poured it into the bucket. It was so hot, my natural reaction was to take my foot out of the water, and as a result, the hot scalding water was directly on my foot. The skin on my entire foot peeled off in the succeeding two or three days, and I had to miss a number of practices and play limitedly in a game. My parents were not happy about that. I eventually

forgave my brother and got the message that I should serve myself instead of asking others to serve me.

21. Not trying out for the baseball high school team until my junior year was a disadvantage for me, so I was not a star player, but I did make the starting team as a junior and played left field. My batting average was not where I liked it to be, but I considered my fielding to be an asset to the team. We had a good win–loss record and went into the tournament with a strong, hopeful team. One of the liabilities was that we had one good starting pitcher whom we relied on. The batting on the team was adequate but not really strong up and down the lineup. We breezed through county and district tournaments and went to the regional, one step away from the state finals. We met a team known as Lincolnshire, down near the Dayton, Ohio, area of the state. We were coasting along with the lead, going into the late innings of the game. The score was two to one, and Lincolnshire had a runner on first base and one out. A hit came out to left field, and I charged in but decided to play it safe and take it on the bounce rather than try to make a shoestring catch. The thinking behind this was that our pitcher was doing well and would probably get the next couple of batters out. Well, the bases became loaded with one out, and a fly ball was hit again to left field in foul territory; I raced over, made the catch, and threw home as the runner from third tagged to go home. My throw was on line but hit the runner and deflected away from the catcher, allowing several runs to score.

Instead of ending the inning, three runs were scored, and we trailed four to two, that being the final score. Lincolnshire went on to win the state tournament and said that we were the toughest team that they played. Small consolation.

22. Here are a few high school stories. I mentioned the tragic death of my very close friend David when he was sixteen and we were sophomores. He was president of our class, and I was vice president. The school year was nearly over, so we continued with me acting as the president until the next year. In the fall of our junior year, we had, as in previous years, an election for officers by classmates. You may recall earlier my run-in with my fifth-grade teacher, Mrs. Burkholder, and following difficulties with her husband, the principal, Mr. Burkholder; this all came back into play. Mr. Burkholder scheduled the election of new officers on a day when our FFA had a field trip, and fourteen fellow classmates and I were not there for the vote to elect new officers. Fourteen of seventy students missing can have a big effect on selections; I did not become an officer in my junior year and, to this day, feel this was a direct attempt by Mr. Burkholder to get back at me. I learned some early lessons in politics that would be replayed later in life. Perhaps before my readers get too down on Mr. Burkholder, I think he had second thoughts about what he had done, and from that time on, he started to try to chum up with me. He promoted me and pushed my candidacy to become president of the student council

in my senior year. He made several other overtures to try to gain favorability with me because I was rather popular in school, and the end result is that he wanted to go as an advisor on our senior trip to Washington, D.C., and to New York City.

23. Mr. Burkholder was not well-liked by many students, which was not uncommon with the principal title. Some friends shared with me a Halloween trick they had played on him. They took a paper bag with animal dung in it, placed it on his doorstep, lit the paper sack, rang the doorbell, and ran. They watched and laughed as he came out of his house and tried to stomp out the fire, stepping in it. I suspect I was blamed for this prank.

24. Another honor bestowed upon me was becoming the editor-in-chief of our annual yearbook. This does not mean that in all cases, you have complete control as those on your staff can subvert some of your efforts. We produced a good yearbook with the help of everyone; however, much to my surprise, when the yearbook was published, there was a picture in there that was entered without my knowledge and caused me some embarrassment.

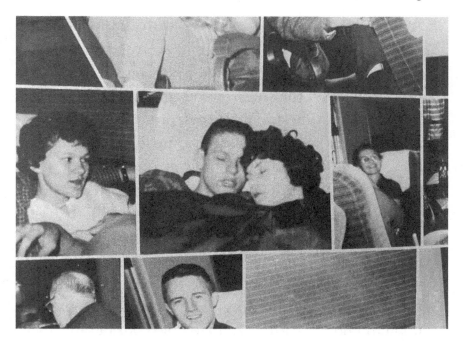

You see, we traveled by train and by bus the six hundred or so miles to the two cities, and some of that was evening travel. It was nothing serious, but during the trip, there was more than just a little bit of time spent with a particular classmate of the opposite sex. The problem was that she had a steady who was a year older, not on the trip, and the star center of the basketball team the previous year. I wonder what it was that attracted her to basketball players . . . Anyway, I was happy with that, but when the yearbook came out and disclosed our two heads together on the bus, with my arm around her and covered with a blanket, it did raise some questions by others. One question I found rather humorous later is why would the editor-in-chief of the yearbook allow that picture in there? I did not allow it; it was snuck in there.

25. A story I regret to this day was with the MYF youth group at the church. My parents were youth sponsors for our group for several years. They were generous and fun for many of the youths in our group. They donated much of their time and resources, provided land to grow sugarcane or sugar beets for income for the group, and hosted a number of events out at our place. I was a junior at the time when new elections were to be held for the sponsors. My parents agreed to serve another year if elected. Can you believe that I campaigned against them? Why? A friend of mine and I loved to go to the gatherings but then, after the meetings, liked to go elsewhere and do things without supervision. I was popular enough with a group to hold considerable sway, and I am most confident that many voted against my parents because I wanted them to do so. When they lost the election, this was very hurtful to them. Later in life, I did apologize to them and came clean with why they had lost the election, and I have felt terrible ever since and for the suffering humiliation they must've felt for many years.

I hope this gives you a glimpse of some of the life of this particular high school student; overall, they were great years, a learning experience, and directions set for my future life ahead.

CHAPTER 5

My Undergraduate College Years, 1962–1966

What an informative time in one's life! After graduation or leaving high school, one is forced to choose among going directly into the workforce, going to a trade school, entering military services, or entering a two-to-four-year liberal arts program. The four-year college program seems to buy some time and broaden your options for the future. Many studies have been done showing the value of college education in the workforce; however, these are based on averages and, there are exceptions to the averages.

It is at this age, eighteen to twenty-two, that the body continues its development into womanhood and manhood, hormones are raging, and decisions knowingly or unknowingly are being made that will directly impact your future. What is it that excites you? What habits are you forming? How driven are you to become successful in all that you do or in one aspect of your life? To what extent will you sacrifice some pleasures now for future gain? Do I really need to forgo some pleasure to study and achieve good grades? Is there a balance in life, or is it "full steam ahead" to pursue the desired success? These are all questions that come into play, and whether we realize it or not, we intentionally or not-so-intentionally make those decisions.

A valued and respected professor told me something that I really liked. Getting good grades was not a problem for me, but getting great grades certainly was. So you might say that I was an average-plus student. I did play sports in college and was active in a number of other areas, including a healthy social life, but hey, this was a fun time of life—out of the nest at home, with no one to look over your shoulder, you do as you please and make your own decisions. Well, what did the professor tell me that was so gratifying to me? When I was down just a bit on a grade I had just received, he told me that he would rather have a solid all-around "B" student than a straight-"A" student with no personality or other life. I seemed to fit that mold and was comforted by his comments.

I remember my father telling me regarding his farming vocation that one thing he certainly enjoyed about that vocation was that he was his own boss and he could do as he pleased without reporting to a higher-up. Entering college was a bit that way; you became your own boss, but like my dad, it was good to take advice and counsel from others.

College years were a very exciting time in my life. It was like my future father-in-law said—"These are the best years of your life." In many respects, he was correct, although I would argue that I also had some other years that were very good years as well. College was a very important time to meet and make new friends of both sexes. Group activities, individual dates, double dating—it was a time when we seemed to have it all. The traditional year began in September and concluded in May, so that left the summer months to either return home or use the interim period for other educational opportunities.

The first two years, I returned home to work on the farm to help earn my college tuition, which was generously provided by my parents. We grew a cash crop of tomatoes, thirty acres, for the Campbell Soup Company. My job was to help supervise the field workers, drive the truck in the field to assist in loading the tomato boxes onto the truck, and deliver them to the Campbell Soup facility in neighboring Napoleon, Ohio, a city about twenty miles from our farm. The land in our area was well suited for growing tomatoes, and the close proximity to Napoleon allowed for a number of farmers to enter a contract with the company to grow tomatoes. During a season, one could achieve anywhere from fifteen to thirty tons of tomatoes per acre. They had to be repeatedly picked, a tough job for which most farmers utilized migrant workers who came up from Mexico and Texas to pick cherries in Michigan and then moved to Northwest Ohio to pick tomatoes until the killing frost came in the fall.

I did not resent doing this because I felt very fortunate to have my college tuition paid for by my parents, and it was the least I could do to help earn my way. There were challenges and difficulties along the way with migrant workers in that one needed to provide housing for them while they were picking your tomatoes. Many of the OSHA regulations were far more stringent than they had for themselves—housing facilities, drinking water, sanitation, worker protection, etc.—but that certainly could be another chapter or book for that matter.

During those summer months, it was refreshing to renew friendships with high school kids who were still in the area as well as family and relatives.

However, I did welcome the fall to get back to school to meet my new friends and become engaged in the activities that were so great during my freshman year.

On to academics. Goshen College, where I went to school, was a liberal arts school known for its nursing, teaching, and premed curriculum during those days. My interest was still in agriculture, and I failed to see how Goshen could lead me to that end. Thus, I inquired what courses I could take that would be transferable to Ohio State University, where I would have more ample opportunity to pursue an agriculturally related field. My thought was to transfer after my freshman or sophomore year to Ohio State. I told my advising professor that I wanted to take courses that would transfer to Ohio State or another school. The advice given was for me to take a fine arts course in my freshman year, which I did, and I gained some appreciation for the arts, but it was far afield from my agrarian background. Many of the other students were fine arts majors, upperclassmen, and, in general, in tune to the fine arts. I did get through the course but received a D in it, and the only courses that transferred were grades C and above.

An interesting side note here that will not make it to the stories section is that we each had to have a project in this class. I took choir training, which means the ability to lead a congregation in song, knowing the hand motions for three-fourths time, two-halves time, and two-fourths time. Interestingly, folks back home knew I took this course in training and expected me to lead the congregation when I returned home during the summer and sing. What a joke!

During my first two years, I also took Spanish 1 and Spanish 2. I have a liberal arts background, and while this would serve me well later, I did not know that at the time, and four semesters of Spanish ate up a lot of my other available courses to take. I also thought that my profession would be in teaching and so enrolled in a number of educationally related courses, but then you do need to have a major, and so while my first love was math, biology won out as my major. Moving through the years, I had sufficient biology courses for a major, but what minor would I have? I had taken a number of math courses, and with my biology major, there were quite a few chemistry courses that were also a part of that.

I came to a fork in the road. I had an equal number of chemistry credits as math credits. I needed at least twelve more credits in each field to classify as a minor. For teaching, what would be a stronger combination to obtain a job—a biology/chemistry degree or a biology/math degree? Since I loved math more, I chose the latter, also thinking there would be more biology/chemistry teachers available than biology/math teachers. All this can lead the reader to certainly understand that I soon found myself course rich but degree poor.

For four years of education, there were 124 credit hours required, and for me to complete what I started, I would need to have 145 credit hours to get a liberal arts biology/math teaching degree. There simply wasn't enough time to get all these courses in during the regular school year; thus, in my junior year, I had to remain in summer school to take three courses. These were each three-week intensive courses, so nine weeks of my summer were spent taking courses on campus. Likewise, graduating in June 1966 with the rest of my class, I received a blank diploma. I had to complete two more three-week sessions following graduation to get the diploma completed. How anticlimactic!

If you want to follow me with the math, I had five additional courses, three credits each. So during my four years, I was able to get 130 credits plus the 15 credits achieved during summer school of my last two years for my total of 145 credits. This plan had some ups and downs. The downs were that it sucked to have to take classes when colleagues were out having fun; the upside was that I was dating a somewhat local gal who would later become my wife, and it was a chance to see her more during the summer.

Cuddle Up With A Book . . .

Winter's the time to cuddle up with a good book, and petite Judy Stealy finds exams double the reasons for cuddling up with books.

As the saying goes, with every cloud, there is a silver lining.

The courses I took had a mixture of learning approaches in that there were a few that were considered rote memorization, such as organic chemistry, and others that required imaginative application thinking. Course learning and course theory have certainly changed over the years. For example, the dictionary was a useful source in those years, as were encyclopedias, where we could look up and get information on certain topics. Today, with the Internet, the iPhone, Google, Alexa, and other search engines, these former sources are obsolete. What will it be like ten years from now? It is hard to imagine.

Athletics were a major part of my life growing up. At Goshen College, we had varsity sports and intramural sports. The intramural sports that I participated in were soccer, softball, volleyball, and flag football. Teams were organized by grades. For example, as freshmen, if we had enough players interested in softball, we may have three teams based on ability: the freshman 1 team, the freshman 2 team, and the freshman 3 team. The freshman 1 team would compete with the sophomore, junior, and senior 1 teams. Likewise, the other teams would complete with similar teams from other classes.

You may notice that I did not mention basketball or baseball. If you went out for a varsity team, then generally, you did not play on the intramural teams. The intramural teams were designed to compete against other students within the college and not against other colleges. Intramural teams were very fun and very competitive. Oh, the pleasure as freshmen that we took in beating the seniors! Being an athlete, I was fortunate to make the number one team in the intramurals in each of the sports I participated in.

I played all four years of basketball at Goshen at the competitive level, my freshman year on the junior varsity team (where I was leading scorer), and then, toward the end of the year, varsity. During my sophomore year, I was sixth or seventh man depending on the position and then was a starter in my junior and senior year. I do remember the pride that my parents, especially my dad, took in the achievements that I had made in basketball. It was when I was either a freshman or a sophomore that the head coach came out to our area on a recruiting trip and told the audience, with my dad in attendance, that if our area could continue to send players like Dick Stuckey to Goshen, we would have a terrific team in the future. His son, Jim, was from Goshen and a great player as well as a great friend on the basketball team.

Although I was not a starter in my sophomore year, it was probably my best year in that as a sub, I averaged over eleven points a game and shot 55 percent from the field. While my points-per-game average increased when I was a junior and senior, in my view, they were not as impressive as my sophomore year. The moral of the story is that while we are striving to achieve a greater level, we have incentive to try and work harder to achieve that goal, and once we arrive, some of that motivation does not remain as strong. This concept will be revisited in later chapters.

Each of my last three years on the varsity basketball team, we had good seasons; we expected to do better each year, but for some reason, we ended up with a ten-to-six record or an eleven-to-five record each year. We had some nice victories over larger schools and, along with those, a disappointing loss or two, but that is life.

For the record, my 15.8 points-per-game average in my junior year was second to my friend Jim, with a leading 18.1 points-per-game average. In my senior year, I dipped to 13.9 points per game and shot a lower percentage than the previous two years. Maybe the social bug and other interests had something to do with that.

My baseball career at Goshen was much more abbreviated when I went out as a sophomore and made second team. However, I soon realized that after basketball season as well as many weekends of home and away games, baseball would be an extension of weekends away, the time that conflicted greatly with social/dating activities. Thus, after a brief stint on the varsity second team baseball squad, I decided to forgo the work and time that that would require.

College years can make a great social life. They can be a time of many ups and downs. You get along well with friends of the same sex, engage in many activities, and generally have a great time—that is, until one of those friends starts competing with you for a special friend of the opposite sex.

Dating can be a fun learning experience. I am sure it was quite different for women than for men. I can only speak from the man's perspective. In many ways, it does seem unfair to me that it was the man who made the invitations to date, not the woman. I understand this has changed considerably since my dating days, and it does seem to me that this is more equitable. I also suspect that some of the same issues exist today that existed in my day. For example, you ask a gal out on a date, and other people see you and wait for the next time that you ask that same gal out. If you do not, what does that say? You do not like the gal? You did not have a good time? You simply want to date other girls? From the girl's perspective, it could be embarrassing to her in front of her peers that the person she had a date with and whom she may really like did not immediately ask her out for a second date.

The danger of asking for a second and third date is that on a small campus, it appears that you are going steady, and it makes it difficult to have a date with someone else. Also, for the girl, she may be in a predicament. She accepts that first date with someone who may not have been her first choice, yet what option does she have? If she accepts a second and third date from the same boy, does this remove her from circulation from other guys whom she may like to date? I think you can see this can be very awkward and, at times, hurtful.

In my own case (and not to belabor the point), dating in freshman year had conflicts for many friends, and as they were going with girls from back home, many of those relationships continued, while others were broken off because of distance and availability. I had dated a number of gals when I left for college but not exclusively, so it was not a problem for me to date other college gals because I had no commitments at home. I did date several gals and then, in the spring of my freshman year, began dating one gal almost exclusively. It became very frequent, with daily dates and get-togethers during the spring of the year, such that my fellow friends labeled me as henpecked and some less appropriate words. The summer came, and we parted, although living only a hundred miles apart, we were able to see each other several times that summer with visits to each other's homes. People assumed a deeper relationship than what actually existed. We did talk about future dreams and aspirations, including some international experiences of mine.

We returned from summer to the campus in the fall of our sophomore year with quite different expectations. My friend expected to pick up where we had left off with daily meals and evenings together; I felt quite different. I longed to see my fellow friends and engage with them after a long summer. My girlfriend raked me over the coals when I did not call for a couple of days. I realize this was hurtful to my friend, who came back with different expectations, but the fact was I was not ready to settle down with only one person taking up that much of my time and limiting my social life.

To make a long story short, as the saying goes, many discussions and many experiments came into play in the next several months. I expressed my desire to date around, and we worked out an agreement that we would give that a try; we would still meet once a week, on Wednesday night, for a date. This worked for a maximum of one month until the final split-up occurred. During that time, I identified five classmates whom I thought I would like to have as dates. The problem was that a couple of these classmates were good friends, and there enters another challenge. After much deliberation, I chose to ask one of the five out. To my surprise, she accepted. She was a beautiful gal, very talented but not an athlete per se. What did I do but invite her to go bowling? Later, she told me she was totally embarrassed and thought I would probably not ask her out again. She was wrong. For the record, I did have one date with one of the other four, one of two who were not close friends of the gal whom I had first asked. I never did ask her other two close friends whom I was considering.

The first date occurred in late September of my sophomore year, and with multiple dates with others, both from her standpoint and mine, by Christmas of that year, we were an item, and by February or March, we were dating steadily.

We enjoyed each other's company; she was not as demanding, and I did not feel as trapped and confined as I had felt previously. She had an on-and-off relationship with one of my classmates back in her freshman year, and as we began dating, sadly, I think he recognized his mistake and did not pursue my new friend further, although he did try on occasion. By the way, his name was Dick, like mine, and he enters a couple of stories later in this chapter.

College came to a close, relationships developed, and our engagement was formally announced on October 23, 1965. The engaged couple dropped notes in mailboxes and disappeared for the weekend to visit a former roommate in Columbus, Ohio. We were married on July 23,1966, and preparations were made for post-college life.

Stories:

1. One story told to me on entering college had particular interest to me based on my farm background. I did not do this but did enough of other things, as you will soon learn. However, several years before entering college, a group of fellows, for a prank, led a cow up to the top floor of the administration building, which was five or six stories tall. What is so unique about this is that what a farm boy would already know is that you can lead cows upstairs but cannot lead them downstairs. Imagine the surprise of administrators coming to work and hearing a "moo" up on the floor above them and discovering a cow as the source. I never heard for sure how they were able to remove the cow, likely with a crane or some other physical device.

2. The next several stories will make one wonder how I was able to remain in the school, and I have asked myself the same question. They were good intended pranks but nonetheless rather stupid. For Halloween, we continued the tradition I had in high school of transporting an outhouse to the main campus of the college, just outside the dining room facility on the big open lawn. A friend, currently a medical doctor with smarts, knew how to cross wires on the ignition to start a truck without the keys. A campus truck was secured, cross-wired, and driven to the countryside to pick up an outhouse and deposit it on campus. This was so much fun, the group of six to eight fellows decided to go out to a turkey farm where there was a pen of sick turkeys and give these turkeys a special pre-Thanksgiving gift by transporting them to the fine arts building on campus. Someone in the group had secured a key to the building, and we deposited three or four sick turkeys into the ladies' restroom within the fine arts building. Imagine the surprise on the professor's face the next morning when she went into the restroom and found the squawking sick turkeys, who should've visited the outhouse rather than the interior toilets as they escaped out into the main area of the fine arts building. This was a major issue on campus, and there was no end to the detective work that went on to find the people responsible for this distasteful event. Finally, nearly all the individuals involved were identified, and the three varsity basketball players, including myself, had to sit out a couple of games for their transgressions. This was

above and beyond the penalties that others received. "Not fair" was an expression I would hear my younger son express on many occasions when he was growing up.

3. The use of secured keys by an individual or two whom I knew must've been most frustrating to the administration. We had a snack shop where we enjoyed going and getting snacks, including ice cream, during the day. "What is wrong with getting an ice cream at night? It is not our fault the snack shop is closed." Thus, on occasion, we went in and helped ourselves to a nice sundae—"no harm, no foul," as the saying goes, until one evening there were about six or seven of us in there, living it up with huge sundaes, the size that my elder son could eat when he came home from college, when the night watchman detected activity in the snack shop and entered. Wow, did we ever disperse! I remember going out the back door into a newly established patio meeting area in the dark, not knowing my way around, stumbling over chairs, and finally finding an exit to break out and run down the long hallway and out into the open. It was a close call, another example of risky business that could've turned disastrous. To my knowledge, none of those involved were positively identified, although I'm sure the administration had a list of suspects.

4. During my freshman year, I lived in a dorm and was paired with another fellow whom I had not met before. We got along fine, but I gravitated to a close special friend from Ohio who was active in sports and planned

to transfer to Ohio State after his sophomore year. We agreed to room together in a special house on the outskirts of campus known as North Hall. North Hall had rooms for about twenty students, and it was a special place that created many memories. There was a group of seniors in the house who lived as a group in the basement, and then there were these sophomores who normally lived in pairs on the upper second floor. A book could be written about North Hall, which, much to our dismay, was demolished about twenty years ago. Some think it may have been taken down to try and remove the memories that were created at that lodging. At Goshen, we did not have fraternities and sororities, but North Hall certainly came the closest to that, and in subsequent years, there were many groups of five or six students who would live together in off-campus housing. The main floor consisted of a piano, some sofas and chairs, and also some candy vending machines. Why do we have to put money into vending machines to get candy? That was the question that one individual in our group certainly had. Free candy should be a right and benefit of living at the house. About every two or three weeks, Dan would hire one of the residents to play the piano loudly while he would turn the vending machine upside down and beat on it so that it would spit out the coins that others had put in to purchase candy bars. He liked to refer to this as a "two-for-one and three-for-one special." Another term was "recycling money"!

5. Another event that happened at North Hall was the frequent secret consumption of forbidden alcohol, which

was against a policy of the college. Two stories are recalled where the "high-priced wine," Mogen David, often showed up behind the hall for consumption by three or four who enjoyed a bit of wine. Did they really enjoy the wine, or did they enjoy breaking the law of the college? How was that Mogen David secured? In some cases, I suspect it was purchased; in other cases, I suspect Dan lifted it from the stores to remove the weight on the shelves.

6. A more disturbing alcohol event that I recall was one evening when three of us were playing cards in the room and consuming 7Up with vodka and peanuts. As the evening wore on, we ran out of 7Up and began the "straight vodka and peanut" combination—not a good combination. We started feeling a bit woozy and uncomfortable. While my roommate and I maintained our interiors, the third fellow was not so lucky—or should I say, the third fellow's roommate was not so lucky. The third person left and went to his room and climbed up to his upper bunk bed, upon which the room started swirling and moving, and he leaned over the side of the bed and pitched his cookies. Unfortunately for his roommate, who left his shoes beside the bed, the shoes became the recipient of his outburst. It's not pleasant but a story that has had long life and still lives to this day.

7. One more story on North Hall. It seems like my departed friend Dan is involved in all these stories. Today I relate this story to very frustrating experiences with many

calls today (when you're phoning a business number and the repeated recordings and transfers are never-ending). Well, this was initiated back in the mid-sixties or before. We had a common phone for North Hall. So if one wanted to talk to someone from North Hall, you dialed the North Hall number and asked to speak with that person. Dan became adept at answering the phone and would go on about a five-minute speech that included something along the lines of "You have reached North Hall. North Hall is a home to many talented individuals. North Hall was established in 1958," and he would go on and on about the history of North Hall. Finally, much to the dismay of the caller, he would end by saying, "Now which of these fine gentlemen would you like to speak with?" He got so proficient that it did sound like a recording and not a live person.

8. While at college, a number of students would get part-time jobs to help them earn some extra spending money. A farm boy had valuable experiences, including a good work ethic that became attractive to a number of employers.

   Three are briefly described here, and with the advent of search engines, I leave it to the reader to look up and learn more about these if interested. Repairing and roofing new buildings plus some normal agricultural farming work was one of them. The other two, I recall, had to do with, yes, turkeys. About twice a week, we went down to the neighboring town of Paris, Indiana, and loaded frozen turkeys into a refrigerated truck. For the last activity, one might say, "Where do these turkeys come from?" Well, I spent many a Saturday afternoon and some evenings assisting with the artificial insemination of turkeys. That is the one I will let you google if you're interested in learning more about AI, not the artificial intelligence that most people associate with AI.

9. At the end of my sophomore year, there was an event called "high school juniors" at Goshen College that my brother Larry participated in. This was for high school juniors who were interested in considering Goshen College for their college; they could experience a long weekend on campus. My brother came, and his freshman advisor was a friend of mine on the basketball team. Larry was a sound sleeper. One evening, after he went to bed and sleep, Fred, I, and several others went into his room, placed some supports under his bed, and carried him out of his room while he was still on his bed. Yes, he occasionally stirred a bit, but his internal voice told him, "It's okay, Larry. You can go back to sleep," and yes, he did as he was never more than half awake. He was carried out of the dorm, across an open field more than one hundred yards, across the railroad track, through some administrative buildings (including that fine arts building), and out onto a large open lawn that was directly outside the main cafeteria. Yes, a train did go by, and we had to put him down and soothe him until the train passed and continue carrying

him. While on the lawn, still in his bed, covered with a sheet, he continued to sleep, and he was left there unattended. The next morning, we got up to go to breakfast, and there he was, sleeping away. People lined up in the cafeteria, waiting to get their breakfast, looked out on the lawn and saw this mattress with the person sleeping away and wondered who that was. Finally, the brightness of the day made him stir. As a crowd of fifty to seventy-five onlookers watched in amazement, he rubbed his eyes, sat up in bed, looked around, trying to get his bearings and find out where he was, finally realized exactly where he was, jumped up, grabbed his sheet around him to give himself more cover than his brief shorts did, and made a beeline for his dorm without his bed. Long after Larry enrolled in Goshen College and attended for four years, the story continued to stick with him. In fact, as a senior, I was often asked, "Was that really your brother sleeping out on the lawn one night?" Yes, it was.

10. Following up on the last story regarding the cafeteria, it was a unique situation when we would check in to go through the cafeteria line to get our food, and frequently there might be fifty to eighty or even a hundred students who formed a line around the cafeteria. As meal eaters came in, they would have to walk through this long line to get to the end. This was a favorite for the guys, to be able to watch the attractive girls who would come in and go past the gauntlet, with all eyes on them as they moved toward the end of the line, so I suspect it was

a bit intimidating for some of the girls but also some of the guys. One joke we played a couple of times on one guy was as he entered and began walking down between the two lines of onlookers, we got his attention and pointed to his fly, indicating that it was open. A couple of times, he stopped and immediately looked down at his fly while others were watching him. How embarrassing! Later in life—in fact, past the age of seventy-five—I learned the phrase "Check your XYZ," which evidently means "Check your zipper." This goes to show that you're never too old to learn.

11. In my senior year, during spring break, a course in advanced biology was created where fifteen to twenty students accompanied three professors to the state of Florida for additional study in marine biology or in land habitations. I was in the larger class of ten to twelve in marine biology. We traveled by vans from Northern Indiana to Southern Florida. On the way, we spent time playing bridge. Two of our professors in our group played a lot of bridge at lunchtime. A friend of mine played and understood some bridge, and I was a novice and became his partner in challenging the professors. The professors had all kinds of bidding conventions that were totally foreign to me. We got the cards. Much to their dismay, these two upstart students were giving them a shellacking. It did not help when I quipped, 'If you just cut the cards one deeper, you would be getting our cards, not yours." It is truly amazing that I did pass that course, which, in my case, was algae identification

and classification. Memorable experiences on that trip were catching and boiling live lobsters for many meals, one student who became a pain in the behind leading to the phrase "Beware of Stan and the barracuda," and a memorable trip of six students taking the college van to Key West, which was about fifty miles west of Pigeon Key, where we were located. The professors agreed to that unescorted excursion one time and one time only. You see, one of the students, not myself, had a tendency to over-embellish in adult beverages, which he did on that trip, and he pitched his cookies on the return. Evidently, despite an attempt of thorough cleaning, either remnants or at least the odors of the transgression remained strongly present. We will leave that story there. I very much enjoy bridge today and do understand many of the bidding conventions.

12. The remainder of the stories involve my lifelong friend and marriage partner to this day. The first story occurred between my freshman and sophomore years when I was a counselor at Little Eden Camp in Onekama, Michigan.

Boy's & Girls Camp — Little Eden — Onekama, Mich. 1963

As a counselor, I was responsible for nine to ten campers who were housed in my cabin. I was dating a girl named Barb during the latter half of my freshman year. A friend who was also a counselor was dating another gal by the name of Judy on and off but mostly on for much of their freshman year. My roommate, Bill, made arrangements to transport the two gals up to Little Eden for the weekend. What a nice guy and a pleasant event! The two of us couples spent a fun time one evening out on the shores of Lake Michigan. Little did we know that my friend's date would become my lifelong date. After the weekend and my roommate and the two gals returned to Goshen, I was disappointed to see my friend hitting on another gal at the camp hours after their departure.

13. One of the most embarrassing times for Judy after we had started dating steadily was a lecture music event at Goshen College that her parents often attended, and on this particular evening, her parents hosted the father's boss of a large firm from Elkhart, Indiana. Prior to the concert, her parents wanted the boss to be introduced to me. Judy made the introduction and introduced me as Dick Zimmerman, not Dick Stuckey. You see, the guy at Little Eden and the guy whom she dated on and off for some time was also Dick but Dick Zimmerman. How embarrassing for her when she made the quick correction! Still, the damage was done. I think she and her parents wondered if this would damage our relationship, but I was so enamored with her that

forgiveness was an easy price to pay to maintain that relationship.

14. As referenced earlier, our dating increased as the college years went on to the point that I proposed in February of my junior year. We informed our parents of our decision in May of that year and planned a summer wedding following our senior year. The secret was well-kept although suspected by many of our friends until the announcement on October 23, the fall of our senior year. It was her idea to notify our friends by dropping notes in their mailboxes before we skipped town for the weekend. I was the one who paid the price. We went to spend the weekend at Ohio State University with my sophomore roommate and his wife. When we returned, I was harassed repeatedly for pulling such a fast one on my friends. For many a night, I would go and retire to my room, and the guys would come in and say, "Do you think we should take him tonight or wait?" This was repeated a number of times, just building up the anticipation and dread of what was to come. Finally, one night in November, it did happen. Against my will, I was extracted from my bed (handcuffed and legs tied), transported to the trunk of a car, and taken away. I was in my pajamas. The destination turned out to be a cold creek of running water. For those who do not live in Michigan or Indiana, November can be quite cold, well past the swimming season. Two guys on my arms and two guys on my legs started swinging me above the cold creek—one, two, and three, and away I went into the

creek. One guy lost control of one of my legs, so it was not a perfect ten-point landing. After retrieving myself from the creek, shivering, I was returned to the trunk for further transport. En route to my next destination, I heard comments—"Where should we take him?" "Shall we drop him off at the cemetery?" etc. Fortunately, that did not happen, and I was transported back to campus, not to my dorm but to the dorm of my fiancée, where I was deposited outside, the horn honking as they drove away. Can you imagine the sight of a soaking wet guy in his pajamas out there in front of the ladies' dorm? How embarrassing! I eventually made the trek across campus of more than a quarter mile and, en route, once again, picked up the attention of the night watchman, who was in his vehicle. His thought? "Aha! I have caught a molester on our campus." For kicks, I made a few trips around, yes, the fine arts building and a few other maneuvers until I became somewhat winded and made a beeline back for my dorm. A car can travel faster than a human, I soon learned. Even though I had a head start, this car came bearing down on me, intent on running me down. I reached the pillars of my dorm just in time, where no car could penetrate. I hurried up to my room for fear that he would get out of the car and start looking for me in the dorm. I have no evidence that this happened, but I do know that I could stay in the room for only a few minutes until I needed to go down to the bathroom in the hallway to pitch my cookies. All that stress had a negative impact on my body, such as too much alcohol would have. The story also continues to this day among many, including my brother, who I think was a part of the action, but I'll leave that to him to either confirm or deny. It was another risky, life-threatening event.

15. Another early-life close call! Goshen College was a hundred miles from the greater Archbold, Ohio, area, where a number of students' homes were. We often carpooled for trips back and forth during the holiday season. During my senior year, I was driving a carload of students, including Judy, who was going to spend the Christmas holiday with me at my parents' home. It was a cold, wintery, snow-blowing day as we entered the Archbold area. I was taking several kids to their homes in nearby Pettisville when we crossed the railroad tracks in the country. Visibility was near zero, with wind howling and snow blowing. There were no safety arms at the crossings. We had just crossed the tracks barely when we heard the train whiz by us. My heart jumped in my throat and stayed there for what seemed like days; I was thinking we could easily have become another statistic of college kids killed by a train. Another near miss!

16. Time to slow it down a bit and catch my breath. During our senior year, one neat opportunity was spending time at a cabin off-campus known as Brunk's cabin. It was there that groups of students could go and spend some fun time together, including an overnight or two. Judy and I were on such an event in our senior year. We were engaged at the time; I transported her to Brunk's cabin. We had an enjoyable evening, and a couple of us

couples stayed up past bedtime. Oh, how nice! We had to go to our separate dorms for the rest the night or, should I say, morning, but the thought was there that the future held the two of us sleeping in the same bed. The next morning, we left to return to Goshen and, on the way home, stopped at a restaurant to have breakfast together. That was like we were almost married. What an enjoyable prelude to what was to come!

17. I remember during the summer session of my senior year getting up and going golfing with my friend. We may have even slipped on the course before it was open, I don't recall, but what I do recall is following golf in Goshen, I got in the car to go to Elkhart, where Judy was. I was running a bit late, as would be the case many times in the future, and so pressed a little too heavily on the accelerator and was stopped and given a ticket by the cop. It was not my first ticket; nor would it be my last.

18. Life has a lot of ironic twists. You may recall that for one of my best friends, I dialed the number for him to call and make a date with my fiancée before I even began dating her. The girl I was dating later became the girl he dated and married. I recall him stating his reservations toward their relationship and the feeling that he expressed of being trapped like I felt near the end of my courtship with her. I encouraged him to rethink and make his stand now rather than later. I suspected he was too far in the process. As you will learn in a

future chapter, my wife and I ended up going overseas immediately after we were married in 1966. My friend got married in 1967, joined the same organization we did, came to the same country we did, and overlapped a year there. He enjoyed the overseas assignment, and international agriculture became integral in the remainder of his life. She did not enjoy life there, and their marriage ended upon their return to the United States. While I dated her, we both shared an interest in international life, and I can only imagine what would happen if that relationship were pursued.

CHAPTER 6

Laos, 1966-1968

Life is moving on. It is time for some life-changing decisions. The college years are coming to an end. Decisions need to be made. What is next? Let's take a closer look at where we are. Some decisions have been made and some steps taken down the road. A college degree is in the near future; it will be in biology education with a math minor. My future life partner has been chosen. Now instead of one person making the decision, there will be two.

What are our options? We could apply for jobs in the teaching field. My wife-to-be is qualified to teach elementary school and I high school. We could apply and go on to graduate school for me to get a master's degree. We could apply for voluntary service in several areas, both overseas and in the United States. The Vietnam War is raging. The likelihood of my being drafted because of my number is low, and my Mennonite religion is opposed to going to war. Thus, going to war does not seem to be a viable, likely action, but is there another way to serve one's country, do some volunteering, give back for which we have been blessed, and try to make this world a better place to live?

What was set in place was that a wedding would take place in July 1966, when both of our degrees would be completed. From there, it was wide open. As we mulled over our futures together, we were optimistic that it would be a life of fun and hard work, a family, and something that would make our family and friends proud. My wife-to-be was the last one out of her parent's nest and I was the first sibling to leave the nest in my family. Both of these events signaled to our parents that life was indeed moving on.

We both felt that we had the support of family and friends as we moved forward. There may have been single friends or two who were not excited about our upcoming marriage and life together, that being a past love or two on each side.

In many respects, I felt that my wife's friends felt like she had made quite a catch, and certainly from my side of the aisle, my fellow friends felt I had hit the jackpot.

Our approach became "Let's look at what could be appealing and explore those opportunities to see which could become reality and then make the decision." The two directions soon became "go on to graduate school to get a master's degree" or "do voluntary service."

The graduate degree program was in a field of biology—plant pathology, specifically—at Michigan State University. My favorite professor at Goshen College had a connection to Michigan State University's Department of Plant Pathology. He was instrumental in several students going there for further education. With his recommendation and those of several other professors, I applied. I was accepted for the fall of 1966. This was definitely one road that was open for me.

What options were there for voluntary service? There was the Mennonite Road through the Mennonite Central Committee (MCC), with options both domestically and internationally. This was the voluntary road that we felt both sets of parents were supportive of the most. Then while we were seniors at Goshen College, there were recruiters who came to campus to interview interested students for positions in their organization. One such interviewer was a graduate of Goshen College and a volunteer with International Voluntary Services Inc. IVS, as it was known, had much intrigue for us; it was founded in 1953 and was a precursor to the well-known larger Peace Corps, established in 1958. Also on the board of directors was William Snyder, a Mennonite who had direct ties with the MCC. So keeping with our philosophy, we applied for both after having decided that if we went with the MCC, we would prefer an international post.

What does one do when one is accepted at all three? My mathematical mind kicked in and said, "The choice seems to be clear with two roads. One is graduate school, and the other has voluntary service with two options." It was difficult and not a given to get into graduate school, especially at your school of choice. Graduate school at Michigan State would be, at most, a two-to-three-hour car drive from our families. Still, we were young, there was a lot of world to explore, and there would always be time after two years to reunite with family. At least, that was the thinking in considering an international voluntary assignment.

Furthermore, my entire life had been going to school; did I really want to immediately invest two more years in education? We were young and without family at this stage, and what better time to do something different and explore? These thoughts shifted us to the voluntary service side of the equation, but before making a final decision, I asked myself, "Would I be forfeiting my chance to go to graduate school at Michigan State?" One way to find out was to level with the head of the department there. I explained my situation, and I asked if my acceptance could be delayed two years so that I could do some service. The surprising response was yes, they would be willing to wait until the fall of 1968, and yes, I was granted that courtesy with the stipulation that in January 1968, I would write and confirm my intention of entering graduate school in September 1968.

With that roadblock crossed, it was now time to further review the two voluntary organizations we were considering. We applied and were accepted by both. We would begin our work in the fall of 1966, and the next question was could we finish our assignment in 1968 in time to go to graduate school in September of that year? The answer to both was yes; they would make every effort to make that possible and did not see a problem. It was a good break for us in that we would be in education, and the normal school year, like in the United States, would have a summer, at which time we could leave a couple of months early if need be. Everything seemed to be working in our favor, and we continued to have to make choices because those choices were not being made for us.

What were the assignments for the two voluntary organizations? The MCC identified a teaching assignment for both of us in Puerto Rico, an interesting place that we had not visited, and my limited Spanish class at Goshen could well be an asset to continue to learn the language. IVS identified teaching assignments in Laos at the teacher training school for Laotian students wanting to become teachers in their country. Laos was a landlocked country in Southeast Asia. It was next-door to Vietnam, where a war was raging. It was a long way from home, a different culture, and something we had experienced very minimally only through books. It was a tough decision to make; we had made the decision for voluntary service over continuing immediate education, and now we had to make a choice between two voluntary opportunities. If we went to Laos, we could always get closer to Puerto Rico in the future. (Fifty-five years later, neither of us has been to Puerto Rico). If we went to Puerto Rico, we would likely never make it to Laos. That was part of the decision and the intrigue of making the tough decision to accept IVS and travel to Laos.

Completing at Goshen College two short three-week courses to complete my degree, planning a wedding, and preparing for transition to international life meant that we had a full early summer schedule. I tackled the short courses, Judy took charge of most of the wedding plans, and I was the lead in preparing for our international assignment. The courses were completed, the wedding took place, and after a short honeymoon at Door County, Wisconsin, we house-sat a very nice property at the outskirts of Goshen, complete with a swimming pool, and were able to entertain guests for the month that we were there prior to our departure to Washington, D.C., for six weeks of training. Judy's training in D.C. was in the program of teaching English as a foreign language (TOEFL), while I was enrolled in the Berlitz total immersion course of learning Laotian as a foreign language.

My training was much more intense but much shorter in duration. I had ten continuous days, weekends included, of essentially living with a Laotian instructor. No, I did not sleep with the instructor, but all meals and times between meals were spent one-on-one with me trying to learn the language. The program was known as the Berlitz total immersion course, after all. At night, while I was sleeping, my wife was the beneficiary of what she described as gibberish being expounded during my sleep. It was, of course, the Laos language. The good thing for me was my training was over before hers, and I had some extra free time in D.C. to explore while she continued her training. In September, we set sail for the unknown. Both our parents traveled to D.C. to see us off, which would be an exciting two years for us and a long two years for them.

Mr. And Mrs. R. Stuckey In I.V.S. Program In Laos

MR. AND MRS. RICHARD STUCKEY

Mr. and Mrs. Richard Stuckey of Archbold, Ohio have accepted the responsibilities of going to Laos for a two year period under the sponsorship of I.V.S. (International Voluntary Services) which originates out of Washington.

Mr. and Mrs. Stuckey are recent graduates of Goshen College, Goshen, Indiana, and were married July 25. Mrs. Stuckey was the former Judith Ann Stealy of Elkhart, Ind.

Mrs. Stuckey will be teaching English as a foreign language to the students while Mr. Stuckey will be teaching science and math at high school level to Lao students who have finished their course in English. Both are expected to learn the Lao language.

They arrived in Washington, D. C. August 28 and will remain there until Sept. 25 when they will board plane and start for their new destination.

During their stay in Washington, they will begin extensive training in the Lao language and upon arrival in Laos more training will be required.

The pur e of the I.V.S. program i. to help with the needs of people overseas where technical assistance and economic aid programs are not present.

The workers must live and work among the people and live at their levels. They will not be able to enjoy the luxuries of home as they were accustomed to.

The program of I.V.S. is based principally upon four things: 1. Help with the needs of the people concerned. 2. Must have their interest at heart. 3. Aid in discovering

Our first stop was in Tokyo, where I found the beds much too short, our biological clocks were totally off-kilter, and our stomachs said, "We wanted food," but in the middle of the night, where do you go, what is open, etc.? Buying a kimono for Judy and seeing a few sights during the two days spent there were enjoyable, but we were ready to move on to see what lay ahead. The next stop was Hong Kong, a delightful, bustling city, and yes, this was closer to the country of Laos both in distance and culturally. While in Hong Kong, we learned that there was heavy flooding in Laos, in particular where we were to live, and our stay in Hong Kong was extended for several days.

Finally, the powers that be decided we needed to move from Hong Kong and get a bit closer to our final destination, so why not travel to Saigon, Vietnam, where IVS had a headquarters for the country of Vietnam? We stayed at the IVS house in Saigon and were there for three to four days, continuing to wait until the floods receded in Laos.

While there, we slept in male quarters and female quarters and so were separated. We agreed that life in Saigon was much more hectic than we had anticipated—very few cars, many motorbikes, three-wheel *samlo*s, bicycles, and pedestrians.

All forms of transportation had horns that worked well.

We were flown to Pakse, a southern town in Laos, as our next stop. This was not necessarily a secure location. The Vietnam War was also going on in Laos. We learned that venturing ten to fifteen kilometers outside the city, one might encounter the enemy known as the Pathet or communist Lao. The day was spent there

when the decision was made to transport the group of a dozen by truck up to the next large town of Savannakhet. This was a real experience for a farm boy, so one cannot imagine what it must've been like for a city girl. The old rickety bus was open air, had an open upper story, and contained an overcrowded number of people and their belongings, including livestock such as pigs and chickens. People were hanging onto the back of the vehicle for transportation, so one can imagine how crowded conditions were on the bus and the various smells that emanated from that moving vehicle. What a six-to-eight-hour ride!

We were happy to reach Savannakhet and have private hotel housing for a couple of days before being helicoptered to Vientiane, the capital city of Laos and the city next to which we would be residing for the next couple of years.

How exciting! En route to kilometer nine, where our home would be on the campus of Dong Dok, we saw the high water marks on the houses where the flooding had occurred;

the roads were passable because they were elevated, but water was fully up to the sides of the road, covering the previously existing rice paddies and making an appearance of a huge sea.

Our new home for the next two years would be on the campus of the university in faculty housing, which consisted of six four-plex stucco French-style buildings. There was an entranceway with a unit on either side of the entranceway and upstairs on either side of the stairway. Our unit was on the second floor, sparsely furnished. It did have a bedroom, an adjoining shower and bath, a living room, and a kitchen with a small table next to it. There was a screened-in narrow porch room that ran the length of the living room. It was quite adequate and clean for two people. yet sparsely furnished

Daily maid service for cleaning was available.

A common scene we saw each morning from our back window.

Transportation was available by bus on a scheduled basis into town. It became a common need for most of the couples and singles in our group to purchase a motorbike for our own personal transportation. I purchased a Suzuki 125 cc.

Laotian women with sarongs and Western women wearing skirts learned to ride sidesaddle as passengers. Helmets were strongly encouraged and worn.

When would school start? Nobody knew, but soon after arrival, we were summoned for teachers' meetings with our chief of staff, Bernie Wilder. Most of the fifteen teachers were from the United States, although there were some from England as well as Australia.

The university consisted of three sections: the French section, the largest, with nearly a thousand students; the Laos section, with three hundred students; and the English section, with two hundred students.

What an exciting time with new adventures! We made fast friends with three other couples. There were frequent dinners together

as well as travel into town for dinner and to the commissary for the purchase of Western-style canned goods. The commissary was used for items that we missed from home; at least those were available and supplemented with local foods that were purchased. The Chinese restaurants in town became some of our favorite eating places as we had not adjusted to Laotian food at that point.

Vientiane, while the capital of Laos, was a dusty dirt-road town with no stoplights and a few taxis and personal cars on the street. Like in Saigon, *samlo*s and bicycles were the more common forms of transportation. The national monument in construction for over fifty years and the morning market were the two most prominent structures in town. There were numerous Buddhist temples, bicycle repair shops, and clothing and retail shops scattered within the city, which possessed a laid-back international airport on the banks of the Mekong River. Rice paddies, with field houses on stilts, were a common sight as one traveled into town.

Rice and fish were the staple foods for Laotians.

As soon became evident, the next couple of years would be more of a laid-back, "bo pen yang" life than the hustle and bustle of life in the United States.

Back to school. Finally, in late September, school gradually opened and began.

Classes were assigned, students were eager to learn, and teachers yearned for their midday break during the hot days to take a short siesta. An older teacher, Dr. Porter—who lived for a number of years in Laos, was well acquainted with the customs, and had adopted a Laotian son—was a tremendous help to me as he and I made up the math and science department for the English section of the university. We taught third-, fourth-, and fifth-year students at the university.

Judy, on the other hand, taught English to first- and second-grade Laotian students.

The students were being trained to return to their rural communities to become teachers there. Fourth- or fifth-grade students could qualify through the American Field Service (AFS) program to do a year in a U.S. high school, generally at the junior or senior level.

There were extracurricular activities that we were involved in, and my being interested in sports soon led me to become coach of the boys' basketball team and also the girls' basketball team. I also introduced the game of softball, which was quite foreign to them. Volleyball was another sport that was common, as was soccer and *kotor*, a game similar to badminton with a low net but no racket and no hands to be used, only feet and other parts of the body to volley the ball back and forth over the net.

The school year ended the way it began; it just kind of petered out, so no one knew when the actual last day of school would be. This made it difficult for planning, scheduling exams, and other activities that one wanted to complete during that year. Oh, well—"bo pen yang."

We tried as much as possible to integrate into the lives of our students by inviting them to parties at our place, which they truly enjoyed, and in turn, we tried to take in some of their activities, such as Baci ceremonies, which were for marriages, the birth of children, travel, and other special events. The religion was primarily Buddhist, and I found it difficult to comprehend, and very troubling to me was that a Laotian mind could believe in two distinctly opposite thoughts and believe both would be true. This was helpful to them when they could accept spirits and evil events with good events—impossible for most of our Western minds.

The currency was the baht. Our pay, which was similar for either of the voluntary services we considered, was $80 per month and a clothing and travel allowance of $125 per year. How far would that go today? Our travel was expected to be mostly during the summer months, the off-season for school.

Contrary to our first impressions before arriving, there was a war going on in Laos before, during, and after arrival, even though the major news media downplayed much of that news. The United States was actively involved in the war in Laos, and Laos remains the most heavily bombed country in the world to this day.

IVS differed from the Peace Corps in that IVS went into war-torn countries; Peace Corps did not. Laos was a war-torn country before and after the period of 1966–1968. IVS was contracted to the United States Agency for International Development (USAID) for support. There were two divisions within IVS in Laos: the education division and the rural development division. While we were there, there were approximately one hundred volunteers in Laos, of which roughly thirty-five were in the education division and twenty or more of those were at Dong Dok (University of Laos) and the others located in some of the larger cities of Laos. The rural development team was scattered throughout government-controlled parts of Laos, often close to battleground areas.

At that time, the Laos government was operated by a tri-government coalition—in short, the rightists, the leftists, and the centrists. Prince Souvanna Phouma was the ruler and from the centrist party. The right-wing group participated, but the left-wing group representing the Pathet Lao were no longer participating in the government.

Nearly half of the population lived in and around its capital, Vientiane.

While those on the education team most of the time felt relatively secure because of their housing in close proximity to cities, the rural development team was under threat much of the time. In fact, during our stay there and shortly thereafter, there were five volunteers in total who were killed. It was a risky business. Some of the members on the rural development team felt at times like they were underpaid spies for the U.S. government when they were asked to report and send signals when there were opposition trip movements in their area. Again, many had joined IVS because they were in opposition to the war and felt that adhering to this request was a real conflict of interest for them. A few did resign, but that was costly because they had to pay for their own trip home and got no further compensation. There are other books on the subject for the reader who wishes to delve further into this area.

Stories:

1. Within three weeks of the start of school, we were teaching one day when planes flew overhead, and soon thereafter, we saw smoke rising from an area between where we were located and the city of Vientiane and the airport. We were told to continue teaching but definitely not to go into the city or to the airport. A coup was underway. Laos was a landlocked country, thus no navy. It did have a third-rate army and air force. The army headquarters was located three kilometers outside of Vientiane, and the air force was located in the town of Savannakhet, about 250 miles away. The army wanted the air force to move their headquarters to the capital of Vientiane. The air force did not want to do so, so finally, the air force brought their planes and dropped bombs on the army barracks headquarters, hoping to kill the army chief. He was not in the barracks at the time and so escaped injury; that is more than what can be said about his home there. It was just the beginning of some bizarre happenings while we were there. Within a day or two, the spat was settled, and life moved on.

2. One of many close encounters occurred while we were returning from the city on the motorbike. As mentioned earlier, that scene consisted of many lower-lying fields on either side of the raised paved road containing rice paddies. Growing rice was a human labor–intensive process. The rice paddies were relatively small tracks of land that had a one-foot-high border around each paddy. The paddies were flooded with water to soften the soil, and then a water buffalo with a one-share plow was put into the paddy and the soil toiled. Then rice was transplanted from the rice nursery by hand and spaced out where the rice plant could grow, mature, and produce the valuable food for the country. When the water buffalo were not harnessed to a plow and driven by an individual, they had the right of way to wherever they wanted to go. It was not unusual to see a small child riding on top of a water buffalo, so you see, they

were team animals and built like a brick wall. We were traveling back from town, with Judy sitting sidesaddle behind me. We were traveling along at about forty miles per hour with another couple or two. I turned my head back and was visiting with Judy, did not see the water buffalo come up out of the field, and decided it was time to cross the road. Our neighbor, riding with us, had a very loud voice that we often disapproved of back at the compound, but it was he who shouted at us because I turned and looked straight into the side of a water buffalo that was in front of me on the road. The water buffalo was in no hurry to cross the road, and to this day, I am not sure how I missed that massive wall in front of me, but I did, and it was a near escape for both of us, one of more to come.

3. Five educational couples decided to take a field trip up the road a ways to a creek and beach for a picnic outing. It was one of those times of the year that the United States determined it was safe to travel more than two kilometers beyond where we lived, so we took advantage of it. We felt like volunteers on the rural development team as we hit our destination, and the sun beat hard upon us. After a very quick swim, we decided we needed some protection and began constructing our own hut to protect ourselves against the sun. We know just a bit now how the cavemen felt when they provided housing and protection for their families [see photo]. It was an enjoyable day, and the memories remain in my mind to this day as a minimum of four of the ten people are no longer with us.

4. Interaction with the students was very enjoyable, and we became very attached to them. We introduced several new indoor games when they visited our homes, such as "drop the clothespin into the jar", and what they enjoyed as much as anything was the Western-style food that we were able to serve.

5. Likewise, we were expected to take part in some of their ceremonies, such as the Bacis, which were held for special events. Weddings, travel, and births were among those things celebrated. Each had its own unique set of containments; however, they did have much in common by having a large bowl with strings attached to the bowl and streaming out to the people, connecting all together, sitting on the floor, and providing a large radial formation. It was somewhat similar to the laying-on of hands that is done at some churches. In addition to the

connective strings, cloth strings were tied around the wrist of a person, one per person, giving them strength or good luck, and so often after one of these events, we may have eight or ten string bands around our wrists. It was strongly encouraged not to cut them off but to let them rot off over time. This depended on how many showers one would take, and they often were on your wrist for seven to ten days. The wedding ceremony was interesting and will be described a bit here. There were eggs included in the bowl as, I recall, a symbol of good wishes for fertility for the newly married couple. However, the fertility would need to wait for a week or two weeks as after the wedding ceremony, the new bride and the new groom returned to their perspective homes separately to live before they could then live together. That would not be to my liking and I'm sure not to yours as well.

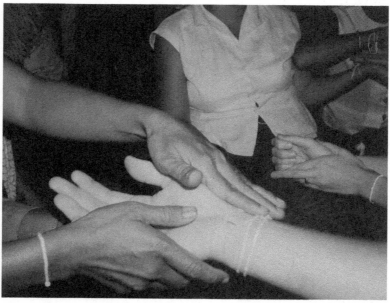

6. Like anytime one has a trip, the first few days seem to go slowly and the last few days rapidly. Thus it was with school. While we were enjoying our time there, looking ahead, two years seemed like a very long time, especially in those times. International phones were not practical, and the mail was slow, taking anywhere from two to three weeks back to the States and mailed through an APO address, yet we communicated that way regularly. More irregular was the encounter with a ham radio operator, who was also the pastor of the international Protestant church that we attended on occasion. Mr. Kleinpeter was proficient with a ham radio. One of our professors back at Goshen College was a ham operator. We got the two together and were able to converse once in a while that way. On several occasions, Judy's parents and even mine, from a hundred miles away, traveled to be able to talk via ham radio. I think they were just excited to hear our voices.

7. I recall going with another couple who introduced us to a higher-end restaurant on the Mekong River for dining one evening. We had an enjoyable meal and, when we finished, was asked if we would like dessert. Hungry for a Western-style dessert, I asked if they had a banana split; they said they did, and I said I would have one. Expecting several scoops of ice cream atop a banana with the typical chocolate, strawberry, and butterscotch toppings, perhaps even a few nuts and whipped cream, you can imagine the surprise I received when the waiter brought back a plate with a banana split longitudinally

on the plate and served it to me. The story was told many times upon our return to the United States, and now you know it too.

8. One of our close friends was a volunteer and, prior to our arrival, married a volunteer who is still volunteering, and he was working with a travel agent, especially for Americans living in the country. Steve helped plan our travel for the 1967 summer and also our return home in the summer of 1968. For the summer of 1967, we decided on a circle tour that included stops in Bangkok, Thailand, Penang, Kuala Lumpur, Singapore, Malaysia, Jakarta and Bali in Indonesia, Manila and Baguio City in the Philippines, Hong Kong, and back home. This trip took a month to take, and it was a wonderful experience to explore many sites. We did spend more than the $125-per-year travel allowance; however, in retrospect, it was very reasonable. For example, our three-to-four-day stay in Penang was in a cute cottage on the beach, complete with our order of three meals a day, each by a French chef, all for the price of $10 per day for the two of us. I contend that type of bargain does not exist today. There are many stories that could be shared on this trip, but I will highlight only a few and will not go into a lot of detail. The rubber trees in Kuala Lumpur and a very modern airport at that time were memorable; the stay at the Raffles Hotel in Singapore, a huge English-style hotel with rooms as large as some homes, and a delicious evening dinner out in the tropical garden immediately come to mind.

The trip to Jakarta was highlighted by a near-sleepless night in a bed infested with bugs and locals trying to rip the watches off our hands as we traveled by taxi. I have had friends who have lived in Jakarta and have had quite different experiences, so it was probably just a coincidence, but the trip to Bali was the most memorable. We arrived at a time when there were no rooms available because of the six-month delay of the cremation of the king and the prince who had recently died. Imagine keeping someone on ice that long! We were stuck at the hotel, where there were no rooms available, when we befriended a lecturer who had spent a year or two in the Netherlands as a foreign exchange university professor (keep this in mind when you come to the Netherlands in 1986–1987). He convinced us to come with him out to the village about fifteen or twenty miles out and stay in a building he had available there. His mother would cook for us, and we would be close to the site where the cremation ceremonies would take place. What a stroke of luck! We did and found that his mother cooked and served chicken with untraditional pieces of the chicken (it seemed the chicken was hammered and served that way), along with ample bananas and peanuts. After several days of this venue, we were ready to return to a more diverse culinary plan. As we had imagined, it was very primitive—not even an outdoor toilet and no indoor shower. The procedure was to squat over a hole to go and ladle water out of the tank onto your body for a shower. We did take a two-to-three-mile walk down to the ocean through a village, where our guide said that the residents likely were observing white people for the first time. Kids would come out into the street after we had passed and just stare at us. It gave us a good feel for how minorities may feel in a largely white community. It was time to move on to the Philippines and watch some of the highline games in Manila and then travel up the mountaintop to Baguio City. There, we were able to stay at the air force base, which was a real deal—a nice cool climate because of the altitude and lodging for $4 per day, including servants who would bring the logs in for your cabin fire each evening. Another couple in our group happened to be vacationing there at the same time. We even enjoyed a round of golf in the hilly terrain and cool climate at the base. Next, we went on to Hong Kong, met a college friend there, had a nice dinner (full course) at a Chinese restaurant, including many delicacies, and then went back to Vientiane. What a refresher and great trip!

9. Being a guest of honor has its privileges and its drawbacks. The soups in Southeast Asia can be quite tasty; just be careful not to ask what is in the soup. On one such occasion, my wife and I were honored guests and served the special soup for our consumption. When I looked into my soup as served, sure enough, one of the delicacies in my soup was a chicken head. It was skimmed, and it was cooked, devoid of feathers, yet contained the succulent chicken eyes and the minimal meat and skin around the bone. I did one of my more famous imitations that evening by taking the chicken

head, sucking on it, and obviously licking my chops at such a wonderful delicacy. Fortunately, I did not find the rat's tail in my soup and did not need to devour that.

10. Here's a frightening and lengthy story, perhaps the scariest story of my lifetime. Another couple was planning to join us on R&R to Bangkok on December 26, 1967. My wife and I were going to go further to the resort area of Northern Thailand known as Cheng Mai. We drove our motorbikes to the airport, complete with luggage, to catch the flight from Vientiane to Bangkok. This was a free U.S.-operated Air America commissary flight that operated about every two weeks and was based on space available. We arrived at the airport and began checking in for approval to fly; the other three passed their test, but I was declined because my health card was not up-to-date on my shots. The shot lacking was hepatitis, and I had received the shot, but they failed to stamp my yellow health card. There was no recourse but for me to go back to the dispensary to get my health card stamped and return and hope I still made it in time for the flight. Brief contingency plans were made if I did not make it back for the flight. Judy would proceed with the other couple, stay in the room overnight at the hotel, and then meet me at the airport the next morning for our seven thirty flight to Cheng Mai. I hustled off to the dispensary; they apologized for their error and stamped my health card, and I returned to the airport, only to learn that the plane had already left. My course of action was to pass the day away until midafternoon, at which

time I would cross the Mekong River in a small transport boat from Vientiane to Nong Khai, the town in neighboring Thailand. There, I would board the all-night train from Nong Khai to Bangkok. It was a hot, humid time of year and prior to the monsoon rains. I got my seat on the train and headed south to Bangkok. The heat was oppressive, the windows remained open, and this train had more stops than Carter has liver pills. There is a saying in Thailand that is very similar in Laos since the languages are similar: "Sa wat dee, pei mei," which translates to "Hello, happy new year." This would be accompanied with a drenching of water from the overpasses of the stops that were made to pick up and discharge passengers. The liquid being dumped on you may have felt refreshing—at least until you questioned where the liquid came from. You see, the rains had not started yet, but that had no impact on the need for water buffalo to urinate. If that wasn't enough excitement for the trip down, there was a train accident ahead of us that caused a delay, and we were running behind schedule. As the sun rose and the train got closer, time was also passing. Judy fulfilled her obligation of getting to the airport and getting checked in but did not board the plane until I was able to do so. Finally, watching my watch closely, I bailed from the train about two kilometers before the airport; it would be the only way I could get to the airport prior to plane departure. Logging my limited luggage, I dashed across the field O. J. Simpson style, got to the highway, hailed a taxi, and went on to the airport. I exited the taxi, ran across the runway, and saw Judy standing there, waiting to board the plane, along with another man. Fortunately, she opted for me, and as the two of us boarded the plane, the other man was heard cursing that I had arrived for my seat because he was on standby and my presence kept him off the flight. I often wondered what his feelings were several hours later when he heard of what happened. What did happen? We had a smooth flight up to Cheng Mai until we attempted landing. It was up in mountainous terrain; there was a low cloud ceiling, and we attempted a landing of the DC-3 flight with thirty-two passengers and three crew members. A descent was made, and then the pilot pulled the plane up as trees were seen below our wings in lieu of the runway. A second attempt was made, and again, it bore the same results, even though we were closer to the trees this time. The third time was the "not so magic" time; we were seat-belted and prepared for the landing—but not the landing we received. A DC-3 plane has a two-seat configuration on either side of the aisle. I was on the aisle, and my wife had the window seat; we were in the third row back on the right side as you face the front of the plane. We knew we were in real trouble when we looked out the windows and saw these trees looming on either side of us, and then as we watched in horror and the pilot tried to veer up and out of the descent, the left wing hit the ground and broke the plane in two. We remained with the front of the plane, the passengers in the seat behind us were in the tail section or between the two parts, and the person beside me on the aisle was hanging upside down from his seat as the split had taken half of his seat fasteners apart from the plane. It was horrific; we looked at each other and were surprised that we were both alive. In shock, we unbuckled our seatbelts and jumped down from the plane, the floorboard being five to six feet above the ground. We walked from the plane through a grassy and wooded area, not knowing where we were going. We saw the tail section of the plane about seventy-five yards away from the front. Additional people exited the plane, and one black woman with two small kids said that her husband was still in the plane. I started to go back to try and assist, but a fire and smoke were ensuing, and my wife said, "No, you can't go back. It may explode." I only made four or five steps back and stopped because the fire had increased tremendously. Sadly, we continued our walk to an opening, and soon, we were met by a pickup truck with an open-back flatbed. The lady and her two kids were ushered inside the cab, and we were invited to sit in the back in the open air. Off we sped; to where, we did not know, but we feared that we would not make it because of the speed and urgency that the driver of the truck possessed. We arrived at the hospital, and there to meet us was a stretcher that they insisted I get on. I declined, saying there were others in far worse trouble than I was who would be coming. They insisted and won their argument. My bleeding face had a lot to do with their decision. With my wife at my side, I was ushered into the hospital, cleaned up, and, within an hour, in the dentist chair to address my missing and partial teeth. They wanted to complete the surgery before extensive swelling occurred. I recall being placed in a room with another dozen passengers. The woman with the two small children was told that her husband was there and had survived the crash, and she desperately wanted to see him, but they would not allow her to do so. Later, we learned that he did not survive the crash; he was knocked unconscious, and with the seatbelt on, he was unable to be extracted and burned in the plane. A little later, one of the passengers entered and was lifted onto the bed, where she had a badly cut leg. Her calf was filleted and cut to the bone, laying open. Soon, a doctor came in and began to tend to her leg. He had only begun, and I distinctly remember and will never forget the look on his face as he examined the leg, and his eyes moved upward to the upper torso and face when he exclaimed, "*Mom!*" and promptly broke down and left the room. I finally was admitted to a room, where I was to spend the next four to five days instead of touring the tourist sites. I recall the kindness of a Methodist minister there who came by every day to see me and spend some time playing chess with me to help pass my time. The swelling on my face and neck persisted, and I drank liquid meals through a straw. After five days, we were permitted to return and given a choice of seats on the plane. We really did not want to fly, but knowing that flying was in our future, especially returning home to the States in another six months, we forced ourselves to do so. They gave us flowers to accompany us. As we arrived back in Vientiane, there were multiple visits back to Bangkok for dental work. It took several weeks for the swelling on the face and the black-and-blue marks to go down as well as on the neck, where I was evidently punched. Judy was one of the most fortunate people in the crash, receiving a hand bruise only. Three people died in the crash, and several had lifelong injuries, including paralysis from the waist down. It was another near-death experience.

11. Rumors abounded back home regarding the plane crash we were in. One of the most dreadful calls Judy's father received could've been handled much better. It was the state department that called and informed her father that his daughter and son-in-law were involved in a plane crash in Thailand and then, after a pause, related that we did not have any life-sustaining injuries and that apart from a few bruises, a full recovery was expected. On my side of the family, my parents later told me that people avoided them on the street because they had heard that we were both killed in the accident, which was one of the rumors. Another rumor was that we were fine but lost a child in the crash. Not true! Rumors are prevalent today, but they were certainly prevalent many years ago as well.

12. Soon, it was time to bid farewell to many people whom we believed we would not see again. Some of our fellow volunteers, we have had various reunions with at intentional meetings in Washington, D.C., and elsewhere. It was the students who were the hardest to

leave. Many of them came out to the airport to wave farewell to us, and we realized that we were losing a valuable connection that would not be reestablished in our lifetime.

There was one exception: a favorite student of Judy's has kept in contact all these years; calls are made on special holidays to wish her well. For many years, he resided in Hawaii, and now he lives in California. Odone is his name. They exchange Christmas greetings each year and call on an average of once to twice a year.

13. In brief, our trip back home consisted of six weeks of travel and many countries visited. The trip out of Laos included stops in Bangkok. We went on to Rangoon, Burma, with a total of six passengers and three crew members on a big jet, which was rather eerie, and then on to Calcutta, India. At that time and to this day, my

memory states that this is the most depressing city I have ever observed. Poverty and begging were everywhere, and particular hurtful was a young child who begged us for money; when we did not give him money, we saw him go back to his parents and get a beating. How sad! We traveled from Calcutta on to Benares, India, where we took in the sights and saw the washing of clothes in the Ganges River,

only to learn on the way to the airport that my camera film had not caught these sights; as I reached five extra pictures, I realized what had happened. Fortunately, the plane to pick us up could not land because of a wet runway, and so we went back to the hotel; the next morning, I was able to get up early again, retrace my routes, and retake the pictures. The next and last stop in India was Agra, the site of the Taj Mahal.

Because of politics, we were not able to fly into Lebanon, as we desired, but to enter Israel, we had to go through Tehran, Iran. We spent the better part of a week in Israel and a day or two in Tel Aviv, but the majority was spent visiting many of the biblical locations. From there, it was on to hot and humid Athens, Greece

,

and on to Oslo, Norway, where I continued to savor the cool temperatures, the great down sheets, and the wonderful meat, potatoes, and gravy that were served there. This occupied about three weeks of our return trip. From Norway, we flew to England to meet Judy's parents on a three-week tour of Europe with Caravan Tours.

14. We went to London, England, Denmark, Amsterdam, and the surrounding sites on to Germany, including Heidelberg and Munich, and then to Salzburg and Vienna, Austria, down to Italy to visit the cities of Venice, Rome, Naples, and Florence, passing the Leaning Tower of Pisa on the way to Monte Carlo. In Monte Carlo, in addition to the beach scenes, I went into the casino, placed a bet, won, and left so I could report that I had beat the system in Monte Carlo. No trip is

complete without visiting Paris, where we saw many additional sights and surrounding areas of the city. My father-in-law had heard a lot about the Moulin Rouge, and he was determined to go there. On an optional night, he secured four tickets, and we went to dinner and a show there. Europe, Paris in particular, was quite different from anything we were used to in the States. The food was good; the show was spectacular, especially for the guys when the dancers wore a few feathers and nothing else above the waist. My father-in-law was surprised, shocked, and a bit embarrassed, and he apologized to me on numerous occasions. We traveled to Belgium, Brussels, Ghent, and Bruges, a lovely city that, unbeknownst to us, we would visit another five to six times in our lives. It was then time to return to the States, greet family and friends, become reacquainted, and accept numerous speaking engagements at churches and other functions regarding our experiences in Laos. We only had a week or two to prepare and move to East Lansing, Michigan, where I began my graduate work in plant pathology. What a two-year experience for two young married people, something we cannot relive! Still, we can recall the memories.

Richard Stuckey

CHAPTER 7

Michigan State University (MSU), Graduate School, 1968–1973

Our return from two years of service in Laos was followed by six weeks of travel to many countries that we had not visited or seen before we entered the United States to begin another chapter in our lives. There were only a couple of weeks to get resettled and relocated to begin hitting the books again. Was I ready for this change? Not necessarily.

Going to Laos, we anticipated a shock to live in such a different culture. We were correct. However, coming back home, we did not expect to be shocked. It felt in two short years that the United States had changed. Oh yes, the hustle and bustle, the sights, and the conveniences were all still there, but the value system, the integrity, and the politicization—the hypocrisy, if you will—seemed different. A closer examination came to the self-realization that U.S. life has not changed; it was our lives that had changed, and we were not prepared for that. So in many respects, the adjustment to returning to the States was larger than that to leaving the States. The value of this realization for ourselves and for others is that when we anticipate becoming shocked or change, that change is easier to accept than when we do not anticipate it but find that it happens.

We got checked into our university married housing unit along with other married couples who had one or more years in school, mostly graduate school. There were several other couples whom we immediately renewed our friendships with from Goshen College who were also attending graduate school at Michigan State, and of course, we met others who became good friends while we were living there. The housing was minimal but doable—one bedroom, one bath, and a small kitchen with a small eating area adjoining a small living room. The living unit was part of a larger two-story building that contained approximately ten units on each floor, and there were multiple buildings to accommodate all those married students. Our unit was on the second floor.

The Department of Botany and Plant Pathology, which I became a student in, was in both the Natural Science and the Agricultural Colleges, one of a few departments that had joint affiliations with two colleges in the university. There were approximately thirty faculty members in the department, roughly half in botany and the other half in plant pathology. There were a few older, senior professors in plant pathology; however, it was a department that was looking to replace them and expand with many new young professors. I soon became one of the active younger graduate students in the department.

I was assigned before arrival, and I agreed to be the first graduate student of a recently hired professor, Dr. Alan Jones, a fruit professor from Cornell University. He was married and had Southern connections in more than one way, being married to a charming gal from South Carolina, complete with a full accent and her speech. I am not sure who was more excited—the professor having his first graduate student or myself, being a first-time graduate student. He was helpful to get me adjusted.

We identified a peach canker disease that was limiting the longevity of peach trees because of fungi, *Leucostoma cincta* and *Leucostoma cytospora*. My master's thesis involved laboratory as well as field research on this particular disease. The lab work was done within the building, of course, but the fieldwork-required field trials were held at the site of the problem, which was close to the Lake Michigan area, where the peaches were grown in the state. The site chosen was in Hart County, a full two-hour-plus drive from East Lansing.

Having a field component to the laboratory research had its advantages. Trips required to the site to do research and, most pleasantly, going during harvest season in August meant that the fruit was ripe, and if you've ever eaten fresh peaches directly from the tree, you know what I'm talking about. Several times, I returned home from the field to a meal fixed by my wife, only to state, "I am not very hungry. I just had five peaches to eat from the field."

During my first year in graduate school, I was involved as a student in the hiring of three new faculty members to join an equal number or more of faculty members appointed within the last two years. This was sufficient to change the composition of the faculty, which was divided largely into two groups: the older established faculty and the new generation. It was easy to bond with the new faculty, they being only three to five years older than the graduate students. Several were also interested in sports as a second vocation, so we enjoyed a number of sports games jointly with and in competition with faculty members.

It was during this time that my goal was to receive a master's degree and then become a high school science teacher with a math minor. The first three or four months of hitting the books were difficult; it seemed I had difficulty retaining what I had read. Perhaps my mind was still elsewhere, either in the United States or abroad, or with the war that was raging in Vietnam and the impact it was having on the U.S. population. The university had become a hotbed for dissent among students in particular objecting to the Vietnam War. I became sympathetic with their cause.

Judy had applied from overseas for a teaching position when we returned and, soon after getting back, had an interview or two. She was hired by the Charlotte school district, a town of twenty-five miles from East Lansing. She accepted and, the first year, commuted to Charlotte, which, during the winter months, became some concern for both of us for her travel safety. She taught second grade. She was well liked, and they wanted her to return; however, a position much closer to home, in Okemos, had an opening in first grade. She applied, was accepted, and took that job, much to the chagrin of fellow teachers and students in Charlotte. She would be on the faculty in Okemos for four years until our next adventure.

After six to eight months of graduate school, I thoroughly enjoyed the environment I was in and made the decision to pursue a PhD while there if given the opportunity. My rationale was that I was back in the academic setting, and if I left to begin teaching in high school, I would likely never return to get my PhD. So while there, why not pursue another several years and get the degree and be all set, so to speak? I also made the decision that it would benefit me to get my PhD with a more experienced senior faculty member. I got along well with my younger mentor; however, there were times when we disagreed, and frequently, the other two committee members on my master's degree program agreed with me as much as or more so than with my professor. This created some sensitive moments.

In the small lab and program that Dr. Jones began with, he did well and began to expand his program. He had a lab technician to assist him with his research and also mine, and then he hired a postdoc from California who fit the description of a radical that some of the folks from California has been assigned. He was fun but clearly way out at times and somewhat undependable, but we do not need to go there.

Master's programs were often completed within a year and a half if there was not a thesis research component. Nearly all students in our department and study had the research component; thus, in two years, I was successful in obtaining my master's degree. During those two years, I had the honor of being named by the department chair as the new graduate student of the year and was awarded a $500 scholarship award. Most students had teaching or research fellowships that created a small stipend and allowed the lower state tuition fees, and in general, graduate school was so much more reasonable than undergraduate costs. It was not enough to live on for the long haul but certainly helped. Having a wife with a job made it so much easier.

Dr. Ellingboe, a respected senior faculty member in the department with an expansive program, agreed to take me on as a PhD student. It was quite a different laboratory setting in that he had three or four other students and several postdocs who worked in this group. He also had research funding that would allow for many expenses to be covered for his students to do the research.

My research was to be primarily lab oriented, and the labs were on site and with growth chambers that were on the north end of campus, closer to downtown East Lansing and also the main campus of the university. I was to research a fungal disease on wheat known as powdery mildew. Host–parasite interactions were those where the pathogen—in this case, the fungus—penetrated the wheat leaves and acquired their nutrition, to the detriment of the wheat plant. In this case, a spore, a propagative unit of the pathogen, would land on the wheat leaf and begin to penetrate the wheat leaves if the host (wheat) did not have resistant genes to prevent the development of the fungus.

The research involved growing wheat seedlings of various genotypes in a growth chamber, harvesting those wheat leaves, placing them in a vial that contained radioactive sulfur or phosphorus, and measuring the success of the uptake of the radioactive solution to the host and then transfer to the fungus. The wheat plants were dusted with spores of the fungus; then a Parafilm solution was applied to the leaves, allowed to dry, and then peeled off and placed in a scintillation container for counting the level of radioactivity that was transferred from the host to the fungus.

This was a time study, and so samples were taken every two hours to obtain a graph that extended to a thirty-hour period. The process only took ten to fifteen minutes for the harvesting but every two hours counting the problem. It ended up that many nights were spent sleeping up at the lab for an hour and a half at a time to collect the data needed. This also allowed an hour and a half to leave the growth chamber lab and migrate to the main campus or go downtown to observe some of the demonstrations that were going on in opposition to the Vietnam War. I was present in the background when the police used teargas to disperse the crowd.

This tended to increase the irate nature of the demonstrators, much of what we see even to this day. The University of Wisconsin was a hotbed for protest, along with Michigan State because of its close affiliation with the federal government and the USAID department, with its involvement in foreign countries.

With my having completed my master's degree and having been accepted for my PhD plus our being married for four years, we decided it was time to start a family—no more waiting until after graduation to get married and no more waiting until completing my PhD to begin a family. After we had made that decision, a mere ten months later, our eldest son, JJ, was born. This created some hardships, but it was well worth the problem. The birth in June was well timed. Very few weeks were necessary to be missed by Judy at the end of the school year, and there were two months before the start of the next year, so very little school was missed on her part. We did find a very nice elderly lady who did babysitting for two to three kids, and Mama Doris almost became a part of our family for the next two years.

Richard Stuckey

School progressed; it was soon time to prepare and take the final oral exam, to be followed by a defense of the thesis. The oral exam was the biggie the students dreaded. There was no exception for me as my major advisor had called on two highly respected and difficult professors to be on my committee, along with the mycologist who was on my master's committee. I do recall the oral exam, generally a three-hour affair of direct questioning by the committee members of the PhD candidate. Although I prepared extensively, I will have to admit the exam was not one of my better days. Fortunately, part of the time, the faculty members on the committee began arguing among themselves. I stood back and let them go at it. Finally, I was asked to leave the room for their deliberation.

It seemed like a long, long time, waiting to be called back in to receive the verdict. When I was called back in, I was

152

congratulated but with reservations. That was the good part. I had passed based on one condition: I would need to do a written part on the subject that the biochemistry professor felt I was a bit weak in and have that written part approved by the committee. This meant another month of work before final approval. To my knowledge, this was an unusual procedure for others who had taken the orals before, but it did become more common after I blazed the trail.

So completing my thesis and looking for new employment became the next order of the day. The international itch reappeared, along with getting a job and settling down. In the process, I was offered two university positions, one in the state of Maine, at the University of Maine. Maine— where is that? In some respects, this seemed like it could almost be an international assignment. The other offer was at Taylor University in Upland, Indiana. This would be close to both of our parents and family and certainly be welcome to our parents.

The other appealing position that was advertised was a tri-university consortium position on a team of scientists assigned to Uruguay in South America for a two-year period. The three universities were Penn State University, Michigan State University, and Texas A&M University. The salaries offered at the two university positions were not great, approximately $10,000 per year. The USAID contract with the three universities would be $13,500 per year. There was another faculty member at Michigan State who applied for that position as well. You will need to go to the next chapter to learn what decision we made.

Stories:

1. A couple of sports stories to start. We attended the University United Methodist Church along with a number of other students at Michigan State. We had a basketball team and a fellow Goshen player at six-foot-one, myself at six-foot-two, for the starting guards of our team. We had a six-foot-eight center, and our forwards were six-foot-four and six-foot-five. In 1968, the starting lineup would be larger than some college teams. We had a competitive city league, and one of our bigger challenges was a team from the Mormon Church that had a six-foot-five starter from Brigham Young and also a six-foot-seven player who took up a lot of space in the center. We won more games than we lost against them, but it was always competitive. We did play in a statewide Methodist Church tournament one year, and we ended up winning that tournament, which included four games played in one day. An added bonus was that my parents and two younger brothers drove up for the day.

2. I recall our intramural university teams, again where we were competitive, and this time, the six-foot-seven Brigham Young player played with us because he was in our department. One basketball game that we did win but with difficulty was against players from the

Michigan State University football team. They were big, they were physical, and they seemed to go in spurts. When they were up, they were difficult to contain, but when they got discouraged, we were able to handle them.

3. Fast-pitch softball was also an intramural sport, and we did quite well there because we had an outstanding pitcher.

4. Individual sports played were golf, tennis, and some very competitive racquetball games, especially at noon. The advantage of being a student or working at the university was that there was some free time where you could manage your own schedule.

5. One of the devious tricks that a fellow student and I played on each other as well as on our major advisor related to the bathroom, which was down the hall from our professor's office and his laboratory. Knowing or seeing the person go into the bathroom and not exit after one to two minutes was a good clue that they were in there sitting down. We would go in, spend a short time at the sink, and then leave and, upon leaving, turn out the lights. That made it quite dark and difficult to finish one's job with any level of security. I suspect the professor had an idea of who it might have been but never did confront any of us. I still wonder if he was chuckling at the joke or fuming when this happened to him.

6. Between my first and second years of graduate school, during the summer, I was contacted to see if I would be willing to be the director of the youth groups at Little Eden Camp. Recall that I went to Little Eden Camp for four years as a youngster and also one year as a counselor. I was delighted to be asked, and upon agreement with my major advisor, I consented. There were three camps, each a week long and back to back, so from start to finish, it was a little over twenty-one days. However, there was a lot of work to line up ten to twelve counselors and some other support staff, such as a naturalist, a lifeguard, an arts-and-crafts person, etc. It took a fair amount of time and coordination to be able to accomplish all this, but I did get 'er done. The camps ran smoothly, and I got high marks from the staff people who were there for the duration—at least until the very last day of the last camp, when I allowed some students to push other students in the natural pool just before they were ready to board buses or get in their cars to return home. This was a mental lapse on my part, but it could've been a bit of payback for when I got thrown in the creek for my engagement (see Chapter 5).

7. As I mentioned in the description of graduate school, the protests were going against the Vietnam War, and I was on the outskirts, observing some of this activity but not directly participating in it. Having been kicked out of high school and deserving of the same fate in undergraduate college, I kept myself quite clean in graduate school. The students did riot downtown, with minor damage

done, marched on the university administration, and actually took over the administration building for a short period, but the university did not close, and the educational process continued.

8. The feature story of this period was the anticipated arrival of our first child. Another couple who graduated with us at Goshen College and were married on the very same day we were were expecting a child on the same day that we were. None of us remember being at the same party nine months earlier. The due date was June 5, 1971. Both ladies became quite large, and they were given the nicknames Waddle and Twaddle, and the race was on to see who would deliver first. Even though Judy was two weeks late, delivering on June 19, she beat her friend by a full two weeks. The other couple were going nuts being that much past due. We had gone to pre-parent classes together and felt we were all prepared, so when the time came, we wanted to be in the delivery room, but I am getting ahead of my story. In mid- to late May, about two weeks before June 5, I was in the laboratory working when I received a call from a lady informing me that my wife had delivered a baby boy. I was in total shock and asked several normal questions: "How did that happen?", "Why didn't she call me?", "Where did she deliver?", etc. The response was that it came on fast, and she called 911; an ambulance came out, got her, and took her to the hospital. In shock, I ran out of the lab, jumped on my motorbike, and made the two-mile trip to our apartment. Sure enough, our car,

a 1969 Dodge Charger, was in the parking lot, so I ran up to our apartment, and no one was there. I grabbed the keys to the car, ran down, jumped in the car, and nearly set a record for the eight-mile trip to the hospital.

I rushed up to the entrance at the front desk and said I was there to see my wife who had just delivered our first child. She asked for the name, I told her, and she responded that Mrs. Stuckey had not checked in. I explained it was an emergency arrival and I was sure she was there because I was called and told that she had delivered. She asked who her doctor was, I told her, and she said, "He has not been here today for delivery." She agreed she would check the recovery room and later came back and said, "No, I think there's been a mistake. Are you sure she didn't go to a different hospital?" About this time, reality began to sink in, and I thought this could be a cruel hoax. Dejectedly, I returned home, went up to the apartment, and entered, and there, I saw my wife, great with child, stepping out of the shower. I had very mixed emotions. I was happy to see that she was safe and yet disappointed that we did not have a new baby. She explained her absence from the apartment and the car still being in the parking lot; she was out in the back with other friends as they had been sunning themselves on a blanket. After thinking about this some more, we thought we knew who might have played this ill-timed joke on us. When we told them the story, they saw how hurt I was, realized the joke had backfired from what was intended, and never confessed to it. To this day, I still suspect the other graduate student who was in the mathematics department was the one responsible for getting a female friend to make that call. In the aftermath, a day or two later, I was still crushed, and I wrote a letter to my unborn child. As anyone knows, the birth of a child is an unmatched experience. This one had a stain mark on it.

9. Life changed after we became parents and had a third person to attend to his needs. It was not just "pick up and go," as it had been before for the nearly five years that we were married. The birth of a child was probably a larger adjustment than getting married. We did a lot of things with the other couple, who had a girl two weeks after our son JJ was born. Rather than get a babysitter, I remember that we often went to get pizza together, put the two kids in their infant seat, and set them on the

table while we had our pizza. Another favorite for us on a Friday evening was to go to our favorite steakhouse and order a steak, medium rare and with Texas toast. What a treat for both Judy and me after a hard week of teaching and graduate school studies!

10. Mama Doris became very attached to JJ during the week when he would go there while Judy was teaching school. We kept in touch for many years after we left East Lansing. What a nice lady, and how great to have a sitter whom you can trust and know loves kids! Another friend, John, came to do graduate work in business administration at Michigan State. He was single, and he loved to come over and see JJ, babysit him if we needed to go out, and in general, Judy thought he was a perfect gentleman. John would vacuum and do any kind of house chores that she wanted done. He set a high mark for me that I never really achieved.

11. The moral of this story is to make sure you ask all the questions that impact your decision upfront or at the beginning. As mentioned previously, in preparation for the birth of our first child, we went through all the preparation classes. We chose a respected doctor for Judy's gynecologist. All went as planned after the hoax incident, and Judy was admitted to Sparrow Hospital in Lansing for the delivery. After Judy was admitted and we visited the doctor, we learned that he would not allow me in the birthing room as we had planned. I wanted to be there to share in the pain, excitement, and

celebration. The doctor said he did not want two people to take care of in the birthing room, his theory being I would not be able to handle the birth scene without becoming a problem myself. My argument that I was a farm boy and had seen many animal births did not hold water with him. Thus, a future father stayed in the waiting room until notified. For first-time fathers, there is a level of excitement that cannot compare with going in and seeing your tired but relieved spouse and the product the two of you have produced for the first time.

12. Here is another closely related story at the hospital stay following the birth. In those days, one stayed for much longer periods in the hospital. Unbeknownst to me, my role would become one of comforter and sympathizer to Judy. Another surprise that her doctor ordered was for her to put a heat lamp on her bottom, with no sitz baths. As I am told, the time after giving birth is an emotional time without having additional applications added. There is no question that Judy, after three to four days of this punishment, was no longer a friend of her gynecologist. Adding insult and the final straw was when she complained, his response was, as he shook Judy's chin, "Listen, little girl. I have delivered many babies, and this is your first"—not the right thing to say to a distressed, emotional lady. The happy ending is that we finally did get home, and Judy enjoyed her sitz baths and was able to heal.

13. We prepared to leave Michigan State and begin our next adventure, and the assignment to be a plant pathology advisor to the Uruguayan Ministry of Agriculture for two years is a subject of the next chapter. Prior to going to Uruguay, we had another six-week-plus stint in Washington, D.C., where I was enrolled in the Foreign Service Institute for Spanish language training. We welcomed getting back to D.C. after having been there five years prior in preparation to go to Laos. This was a nice interim between graduate school and finals and the start of a new job. The language training was not Berlitz total immersion, so it was much more tolerable. It was a time to become more familiar with Washington, D.C., and some of the many fine restaurants that it had to offer. Soon, we were off to Montevideo, Uruguay, to meet the other four to five members of our team who represented various disciplines. Upon the completion of the two-year term, I was offered up to one year of employment at Michigan State University until I located another position.

CHAPTER 8

The Uruguay Years, 1973-1975

Finally, it was time to leave Washington, D.C., and all the training experienced and head to our new destination in Montevideo, Uruguay.

Serves Agriculture In Uruguay

Mr. and Mrs. Richard E. Stuckey and son, Jeffrey, left Oct. 24 for a two-year overseas assignment in Uruguay, South America.

Richard, son of Mr. and Mrs. Chauncey Stuckey, his wife, Judy, and their 28-month-old son, Jeffrey, returned Oct. 12 from Washington, D.C., where Mr. Stuckey was studying Spanish for eight weeks.

As an assistant professor of Michigan State University, Mr. Stuckey will work with the Uruguayan Ministry of Agriculture.

The project in Uruguay is directed by a team of professors from the Universities of Michigan State, Penn State, Texas A&M, and is designed to help Uruguay export agricultural crops.

One of Mr. Stuckey's responsibilities on the team of scientists is to "advise" the Uruguayan Ministry of Agriculture with problems concerning fruit and vegetable diseases. He will also select students to continue their study of agriculture in other countries, including the U. S. Students after studying in a foreign country, will return to Uruguay to work for the Ministry of Agriculture in areas relating to agricultural problems.

Mr. Stuckey received his Ph. D. in plant pathology in August of 1973 at Michigan State University, East Lansing.

The Stuckey's address will be: USAID-Montevideo, American Embassy, APO New York 09879

Mr. Richard Stuckey and family are in Uruguay where Mr. Stuckey is helping in agricultural exports.

Once again, we had a slightly deviated route for international travel than we had planned. The first stop was to Anchorage, Alaska, and then on to Bogotá, Bolivia, from there to Asuncion, Paraguay, on to an unscheduled stop in Buenos Aires, Argentina, and finally to Montevideo. The

Bogota stop was airport only, but at a twelve-thousand-plus-foot altitude, it was an adjustment for the four to five hours we spent there. Because of the altitude and less oxygen, we both developed headaches and were eager to leave for Asunción.

The unscheduled stop was to Buenos Aires for three to four days. Why? We knew there was some unrest in Uruguay with the insurrectionists, the Tupamaros, but we were the recipients of the crackdown that occurred where hundreds and thousands of protesters, many with the universities, were rounded up and jailed, and the universities were closed by the military government. It was deemed that our small family with a two-year-old child should stay a few days in Buenos Aires until things settled down just a bit. Fortunately, we had friends from the Michigan State graduate school who were working in Argentina, and we enjoyed spending time with them. Also of note, which we were not aware of at the time, was that many of the American businesses that were operating in Uruguay had moved their families to Argentina for safety reasons, and the businessman merely commuted during the week into Uruguay.

Initial impressions were that it was a world apart from Laos. Uruguay did not seem so foreign; I could actually understand much of the language, and their way of living was not diametrically opposed to what we were used to in the States. There were houses and jobs for the people living there. There were cars on the streets, although many older cars were from the 1920s, what we would consider old classics. There were stoplights and intersections. There were multistory buildings. They had real food and did a lot of barbecuing. Their eating schedule was a bit off, but we generally got used to it, the dinner hour not beginning until eight thirty or nine in the evening. Mid- to late afternoon was a time for coffee or tea and rolls or what we would call a very light meal.

This time, I was working much closer with USAID than when we were in Laos. Both assignments were contracted to USAID for support, but the support for this assignment was nearly unlimited. We were provided housing, allowed to ship a car to the country for our own use, provided a work vehicle, and were on a decent salary. All these things made life more comfortable. The house secured was rather dark, on the first floor of a three-story home, with the gate in front for security, and it extended quite a distance to the back, which contained an open backyard.

We were given the opportunity to hire a maid at our own expense, but for $50 per month, it was quite a bargain. There was a live-in quarter in the house for the maid, and her duties were to live with us, clean, take care of our child, and cook when requested. All these things lead to gradually spoiling a wife. After two years of this, it would be a rude awakening returning to the States, where many of these services were not provided nor affordable, but as they say, "Enjoy the moment."

It was exciting to meet the other team members on our team. The chief of the party was an older horticulturalist, Dr. Chet Hitz from Penn State. Dr. Ron Morse was a young horticulturist, also from Penn State. I was a plant pathologist from Michigan State and also young at the time. Dr. Oscar Tobada was from Spain, married to a proper English lady. Oscar was an older communication specialist from Michigan State. The fifth member was an economist from Texas A&M University who worked in the animal rather than plant sector like the rest of us did. Dr. Jim McGrann had prior experience working in Argentina, knew the language well, and was married to a lovely lady from Yugoslavia. So that was my family of team members for the next two years. I got along well with all them with the exception of Dr. Hitz on occasion. All other members of the team had their moments with Dr. Hitz as well. Thus, I concluded it was more his fault than my fault.

Our team had a senior USAID man, Dr. Stevens, assigned to us among his other duties, and it was Dr. Hitz, the leader of our group, who was in direct contact with him, but over time, a direct relationship developed between several of the other team members, myself, and the agro-economist, Dr. McGrann and Dr. Stevens. We all came to the conclusion that Dr. Hitz was a good pomologist in his day who was being sent to Uruguay to put him out to pasture.

We all had offices in the U.S. Embassy, a fortress-like building, and also at a very meager office building at the outskirts of town in the area of Sayago.

The office had several rooms, and I shared a room with a short-term entomologist from Michigan State, Dr. Howitt, who was there for three months, a couple of times, while I was there. We were promised a new facility and a modern experiment station twenty-five miles out of town, known as Las Brujas, "The Witches." This was finally completed about six months after my arrival and had much nicer office space as well as a laboratory and lots of ground for field experiments. The disadvantage was that the commute was much longer each day. The advantage was the rural scenes along the way and famed Uruguayan gauchos.

We were expected to spend four to four and a half days a week at the experiment station and a half day or so at the embassy doing U.S.-related business. In addition to our team of scientists, we also made friends with a number of the embassy personnel and their families who were there.

I was assigned to counterparts Carlos Moscardi and Stella Garcia. They worked with me and reported to the chief of the plant protection unit, entomologist Dr. Carbonel, who reported to the experiment station director, Dr. Curotto, who ran the operation with a tight fist. There was a gasoline shortage, so each month, we got vales for the purchase of gas, and we had to be very careful in our management to get our work done. This often meant carpooling from the city out to the experiment station so that more gas would be available for field experiments off-campus.

Stella was the more trained and senior of my two counterparts. Carlos was younger, more energetic, and his behavior more like a bull in a China shop. Carlos did get things done and became a valuable member of the team. I had very good relationships with my two counterparts, Dr. Carbonel, and Dr. Curotto for much of my tenure. Both were much more appreciative of my efforts than they were of Dr. Hitz, whom they tolerated out of necessity.

My relationship did sour a bit when the entomologist and I both challenged the poor rating given to Carlos. Our thinking? It is what bosses do to support their people who are valuable to their program. Evidently, his Uruguay bosses did not see it the same way, saw it as outside interference, and did not take kindly to our involvement and pushing for more monetary support for one of their employees. Looking back, I can understand their resentment. All in all, we got along well, and I became good friends with Dr. Carbonel, especially when I would participate in their morning ritual of drinking hot *mate*.

My particular assignment in Uruguay was to improve the quality of fruits and vegetables so that they would be exportable. The major crops that I worked on were apples, peaches, potatoes, grapes, and onions, in that order. Alarm systems were developed for the first three crops mentioned. By "alarm systems," I mean the attempt was to reduce the number of fungicide sprays to the crop to the critical periods of when the weather and host indicated that an infection could occur. This practice could reduce by over half the number of sprays applied and yet produce equal- or better-quality fruit. Trials were done on grower farms and results communicated in publications that were disseminated to other growers. Meetings were held directly with the growers to explain the program. For the most part, the information was received enthusiastically.

Uruguay is a small country that was once the pride of South America for its education and development. It was known as the "Switzerland" of South America. There were nice beaches and resorts, a good agrarian industry, and a favorable climate for production and for tourism. In addition to the excellent climate for the production of fruits and vegetables, the northern part of the country was well suited for citrus growing. Parks abounded in the city, and people loved to be on holiday and visit the parks. Summers were excellent times to take holidays.

Stories:

1. As I was a lover of food, it did not take long for me to take to the Uruguayan culinary. They had great-sized servings of beef; one in particular was known as the entrecôte. It was a huge T-bone steak. When I mean "huge," it was not unusual to be served a thirty-ounce T-bone, and they had great French fries to go with them. Their pastries were good, as were their desserts; especially, the flan remains a favorite. The flan is custard served with a somewhat rich topping that one could say resembled caramel sauce. Uruguay followed much of their European descent by treating eating as an event

to be enjoyed and with no hurry. Fast food had not caught on yet as it was raging in the United States. A late breakfast, relatively substantial lunch, midafternoon tea, and pastries and sandwiches were often enjoyed. A typical dinner consisted of cantaloupe and ham followed by a soup and then the entrée, coupled with many sides and a salad, finally followed by the flan dessert. I remember being invited over for dinner to be served chicken and wondered, "Why not the famous steaks for which Uruguay is noted?" It was brought to my attention that chicken was the delicacy in Uruguay, not steak. This was quite a difference from my growing-up years in the United States. Let it be said that going hungry was not a worry for me for the next couple of years.

2. Transportation in the capital city of Uruguay, Montevideo, was largely by bus, taxi, horse, or bicycle.

A few had their own cars. The bus was a cheap form of transportation but not the fastest as one would have to wait for the bus and know what route the bus would be taking to make sure they got to the right place. One interesting aspect of riding on the bus, which we did on several occasions, was that the passenger would hiss at the driver when he wanted the driver to stop. For example, the bus driver had a route with very few scheduled stops, and if you wanted to get off between stops, you would make a hissing sound between your teeth. At first, I thought this was very rude—but not deemed so in Uruguay. In fact, if you were at the restaurant and wanted the waiter's attention to get something, you hissed at the waiter. Actions have different meanings in different countries.

3. The U.S. Embassy in Montevideo was a fortress, a huge three-to-four-story structure consisting of tons of concrete that stood out either as an eyesore or as a well-built, fortified structure seen when traveling along the beach highway.

While much of our social functions were with our team and their families, we did become friends with other Americans in the country, most working for the U.S. government. For example, there were the marines, who had a house where I would join them on occasion to play poker in the evening. There were the workers in the "communications" department of the embassy who also played poker at the marines house and whom I became friends with as well. The communications department is another term for the spy department. One thing that several of the communications department personnel and I had in common was that we purchased a motorcycle, a very nice CB360 that was fun to use to travel in the country and other places. The ambassador to Uruguay was a motorcycle fan and also had one.

4. One of the perks of working with the government is a shipment of vehicles at no cost to the site. Our new 1973 Ford Pinto station wagon was sent by ship to our destination for our use while in Uruguay. The Pinto cost us around $4,000, not that many miles were put on our car while we were there, used mostly for driving around town and, once in a while, to Punta del Este, a resort city eighty miles to the east of Montevideo. Gas prices were extremely high, a little over $3 a gallon, compared to the approximately $1 per gallon stateside in those days. The new white Pinto station wagon did stand out a bit, but there was an influx of cars from other countries for diplomats who lived in Uruguay. Like the elevated gas prices in Uruguay, car values were also greatly elevated. At the end of our tour, we were allowed to sell our cars but were instructed to donate any profits received to a charity. We sold our car upon leaving for $11,500. Imagine a used two-year-old car receiving three times

the new price of the car. The new owner paid $2,000 of the $11,500 to the government, and I received a check for $9,500. When I subtracted the $4,000 cost, I had $5,500 to donate to charity, which I did. I am not sure how many others did the same since the policy did not seem to be enforced.

5. It was about five to six months after arrival that I broke down and bought the CB360 motorcycle. It was a nice machine and far better than the 125 cc Suzuki I had in Laos and also the similar Kawasaki motorbike I owned and operated while in graduate school at Michigan State. Besides, a number of my embassy friends as well as the ambassador had motorbikes. A couple of neat trips stand out. One was the long weekend trip by six of us with bikes that we made up to the northern city of Salto, the citrus-growing region of Uruguay. This was a guys' weekend up there, and we had a good time partying and playing cards. On the way home, we came by the town of Colonia, our sister experiment station, which dealt with the animal sector rather than the plants like Las Brujas was noted for. I do recall making the trip back from Salto and riding through driving rain, which is something one on a motorbike does not like to do. We did stop at a hotel for a while and asked to come in, dry off, and rest a bit while on our journey. They were accommodating, and to this day, I have to think whether I would welcome six-drenched cyclists coming into my lobby and messing it up.

6. Another motorbike trip that I recall was traveling with the ambassador, Siracusa, to Punta del Este. His favorite drink was the Bloody Mary; of course, he had a security detail that traveled with him wherever he went. So as we traveled to Punta del Este, a black official sedan followed us. It did feel important traveling this way, although the privacy was lacking. I do know that the car was large enough to house more than sufficient Bloody Marys. A couple of stops on the way provided a refreshing drink of a Bloody Mary. I also recall several parties at the ambassador's residence, which was a far cry from the housing that we lived in. Of course, the Bloody Marys were very prevalent there as well. One motorbike trip I did not go on and would've loved to do was a two-week trip into Southern Brazil that was made by twelve to fourteen Americans who owned motorbikes, including the ambassador. Southern Brazil is where a lot of the fruits and vegetables are grown in the country, and I could've weakly justified the trip for that purpose, but taking two weeks and "not doing my job that I was sent to Uruguay to do" seemed like a poor decision to make. My Uruguayan counterparts would not have been impressed by my rationale.

7. I was given and encouraged to do a lot of travel to other research stations in other countries. For example, I went to Lima, Peru, to visit the International Potato Center and consult with them. You see, we had a potato effort in Uruguay where there was a serious virus problem and a bacterial problem. Solving the bacterial problem

was easier than the viral problem. There were soils that contained the bacteria, and so eliminating potato production in those land areas and quarantining the other land areas made control of this disease, known as ring rot, doable. Insects, on the other hand, vectored the virus, and there was a cultural practice that hurt the control problem significantly. Potato growers traditionally would select the smaller tubers to replant their potatoes. One of the effects of virus-infected plants is to produce smaller potatoes, so this practice became a continuation of the problem. The smaller potatoes were safe enough to eat, and thus, a communication effort was made to educate growers to take their larger potatoes, cut them up into several pieces to use as replants for potatoes, and consume the smaller potatoes. I think of this even today as I see the small red potatoes that are very tasty when cooked with green beans, onions, mushrooms, and cut-up bacon or sausage. My kids and I referred to this as the "five-cent meal." You will need to go to the next chapter to find out what that is about. Another trip besides going to the International Potato Center in Lima, Peru, was to visit the experiment stations in Argentina and Chile. The Argentinians had a network of many agriculture experiment stations around the country, each noted for the specific reason of producing and protecting those crops in that region. With Stella Garcia as my counterpart, the two of us traveled to five Argentinian experiment stations. The most remembered was the Mendoza site, where viticulture, wine production, was most noted. From there, it was on to Santiago, Chile, where we visited their fruit production station and the university. One of the saddest things learned on these trips is that the workers were paid very, very little and were forced to take additional jobs outside of their work to make ends meet. I believe their salaries equivocated to about $125 a month, if I recall correctly. That compares to my salary of over $1,000 per month.

8. While values and customs in Uruguay were more similar to the United States than what I had experienced in Laos, there was one mind-shattering practice that took quite a while for me to get my arms around. You see, growing up, I was taught conservatism, saving money that you could use for a rainy day rather than spending. Carlos and Stella would go to the bank to cash their check on the day that they received it and spend or commit that money immediately. For example, they would purchase a refrigerator with 10 percent down on the equipment, with an additional 10 percent paid each of the next ten years. After visiting with them and studying the situation, I was convinced that a different mindset needed to be used in Uruguay. You see, the two years that I spent in Uruguay, the inflation rate one year was 108%, and the second year, it was 76%. This creates a whole different, dynamic use of the funds that you have. As they would explain to me, with that kind of inflation the last few years of extended payment, one would be paying an effective rate of pennies on that purchase. On the other hand, if they saved their

paycheck for several years, it would buy very little. Their argument made a lot of sense. Another example is to not be judgmental until you have all the facts.

9. Back on the home front, Judy was enjoying her time with her friends and with their collective kids by going to parks and getting together for play dates. It was a great time where she could be with her son and also have free time while our maid looked after our son. What I am not sure that we knew when we had left the States was that there would be a sibling

for our two-year-old son who would be born in Uruguay. As I would later say, our younger son was born in Uruguay but made in the United States. Dr. Stanham was a British gynecologist who was Judy's doctor and quite a far cry from the one she had in Lansing, Michigan. I was able to be in the delivery room when that time came to see our second son, Jon, born. While JJ was two weeks late, the birthing process took place somewhat rapidly when he just decided to leave his protective environment. Jon, on the other hand, was showing some of his stubbornness at a very early age, and when the due date came and Judy was admitted to the hospital, a prolonged delivery procedure ensued. Finally, getting well into the evening and insufficient process being made, Dr. Stanham decided to begin the induction system, which he did. Jon had no choice, and the birth proceeded. In the nursery with other Uruguayan-born babies, he became known as El Rubio, "the blonde one." It certainly made it easy to pick him out and to make sure no unintended exchanges were made. The new arrival on March 29, 1974, created additional work for Negrita, but she did not complain. She fell in love with both of our boys.

It was very convenient for us to have her get up during the night to change his diaper. Likewise, when he needed milk, there was not a whole lot I could do, so I lucked out in both cases.

10. The trip of all trips occurred without my participation. You see, the two sets of grandparents desperately wanted to see their grandson, whom they hadn't seen for a year, and also the newly born grandson, whom they had not seen. They agreed to pay for a trip back to the States for Judy and the two boys. This was done during the summer of 1974, a mere three months after

Jon was born. Judy and the two boys headed back to the States for a month of visitation between the two sets of grandparents. I stayed in Uruguay and continued work with my job. Upon their return, I flew to Rio de Janeiro to meet them, where we spent several days in Rio, and then the four of us traveled to Iguazu Falls, the most amazing falls I have seen. We had several days staying at the "Pink Hotel," Das Cataratas. (Ironically, this is the same hotel where we stayed in 2020.) Finally, it was back to Uruguay to complete the final year of my contract.

11. Going-away parties and utilizing my month reports to produce a final report, along with recommendations for the future, were a part of the closure activities prior to leaving for the United States once again. Some of this time was also used to search the employment market to see what jobs might be available. I was comforted by the fact that I had a year of employment at Michigan State while looking for a more permanent job. Several feelers went out, but in the interim, I was going to be assigned coordinator of the field scouts in a large integrated pest management program conducted by Michigan State across the state of Michigan. This assignment would be working with a team of scientists, multidisciplinary, and leading the effort in collecting reliable information from the field for making decisions on treatment for productive agriculture. The program would be administered through the entomology department at Michigan State

University, although I would be a member of the plant pathology department.

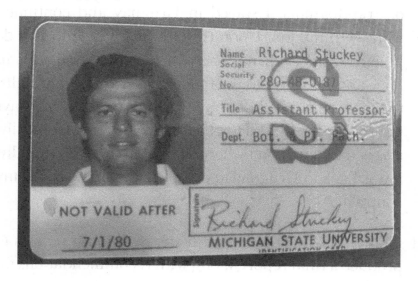

It sounded like an exciting program and one that I would be well suited for. It was and provided me the opportunity to continue my job search. Coming back to Michigan State, I had a salary based on a 10 percent raise my second year in Uruguay that exceeded other starting faculty members and closely approached those who had received tenure at the associate professor level. While I got along with other faculty members, I wondered if there was ever a resentment for the salary I was receiving but did not feel that resentment if it existed.

CHAPTER 9

The Road to Lexington, 1975–1989

[This is with the exception of one year, 1986–1987, which is presented in chapter 10.]

I arrived back at Michigan State University in time to go and attend the American Phytopathological Society (APS) annual meetings and continue my in-person job search. At this time, I was looking mostly for a university position. There were two positions that had particular interest. One was at the University of Wisconsin in Madison, and the other was at Penn State University. It was with some interest that I came to know the third position, advertised as a university extension person at the University of Kentucky in Lexington.

While at the annual meeting, I interviewed a couple of faculty members from Wisconsin and learned I was one of four or five students they were interviewing for an on-campus interview. I did not get the opportunity to interview on campus with the full faculty. Though that door seemed to close, I did speak with the chairman of the Department of Plant Pathology at the University of Kentucky, and he encouraged me to submit my application, which I did. The Penn State position, I had already submitted an application for. For some reason, Penn State seemed to be dragging their feet and not moving forward very rapidly with interviewing and hiring.

I was invited to interview at the University of Kentucky. My reservations were severalfold. The position was for an extension plant pathologist, and I was more interested at that time in research than extension work. I was counseled that I could do as much research as I wanted, and it would be looked upon favorably with an extension appointment. That appealed to me, kind of like extra credit, where you are not expected to do something, but if you do, that will be beneficial. A second reservation was that there was one faculty member in particular and perhaps a couple who had an ongoing feud with a faculty member at Michigan

State, and up to that point, I had heard only the side of the Michigan state professor; he was actually a member on my PhD committee. A third concern was that I had not heard as much about the plant pathology department at the University of Kentucky and held them at a slightly lower level than the departments in Wisconsin and Pennsylvania.

I had a very successful interview at the University of Kentucky and was offered a position there. Continuing correspondence went well while I took the two-week period to consider whether to accept the offer. In fact, even though I told the department chairman I was leaning their way, he told me that the dean of the college had told him, if I did receive a better offer financially, to let him know because he wanted the opportunity to counter. This played well into my mind because it assured me that they really wanted me to come there.

During this period, a visitor from Penn State came to the Michigan State campus and visited me, and when I told him I had an offer and I was leaning toward accepting it, he was shocked. He said even though the position at Penn State seemed to be moving slowly, he was very certain that they were counting on me being a prime candidate. He went further to say that if I was not a candidate, they may cancel or re-advertise the position. This told me that I had the inside track for that job, but that job was still out in the bush when I had an interesting job offer in hand.

It was in the last week prior to my accepting the position that the waters got muddied. A respected professional plant pathologist at DuPont contacted me and encouraged me to come to a hastily arranged interview with their company in Wilmington, Delaware. Taking the philosophy of "What do I have to lose?", I accepted the interview and flew out the next day for an interview. The interview went very well, and of particular interest was that the research job was offered on the main campus at Wilmington. I met with the higher-ups, including the international marketing manager, who appeared to be about five to ten years from retirement and, noting my international experience, offered that his job might be one that I could be interested in the future should I come with the company. That afternoon, before leaving, I was offered a position with DuPont. Interestingly, my offer at Kentucky was for $18,500 starting, and this offer was for $18,600. Sometimes progress moves painfully slow; other times, it can happen overnight.

So another road was open and created a difficult decision that would have major bearing on the rest of my life. Lexington was a more desirable place to raise a family. A university appointment could lead to an industry job offer later more easily than vice versa. Promotions and an unlimited budget would be more likely within the industry, but the job security would be less. There could be more travel and international travel with the industry position offered in the future.

While considering these pros and cons, I did get back to the department chairman at the University of Kentucky and told him that he wanted me to contact him if I received a better job offer, and so I was doing that. I also told him that I was leaning their way but was just following his instructions. Within a few hours, he came back to me and said that the dean of the college had increased his offer to $19,000. I thanked him and told him I would let them know in a couple of days. I think the business moral of the story is work fairly with those you are in negotiations with, be honest, and do not push the envelope too far.

DuPont came back and wondered if I would not be coming their way and sure hoped that I would be. Ironically, it was one of their employees, who was a fellow graduate student of mine at Michigan State, who helped make my decision not to accept the DuPont offer. He cautioned me that he was mostly happy there, but one of the things that were different from university life was that at five o'clock, they locked up, and you left, and it did not matter if you were in the middle of your research work. This was contrary to our university study, where the end of the day was very arbitrary and may go into the evening or could end at 4:30 p.m. It also signaled to me that I wanted to work hard and did not want to be constrained with office-like hours.

Thus, I accepted the offer at Kentucky, and we were on our way to Lexington for house hunting and making arrangements to begin a long tenure there. The official start date would be December 1, 1975, although I would not be expected to be at work until January. This was offered as a way to help cover some moving expenses. Our parents were generally pleased with this decision, meaning that we would be closer to home, only a five-to-six-hour car ride away, making weekend visits reality.

When uncertainty exists, time can move slowly, but looking back, from our arrival back at Michigan State around July 1 to getting started and well-grounded in my temporary job there, doing a job, and accepting a new appointment before the end of October meant that a lot of grass did not grow under my feet.

Traveling to Kentucky with Judy's parents over the Thanksgiving weekend in the search for housing, we found one we liked. We were thinking of purchasing a house in the $35,000 range, but for this one, we had to move to $50,000 to purchase it. It was on a quiet cul-de-sac street, backed up to an elementary school, in a good neighborhood, and about three miles from the university campus. We were able to close prior to our move to Lexington so that we could move directly into the house. Many memories would be created there over the next five years until we moved into a larger house in a different neighborhood.

Work proceeded as advertised and was very satisfactory. I had good rapport with fellow faculty members in the department and also made good professional and friendly relationships with faculty members in other departments. I loved working across departmental lines. An esteemed faculty member who had been promoted to become department chair of the Department of Horticulture held the job I inherited. So he was across and down the hall, and I took advantage of conferring with him on several occasions during the first three to four months.

The University of Kentucky had a main campus at Lexington and two major experiment stations in the state. One, Quicksand, was in the eastern Appalachian area with a fruit, vegetable, and lumber focus on small hilly plots of land. The other, Princeton, was in the western part of the state and focused on agronomic crops, along with some of the fruit that was grown in that part of the state. The agronomic crops were corn, soybean, and small grains of wheat and barley. These were the crops under my purview and a reason that so many trips were made to that part of the state. For the first several years, the smattering of fifteen to twenty faculty members located there did not have a plant pathologist. This changed four years after my arrival, when we hired a plant pathologist and opened a diagnostic lab for the western part of the state as well as the one that we had in Lexington. My colleague John Hartman and I were in charge of the diagnostic lab in Lexington, where we received close to four thousand plant specimens per year for diagnosis and control recommendations. We hired a lab diagnostician to help run the lab, and with time, most samples were diagnosed by the diagnostician.

Making new friends and searching out several acquaintances who were living in Lexington were enjoyable times. Judy and a Goshen College friend several years our junior began searching for churches to attend. They had a visit by the pastor, Reverend Blondell from the Disciples of Christ Christian Church, and they were very impressed to learn about this church, Crestwood Christian Church. We began attending there, made many new friends, and became involved in a group known as the "lost and found" group, a Sunday school group, and the WHO group, which was a social group of friends. The WHO group was named to represent "Wives, Husbands, and Others"! To this day, we remain close to our friends at Crestwood Christian Church.

We transferred our membership from the United University Methodist Church in East Lansing to Reverend Blondell's Disciples of Christ Christian Church. It was a large church that had around one thousand members. The "lost and found" group consisted of around fifteen couples, mostly with young kids, which made it a fun and valuable group. While most of us were in a Sunday school group such that we met every week on Sunday, there was also the group social function at least once a month and the frequent get-together during the week with a smaller subset. The smaller subset consisted of four to five couples whom we became very close to, and we did a lot of things together. You will learn some of them in the stories section of this chapter. Judy sang in the choir and was a member of a talented women's trio that did special numbers frequently at church, along with a few solos that she would do now and then.

My activities at the church included serving on the board of directors as vice chair and chair, on the education committee as organizer for speakers for our Sunday school class and youth sponsor for many years, and on the search committee for an assistant pastor. The church was only one mile from the university campus, and a number of faculty members and leaders in the community were also members of the church. One such member was Joe B. Hall, coach of the basketball team at the University of Kentucky. Reverend Blondell and I shared several things in common, one of which was our love for sports.

My sports activities were both active and passive. The active part was that for many years, I played on three softball teams while in Lexington: one on the church team, another for the animal science department team at the university since our department did not have a team, and the third a more competitive travel team, Tucker and Associates, who had several team members who should have been members of the church as well. The travel team entered tournaments, mostly in the broader local area on weekends but generally only once a month. I also played basketball with faculty members at noon, including several times with Cliff Hagan, a former pro with the St. Louis Hawks, who continued to sharpen his elbows on me to perfect his famous hook shot. I also played soccer with other faculty members frequently during the noon hour. Refereeing soccer games for the youth in Lexington was also an active sport.

On the passive side, I coached a number of soccer teams, on most of which I had one or the other of our two sons playing.

They both excelled in soccer and made traveling teams, so many of our weekends, we traveled to weekend tournaments, many in neighboring states.

Passive also included going to nearly all the UK home basketball games as a season ticket holder and also to many home football games. I was a part of the cooking crew for the famous pork chops served during the homecoming weekend of the football game. Again, the animal science department in the College of Agriculture and the friends I had made with the faculty members there gave me that honor to help host this annual event. Basketball tickets were highly competitive, and I was fortunate to win a lottery of a few additional seats available when they moved from Memorial Hall to Rupp Arena in 1976. I kept those tickets until around 2014, even though I had left the university twenty-five years earlier. I sold them at face value to one of the couples in our "lost and found" group who appreciated receiving them. During all that time of thirty-five-plus years, we never moved up from our original seats.

I was the beneficiary of many awards during my tenure at the University of Kentucky that I treasure to this day. I was given authorization to travel to many regional and national meetings. The ironic aspect is that you want to allow your employee to further their experiences in education and, at the same time, gain greater recognition as the employer. This certainly did happen in my case, but in the end, it was this recognition that ended in my leaving the university and accepting another position. Some of the awards and honors received internally included the rapid promotion from assistant to associate to full professor, a stature that not all faculty members received at the university.

I served on numerous extension committees and on program-planning groups. I had the honor of serving as president of the Association of Kentucky Extension Specialists. This group consisted of over five hundred specialists at the county and university level. There are 120 counties in the state of Kentucky, and each county had anywhere from one to three or more extension agents; it was the responsibility of the extension staff at the university to support their activities to the people in their county. This could be by providing the educational materials needed in most cases and also occasional visits to the county to give classroom-type training and lectures or participating in field days. Another honor was being chosen by the dean to serve on a search committee for the extension director position in the College of Agriculture. He did this after inquiring if I was planning to apply, and if so, then I should not accept being on the committee.

I was invited to be a speaker in the gathering of all extension personnel in the state for a meeting that was held every five years. I was heavily invested in integrated pest management, a multidisciplinary team approach to solving pest problems to allow crops to increase production. This team traveled around the state and also had on-site meetings for integrated pest management scouts who would actually go out in the field and collect data on the pests. For some of these controls, there were cultural practices that could be employed, and for others, pesticides were required to be applied to prevent crop loss. This led to another area where I was an integral team member, and that was in pesticide applicator training programs that were sanctioned by the state. Someone who was in the business of pesticide application for others had to have a license, and this means they had to pass a state test, so our group provided the training for those applicators to become certified. One year I received the "extension specialist of the year" award, truly an honor, and I served on many internal panels and study groups on the future of extension.

On the awards external to the University of Kentucky, these range from regional to national. One of my crop responsibilities was soybeans. There was a group started that was known as the Southern Soybean Disease Workers, which comprised the fifteen states in the southern United

States that were growing soybeans. So these were my colleagues, plant pathologists in other states, ranging from Virginia in the east, across Kentucky, Missouri, Oklahoma, and Texas, to all those states south and east of this border. There was an annual meeting held in March at Fort Walton Beach, Florida. I made the mistake of taking my family to one of those meetings, and every year thereafter, they wanted to go with me as well. In addition to the annual meeting, there were several planning meetings during the year for the officers of the group. I was on the planning committee and then became secretary and president of the group. It was a useful group but required much travel. Interestingly, I followed the position of a plant pathologist from Texas A&M who later became the extension director at the University of Kentucky. The world was actually becoming smaller even in those days.

Another honor was being chosen as a member of the national integrated pest management task force, which consisted of a six-member multidisciplinary team of scientists. This task force had annual meetings in Washington, D.C., or on site at various states to evaluate their pest management programs. This program was very beneficial to me from the interaction with other leaders in their disciplines and also to become familiar with other programs across the United States. We visited pest management programs in Georgia, California, Wyoming, Nebraska, Arizona, Michigan, New York, and Oklahoma, among those that I immediately recall. There will be stories to tell on some of these trips, you can be assured of that.

As a result of that and other exposures, one thing led to the next, and I was invited by Purdue University to be a team member to make international visits to four countries in Latin and South America. This took place for the entire month of May 1980. We visited **IPM** programs in Guatemala, Costa Rica, Columbia, and Peru.

In many respects, we were treated as dignitaries and wined and dined well. The latter three countries had international agricultural research centers for specific crops located in the countries. You can be assured there will be stories on this trip as well. Team members included a member or two of the IPM task force as well as a colleague, Dr. McGrann, who served with me in Uruguay some five to seven years earlier.

One annual assignment I had was to travel to Purdue University to cover for my field plant pathologist counterpart, who took his spring family vacation every year to Sanibel, Florida. Purdue had a weeklong program for IPM training for international students, and I became the plant pathologist on the training team for the international students. Past international living and experiences helped me relate to those students coming to the United States, many for the first time. Much of my fieldwork involved evaluating fungicides and nematicides for the control of plant diseases. I was chosen to be the chair of the task force committee that evaluated Temik, also known as aldicarb, for review for the Environmental Protection Agency (EPA).

I was also active in my national scientific society, the APS. While serving on a number of committees and giving papers at annual and regional meetings of the research that I had done, I was enticed to become business manager of the annual publication, known as *Fungicide and Nematicide Test Results*, for six years. Judy was a big help and became my bookkeeper in receiving funds and mailing out the publications. We had one bedroom that served as an office and contained many back volumes of the publications that would often be ordered along with the current-year publication. It was a good experience in running a business.

Classroom teaching was a small part of my assignment, but for all the years there, my colleague John Hartman and I taught a graduate-level course in plant disease diagnosis and control. It worked well to co-teach this class as frequently, one or the other of us would be on travel or not in the office. When we were, we co-taught, and when neither one of us was present, a fellow faculty member would conduct the class. Our approach was to have each student identify two different crops and follow each crop through the season, reporting on the diseases that they had found and what control measures would be recommended. They would present their findings each week to the rest of the class and be subjected to questions from other classmates or from the professors. In some ways, it was like a PhD prelim. The course was popular not only for plant pathology graduate students but also for entomology, horticulture, and agronomy graduate students. In diagnosis, there can be nutritional, insect, or chemical injury that can resemble a disease problem.

As I was working in the field of integrated pest management, it would only be natural for me to look at reducing the use of pesticides on crops. I also had a fairly large testing program of fungicide use on wheat as well as fungicide and nematicide use on soybeans. Traditionally, other than seed corn, fungicides were not used on corn; the same cannot be said about insecticides. The fungicides tested were largely those that were close to registration for use, but we included some numbered candidates as well. So for some of these, care was needed to be taken with handling these pesticides. My assistants and I would plant a small field of a susceptible variety and then create smaller subplots where the twelve to fifteen test materials could be applied and replicated four times. The treatments would be applied including a control, without treatment, and oftentimes a registered labeled material that was known to be effective. Disease development would be monitored and recorded during the middle to late stages of plant development, and then the plot would be harvested and results correlated.

To provide the service, I was given small grants from the companies that were looking to register their products.

Generally, $500 per treatment was the going rate for my services, and in this way, $5,000 or more were generated to do the work for the service. For many years, I would have four or five such plots conducted. This small source of funds was well received by my department and the college as they were largely discretionary funds that could be used for many purposes—teaching supplies, equipment or laboratory products, etc. As long as I received what I needed to conduct these trials, I was very willing to have the remainder go into a departmental fund for the chairman's use. This was good politics in that when I requested something within reason, it would generally be granted considering what I was contributing to the department. The companies would use the data they received from the trials I conducted for their use to proceed with registration for their product.

While some of my counterparts in Southern states were recommending fungicide applications to soybeans to increase yield, I found that it was not economic for soybeans growing in Kentucky on a year-to-year basis. However, one specific area where fungicides could be beneficial was the soybeans being grown for seeds. Thus, the yield component was not there, but the quality component was dependent on several parameters, such as the variety planted and the date planted. Early planted beans were more susceptible to diseases. This work was done in collaboration with fellow faculty members in the Department of Agronomy.

In similar field research trials, the impact of virus-infected beans on the quality of the seed produced was researched, and this produced a number of research papers as well as the research described in the preceding paragraph. This research was conducted with one or two research faculty members within our department.

The natural extension to the above work led to the development of predictive systems that determined when to apply fungicides to field crops. To make it simple, we developed a point system where different points—one, two, or three—would be added and the sum totaled so that if you received more than fifteen points, then you would know that you should apply the fungicide. This made it rather simple for the farmer or the field scout to take a little survey, fill in the blanks, and total the amount to determine whether or not the fungicide application was needed. (In 1989, I was invited to present a paper on this work at the World Soybean Conference held in Buenos Aires, Argentina. It was also an opportunity to leave a few days early, stop in Uruguay, and check in on the counterparts and other faculty members at Las Brujas.)

Another vital aspect was to determine the most appropriate time of plant development to apply the fungicides for disease protection. This was true for soybeans and even truer for wheat. There was a points system developed for wheat as well. Traditionally, producers did not apply fungicides to soybeans or to wheat production, but our Kentucky farmers had read about the one-hundred-bushels-per-acre yield in Europe on wheat, and their averages in Kentucky were more like fifty to sixty bushels per acre. Why the difference?

A group of Kentucky farmers decided to travel to England to visit with consultants and farmers there and determine why they were getting larger yields. They soon noted that English farmers put on much more nitrogen on the crop to help it grow. They also observed that five to six fungicides were applied per growing year. Well, the Kentucky farmers did put extra nitrogen on the crop but did not use fungicides. So they decided they would increase the level of nitrogen but would not go with the fungicide program. This procedure resulted in a very lush crop with a high internal relative humidity that was ideal for disease development, especially powdery mildew and Septoria diseases. This is where I came in, along with an agricultural economist, to advise that if you were intent on growing high-yield wheat, then you should consider a single or double, not five or six, applications of fungicide and, with our research, the appropriate time to make those applications.

One other factor that was often ignored or not considered is that the growing season in Europe is much longer than in Kentucky. In Kentucky, at grain fill in mid- to late May, the weather suddenly turns dry and hot, and this shortens the grain-filling period. England, on the other hand, remains relatively cool with plenty of moisture, which allows for larger kernels of grain to be produced. The moisture and cooler temperatures are also conducive to more disease development, thus their use of additional fungicide applications. The results and recommendation for our Kentucky farmers was that if they wanted to bump up the nitrogen just a bit, that might be fine; they would settle for seventy-bushels-per-acre yields, and that may be the most economic. If they wanted to go for very high yields with lots of extra nitrogen, then they should be prepared to apply a single or double fungicide application. Interestingly, it was this work that was the impetus for my applying and being accepted for a sabbatical leave in the Netherlands.

Well, I could go on some more but will close with one more honor, and that was being chosen to be an author on a National Integrated Pest Management of Wheat publication. Participating in this and making presentations to the extension service in Washington, D.C., as well as the wheat power brokers there began the process of my recruitment to take the position of director of the National Association of Wheat Growers Foundation (NAWGF). This was the job that lured me away from the University of Kentucky in 1989, another fork in the road that created more life experiences.

In reading this chapter and some earlier chapters, the reader could consider this very braggadocio. It is not intended to convey that. I was also invited to be the primary presenter of an agricultural workshop in my home town

Agriculture Speaker Stuckey Has Homecoming

by Judy Winnett
Buckeye Staff Writer

Richard Stuckey recognized over half the faces in the crowd.

It was almost like coming home, even though he's lived away from Archbold for about 25 years. Stuckey looked over the group he was to address during the day-long seminar sponsored by Zehr & Co. at Ruihley Park Pavilion Friday.

His father, Chauncey Stuckey, was there. His brother, Ron Stuckey, Archbold High School vo-ag teacher was there with students eager to hear the visiting plant expert. Stuckey's uncles, old neighbors and farmer friends surrounded him.

The welcome was warm.

Stuckey was selected as guest speaker for his expertise as Extension specialist in plant pathology at the University of Kentucky, Lexington, Ky. Groups of about 80 assembled in morning and afternoon sessions to hear him. About 125 persons attended the lunch according to Archbold Plant Manager Elden Badenhop.

It was a bonus that Stuckey was an Archbold native with farming background that familiarized him with particular soils and plant problems found here in Fulton County.

Birthday

For Stuckey the invitation to come was almost like a birthday present. His birthday was the day following the seminar and he could celebrate it with his parents this year.

It was his 42nd birthday or he's in the middle of his 10th year depending how you count a leap year birthday, as he was born Feb. 29, 1944.

At the seminar Stuckey discussed disease problems in corn, soybeans, wheat and alfalfa production. He shared the podium with various product representatives who discussed pesticide and fungicide management relating to their particular products.

In informal discussion following the seminar Stuckey said the only product he wanted to promote was education.

He became involved with the whole agricultural-education scene at an early age by farming with his father. After graduating from AHS graduating in 1966. There he was

(Continued on page twenty)

A plant pathology workshop turned into a family reunion of sorts for Richard Stuckey, left, Extension professor at the University of Kentucky. He visits with his uncle, Orville Stuckey, center, and his father, Chauncey, during the Friday workshop sponsored by Zehr & Co. Stuckey was the guest speaker for over 100 area farmers who attended to learn about disease control.—Photo by Judy Winnett

Rather, with good decisions, hard work, and a smattering of luck as well as being in the right place at the right time, much can be accomplished. Networking and collaborating, not burning bridges, can play a big part in one's future opportunities.

Stories:

1. Our eldest son, JJ, at a young age, had an obsession of being very strong-willed and wanting to do things on his own, but when given the opportunity to do that, he waffled, and he wanted his mom to do it for him. A prime example was that he wanted to put the toast down in the toaster. As soon as his mom would allow him to do it, he then wanted his mom to do it. It was the same with

plugging plugs into a socket. We were thankful that he was inquisitive but did get a little tired of the tantrum. "JJ do it. No, Mommy do it. No, JJ do it." Sometimes it is difficult to have patience and understand kids; however, their determination is admirable.

2. Jon, the younger son, also had memorable events. One of his that I recall was the call for dinner; he would come to the table, look over what had been prepared, some favorite dishes, and state, "What's the main course for dinner?" He would frequently take the food and put it on his plate, and if it wasn't to his liking, he would say that he was full. Then moments later, he would want dessert, and when questioned about being full, he would claim that his dessert pocket wasn't full. Another antic after eating was that he would often say that he was tired and lie down on the carpeted kitchen floor until the entire cleanup was done. We tried to teach both of our boys that after a meal, they didn't just leave the table, but at a minimum, they needed to help set the dishes over to the counter nearby. Of course, by this time, Jon decided he was "too tired" to set his dishes over and so quickly lay down on the blue carpet we had in the nook and claimed that he needed to sleep. Such a guy!

3. Lexington, Kentucky, was a six-to-seven-hour car drive back to Judy's parents in Elkhart, Indiana, and a five-to-six-hour car drive back to Archbold, Ohio, where my parents and family lived. We went back for holidays and several other times during the year. With two kids

in the car, oftentimes picking on each other, I wanted to get to the destination as soon as we could. That plus a known heavy foot got me in trouble with the law now and then. On one such trip back from Indiana, we were passing through a known speed trap, Seymour, a small town south of Indianapolis. The sixty-five-miles-per-hour interstate speed limit was suddenly changed to fifty-five miles per hour for no apparent reason other than to give unsuspected travelers a ticket for speeding. Of course, that system happened to me. I generally try to stay within ten miles of the speed limit to avoid getting stopped, so traveling at seventy-five in a sixty-five would allow one to get by, but when they drop the speed limit to fifty-five and you're not paying attention, then you're doing twenty miles per hour over the speed limit. Traveling along, we heard the siren behind us and the flashing red and blue lights on the police car—not a good sight to see in your rearview mirror. I pulled over; the policeman got out, walked up to the window, and asked for the registration and driver's license, the whole bit, and then began writing out my ticket. Evidently, the two boys were wide-eyed and very observant. Later on the trip home, I received a drawing from my elder son that had a police car with red and blue lights parked behind our car with four people in it and a caption below it that read, "Daddy, don't ever do that again."

4. One of the neat practices in Kentucky was that a pint of blood could be donated to remove or prevent points going on your record for speeding violations. This was

used many times over the fourteen years that I lived in Kentucky. One time I went to give blood, JJ went with me, and while I was used to the sight of blood, had given many pints, and had also grown up on a farm, JJ had not. He fainted while observing the blood draw. He knew right then and there that he would not enter the medical field as a profession.

5. I recall one particular trip. As we were traveling north to Ohio in our 1975 Ford Pinto station wagon, the boys were excited about the upcoming holiday and just couldn't keep their hands off each other. This had happened on trips before to the extent that we had made a plywood board to be placed between them for separation. On this particular trip, even that was not working well. So I warned them that if they did not behave, I would need to pull off the side of the road and stop. They did test me, and I did pull off the side of the road, and they said, "Dad, what are you doing?" I said, "I am waiting until you boys are able to behave because driving with such distractions is dangerous." We sat there for what seemed like fifteen minutes, more likely five minutes, and went on our way. I recall there were several additional times on that trip that I needed to pull off the side of the road. By that time, they knew I was serious, and it was infrequent that I had to stop on future trips.

6. Weather factors can make traveling dangerous as well. One Christmas holiday, we were traveling up to Elkhart,

Indiana, when north of Indianapolis, we ran into a real whiteout blizzard. It was windy! The snow was blowing totally sideways, there was nearly zero visibility, and it was piling up on the road such that you could not see the road, just some tracks to guide one, and even those were filling up. There was no exit that one could see to pull off and be safe. We moved ever so slowly along at five to ten miles per hour for many miles, fearful for our lives. We didn't know when we would run into a car or when a car would run into us or when we would run off the road. It was a very harrowing experience, and I'm not sure how we made it to this day. This is one memory that I would like to forget, but memories do not seem to operate that way; you remember the good, and you remember the bad.

7. We were fortunate to have two families with children living in our cul-de-sac in our early years in Lexington. The Kirbys had a son slightly older than JJ and a daughter a year or two older than Jon. The other neighbor had a son younger than JJ. The three older boys ruled. One of their favorite games was playing out *Star Wars*, and the older boy, Scott, always wanted to be the hero and the star player. This was sometimes frustrating to JJ, and of course, Jon, being the younger one, would take whatever he could get, just excited about being a part of the group and being included. The kids got along well, and the parents were just glad that they could play and occupy much of their time together, which gave the parents a short vacation.

8. After five years, we moved from the cul-de-sac and 1,600-square-foot house to a large three-story house with 4,500 square feet or more.

It had a full-furnished basement with a bedroom, a bath, and a long extended living area that was called a bowling alley with a large bar with stools. There was an external door that led directly to the outside and an upper stairwell to the backyard.

The main floor consisted of a guest bedroom, a living room, a dining room, a kitchen, a family room, and a screened-in porch. The upper floor consisted of four bedrooms and two baths. The house was set up on a hill and so had a steep front yard, difficult for mowing grass, but had a backyard that was mostly flat and good-sized. It was here that the neighborhood kids gathered to play soccer and softball. We were glad to host gatherings because we knew where our kids were and that they were safe—well, mostly safe. Occasionally, I would go out and play with them, but oftentimes they were there when I got home from work and playing by themselves, which was great. One of the neighbor kids who was not so athletically inclined at that time was being introduced to softball. I recall one day he went up and swung the bat, and one of our kids' heads got in the way, and he cracked it pretty good. He did feel bad, but it was time for some instruction on being careful around equipment and people.

9. It was at this location that several events occurred that every member of our family, not only myself, remembers well. We had just hired a new faculty member in my department at the University of Kentucky who was to be stationed out in the west part of the state at Princeton, Kentucky. I would be working very closely with the new professor. We invited Wayne over for dinner one evening when he was in town. It was one of the worst displays our two kids put on for any guests that we've ever had. I don't know what got into them, but they were impolite and discourteous and misbehaved. They would probably describe their behavior worse than I have. Fortunately, Wayne had a family of his own and small kids, so I think that he did understand. He later explained to me that he thought nothing of it, which made me feel just a bit better.

10. Another incident was when my brother and his wife were visiting us and we were having a nice dinner inside and visiting afterward like adults do. JJ wanted to go out and play basketball or shoot hoops, as he would call it, but the car was in the way. We had a flat driveway atop a very steep incline from the street. We had posted a backboard and basketball rim above the garage door. From the two-car garage, one could back the car out a ways, turn it so that one could face the long incline, and drive safely down to the street below. This worked well except in inclement weather during the winter, when there might be some ice or snow, and in those days, we parked the car on the street rather than the garage. Back to the story. JJ was fourteen years old at the time and had not driven a car, at least to my knowledge. He wanted to have the car moved so that he could shoot hoops. So I told him he could back the car up and gave him the keys, half-thinking that he would not take up the challenge, but he did. He got in the car, started it, and backed it up, but in his excitement, he did not make the turn necessary, hit the gas and not the brake, and backed right off the driveway, almost into the neighbors' house. He came back into the room quite pale and was nearly speechless. We walked outside to see the underside of my 1976 Brohm Plymouth car looking like it was ready for takeoff in the space program. With my brother and the neighbor, who came out, also with a drained color, and Judy in the driver seat since she was the lightest, we pushed and pushed to try to push the car out but could not do so. Finally, there was nothing else

left to do but to call the tow truck. "Hello. Can we help you?" "Yes, I need a car pulled from a small ravine." "Where is your car?" "In my driveway." "Where do you live?" "2152 Lakeside Drive." I was sure hoping the neighbors were busy doing something else when the tow truck drove up, hooked up to my car, and pulled it back up onto the driveway. As a side note, Judy remembers this incident very well, and she recently told me she believes this is the angriest that she has been at me in our life for giving the car keys to fourteen-year-old JJ while we were entertaining company!

11. Both boys played soccer competitively and in high school. There was a dog named Henry that liked to hang around with the kids at soccer practice. One after one, the kids would take Henry home with them to see if their parents would allow him to stay and they would adopt the dog. That worked for several days for several families, but in the end, Henry always returned to the practice field. I figured our turn was coming, and sure enough, one day here came Henry, home with the boys after their practice. "Dad, can't we keep Henry? He's a good dog." "Who is going to feed him and pick up after him?" "Oh, we will, we will." Again, these responsibilities seemed to fall more and more on my lap. I was a runner at the time and would run five miles or more a day during the week and longer on weekends. I agreed to take Henry along on a run. Henry was more interested in squirrels and investigating during the run I had done so many times before. I can't blame him, but

when he ran off to explore and got on the wrong side of the fence that I would have to backtrack to get him around to the proper side, it became old, and Henry no longer went on runs with me and soon was back at school at the soccer practice field. I just hoped there were some other boys willing to take Henry because he did need a home, and he certainly must've felt unwelcome after being returned so many times. Such are the cruelties of life!

12. My frequent travels in state and out of state and long work hours resulted in Judy being at home with kids for extended times. She was ready to turn the kids over to me when I got home. There were occasional disagreements, and one day I came home to hear two versions: one from adult, one from child. Perhaps JJ felt that the full story wasn't being told or that I was taking the side of his mother without hearing the kids' side, so one day JJ secretly taped the dispute between Judy and Jon and offered to play it for me. As I recall, Judy did not want me to hear the tape. Judy was a stickler for kids going to bed at the appointed hour, so when she had choir or an evening meeting and I was with the kids, I liked to play games with them, and when she got home and they were still up, she was not happy. She claimed and was likely correct that kids without appropriate sleep would be grouchy all of the next day. Once again, she was probably right because I would be at work and was not with them.

13. I felt fortunate that while our kids did get into some mischief, it did not compare to what their father had done in his younger years, and they were mostly honest with us. At least, that's what we were led to believe. I mentioned that we had a three-story house with a guest bedroom on the main floor as well as a complete furnished lower floor with a bedroom and bath, where our elder son stayed. The four bedrooms on the top floor were occupied by the younger son and us. We always wanted our kids to come and tell us good night if they were out after we went to bed. This story happened one particular Saturday night when our elder son came home around eleven and said, "I am home." We thanked him and acknowledged him letting us know. What we didn't know was that he went down to his basement room for about thirty minutes and then left out the back stairwell door to rejoin his friends.

When we went to church the next morning, we did not observe how tired he seemed but became suspicious when friends and the mother of one of JJ's friends visited with Judy to inform her there was a good chance her son was out with a group of guys well into the morning hours. On the way home, JJ received an unexpected grilling; he immediately confessed, said he didn't want us to worry, and went down to his room to retrieve a note in the wastebasket that he had left on his bed in the event that we got up and came to look for him. It would explain that he had left on his own will and that he loved us. It was hard to punish a boy so honest and loving.

14. My parents came down to pick up our two boys to take them back to Ohio for several weeks on the farm.

Driving up I-75 to Cincinnati and crossing over the Ohio River and onto I-75 in Ohio, my parents got the biggest kick out of six-year-old JJ when he observed all the cars going south and inquired, "Why are all the people moving to Kentucky?" Another part of that conversation occurred when my parents were speaking in low voices to each other; JJ piped up and said, "You don't have to whisper. We know all about the birds and the bees."

15. Many years we were able to return to Northwest Ohio for the annual fall butchering day where my larger family would do an actual butchering of two hogs for a museum. Crowds from miles away would come to

watch this once common farm practice that was fast disappearing.

16. We were close friends with a number of couples in Kentucky; one in particular were the Nickels, who had two boys, one each slightly older than our boys. They

spent a lot of time together and overnighted at each other's places. One night our eldest son, one year older than their younger son, was overnighting at their place. They got a bit rowdy by throwing socks and other objects over from the upstairs balcony down onto the main floor at each other. During the course of the night, they got into the ice cream and had a good-sized dish. The problem was they became distracted and forgot to put the ice cream away. I can just hear mother Pat Nickel, when she got up in the morning, having a fit over the liquid ice cream that was all over the counter. These were fun times and fun stories with family growing up in Lexington, Kentucky.

17. Other close friends of ours are the Wakefields. Don was a medical doctor and frequently had medical meetings in places with lots of free time. So we eagerly agreed to their invitation to join them in Snowmass, Colorado. He would have meetings for half a day, and the other half a day, we would all enjoy skiing. The year was 1984. How do I know? Because it was Judy's fortieth birthday. I met a friend in Lexington who was very good at limericks and had a special limerick and card, business size, printed up for me. It was as cheap to print five hundred as it was for one card, so I had five hundred printed and thus had many available for distribution. It all started on the plane when I confided in one flight attendant about the plan. She thought it was great. I slipped her a couple of cards, and after a period in flight, she came over to Judy and said, "I believe you dropped this card" and

handed it to her. Judy said she did not think she did but took the card and saw forties all over it with her name on it and a limerick describing how she was an animal in bed.

Judy Stealy Stuckey
January 20, 1944

Forty's an age we all dread,
But Judy is still way ahead.
When in a tight squeeze,
She brings Dick to his knees
'Cause she's still an animal in bed!

2152 Lakeside Drive
Lexington, KY 40502
Telephone
606-266-4810

I believe she knew she had met her match when she saw that card, and try as hard as she would to confiscate the card, it was impossible because they just kept showing up everywhere that weekend—on the ski slope at Snowmass, in the restaurants, in the living unit—and there were still enough for the return flight and distribution when she got home. While these are memories of mine, I am sure if you ask her, she will remember this one very well.

There are many stories of work in Kentucky, but I will share only the top dozen in no particular order.

1. We had four extension plant pathologists in our department. We often did training programs together; usually, it was just one or two, but in these particular several days, all four of us were called to Owensboro, Kentucky, to do a training program. To cut costs, we shared rooms, two to a room, each with two double beds. This night, we had an adjoining room that had an internal door for passage to each other's rooms, very convenient if used for appropriate purposes. My colleague who was also considered a jokester by many was my roommate. We were out later than the other two that evening and, upon returning to our room, wondered what we could do to mess up their room a bit. We checked the internal door, and it was unlocked, so we entered while they were sleeping, found our way around, and moved a few things like shaving cream. I don't remember all of what we did, but one thing I do remember that remains for many years in the retold story was placing one of our colleagues' shoes in the refrigerator. He got up earlier than we did, searched and searched for his shoes, could not find them, and finally did encounter cold shoes in his refrigerator.

2. We had an interdisciplinary team of scientists to go out and do integrated pest management training. Frequently, it was an entomologist and me who would travel in a pair around the state, doing the training. The schedule could be fast and furious, with little time for breaks and eating. We kept the fast food businesses in business eating on the run. One day we drove through

McDonald's, ordered our burgers and fries and drinks, and were ready to be on our way when my partner said he needed to visit the restroom quick before proceeding. While he went into the restroom, I reached into my sack of food, pulled out one of the hamburgers wrapped up, took a big bite out of the hamburger, and then wrapped it back up and placed it neatly inside the bag. We started down the road, eating as we were driving. He was driving the car. I reached into my bag, pulled out my wrapped hamburger, opened it very visibly, and then exclaimed, "What the heck?" looking in disbelief and showing my hamburger with a big bite out of it. My entomologist friend about had a fit, and he said, "Do we turn back the couple of miles we had gone and take it back to get another one?" I said, "No, we don't have time. I'm hungry. I'll just go ahead and eat it." His jaw about dropped to the floor, and then I burst out laughing, and I left him in on the joke. I'm not sure if he has forgiven me yet or not. In fact, this person, who died of a heart attack while riding a bike in his early fifties, became a major factor in my deciding to retire early!

3. I played another joke on a number of my colleagues who drove state-owned vehicles or their own cars and occasionally parked on campus in fifteen-minute parking areas near our laboratories when we were coming and going from the university. We came across some small harmless firecrackers, but they did make noise. So when the colleague forgot to lock his car, I would sneak into the car on the other side and tie a string to the inside

door and to the steering wheel or some other fixed part. Imagine the surprise when the unsuspected driver came to his car, opened the door, and *bang!* Sometimes they nearly jumped out of their boots. Of course, it wasn't too long until I was receiving the blame for those that I did and also for those that were done by others. If we could, we hung around to where we could watch it happen, but sometimes the wait got too long, and we had to go about our business, yet knowing that it happened made us chuckle.

4. One of the popular ways to provide information to state residents of Kentucky was to conduct field trials across the state. There would be field days either where the trials were held or as educational seminars. The field trials were valued by the growers in that they were conducted in their area; they could visualize and see the results and were not just some laboratory study, sort of like where the rubber meets the road. On one occasion when I was in Western Kentucky, where many of my field trials were conducted, my colleague, the guy whose shoes ended up in the refrigerator, invited me to go and record data from his field trial. His primary crop was tobacco, a very important cash crop for many Kentucky farmers. We parked the state car and made the walk back through a couple of fields to his plot, at which time we looked up and saw a person standing with a shotgun in front of us about 150 yards away. It was clear he did not want us there, and it was enough to convince us that we needed to come back another day, if we needed to

come back at all. Marijuana was an illegal drug then but grown; it was an indication that we had stumbled too close to one of those locations and it was time to leave. We complied.

5. When I arrived in Kentucky, there were only four or five counties known to have infestations of a nematode that attacked soybeans. This nematode was the soybean cyst nematode. A part of my work was to work in consultation with the research nematologist in our department. I would take soil samples from suspected fields and bring them to the lab to have them assayed for the soybean cyst nematode. I would also conduct some field trials using differential varieties for resistance as well as test the effectiveness of different nematicides for control of the nematode. Because of the location where the nematode was quite prevalent, it would require some overnight stays to perform the field studies. My brother-in-law, Ron, and his wife, Lorraine, Judy's sister, came to visit us once or twice a year. We enjoyed their visits, and Ron would often accompany me when I needed to travel out in the field if he was in town. We went to a new state area to search for the nematode near Bowling Green, Kentucky, and I stopped at several fields that had typical symptoms, stunted and yellowing plants in circular or elongated areas of the field, to inspect the plants to see if indeed there were cysts of the nematodes on the roots of the plants. If we found the cyst nematode, we went up to the house and informed them of the bad news. Ron seemed to get a kick out of this. I received

some satisfaction from knowing of the new find but sorry for the farmer. By the time I left Kentucky, there were over thirty counties infested with the nematode.

6. During the summer, meetings were often held outside, on site, at the field, or at the experiment station. Kentucky is known for its mild winters relative to some other states, but it did get cold and snow sufficiently that winter meetings were all held indoors. I recall one February we had meetings over in Louisville, Kentucky, for three to four days consecutively, so we overnighted even though it was only eighty miles from home. While we were there, a winter storm came through, complete with blowing ice and snow. When I got up to leave in the morning, I could not unlock my car; the lock was frozen shut. Lighting a match or using a cigarette lighter to try and thaw out the area was of no avail in this particular case, evidence of a severe frozen lock. This delayed departure for several hours until we finally got the lock unfrozen. It was very unpleasant working outside in that kind of weather. On another occasion, at a winter meeting in Henderson, Kentucky, I recall a winter storm going through the area and shutting down travel and traffic for three days, so I was stuck out there for several additional days before being able to return home. In Kentucky, these events were infrequent, but when they occurred, they became very memorable. So much for the reputation that Kentucky had a mild climate! When we first moved to Kentucky, we were advised not to even bring a snow shovel. Not only did we

purchase a snow shovel, but also, we purchased a snow blower, which we used numerous times!

7. We had a good group of faculty members, and about half, seven to eight, enjoyed playing a monthly game of poker, one evening each month. I was among them. We often imported one "sucker" from the horticultural department to join us. We rotated homes to host the poker event and, of course, had food and drinks to accompany the game. There were a number of nights that I felt I had to eat and drink a lot to try and cover my betting losses.

8. In the late seventies, with our youngest son four to five years old, we decided with having two sons, we had a complete little family. There were two common practices that could be employed to prevent additional children being born. One was to have the lady's tubes tied, and the other was to have the man have a vasectomy. Judy figured she had done her due diligence by giving birth twice, so it was my turn to do my part. I agreed with her rationalization. At the time, I was youth sponsor for the youth group at church, and approximately three or four days after the operation, I thought I could play a little volleyball but take it a bit easier. I'd been warned to lay low for a number of days and had complied for the first three days and felt much better and so thought I was ready to go. The swelling was down, and everything seemed to be well on the way to recovery. The next day, I was scheduled to travel to Owensboro, Kentucky,

for an evening meeting and then on to the Purchase area of Kentucky for a breakfast meeting the following morning. I made it to Owensboro and, with some discomfort, was able to conduct the evening meeting in conjunction with a sponsor from the chemical industry. As I recall, both of these lectures were on the soybean cyst nematode referred to earlier, and the chemical representative hosted the meal at the delicious Moonlight Inn barbecue restaurant. He and I decided to travel to Paducah, Kentucky, to overnight and be much closer to Mayfield for the breakfast meeting, which he would also host. Well, more traveling after a big day was not popular with my body. We were following each other with our CB radios on (to avoid cops and speed traps) and were on the Pennyrile Parkway, ready to fly, so to speak. Conversing occasionally, we were making good time and approaching the outskirts of Madisonville when I asked my traveling partner ahead of me, "How is it looking up there?" and the response I received was "Bring it on. It's clean and green." So hurting more and more, I increased my speed by five to ten miles an hour to around eighty on the sixty-five posted parkway speed limit. Another two miles down the road, I was pulled over, taken into the courthouse, and delayed for ninety minutes to talk my way out of spending the night there. I arrived very late at the hotel; my traveling companion was there, and he said he did not reply to me on that request I had submitted earlier, so it was the cop who had encouraged me to bring it on. I wanted to fight this in court, but Madisonville is three and a half hours away from Lexington; it would've taken a day to travel out there to court and fight the case, where it was not a sure thing that I would win. My immediate concern was getting in the bathtub and soaking for thirty minutes. I did make it to the breakfast meeting, made a leisurely return to Lexington the next day, lay low for another several days to allow the healing that had begun, and went into reverse for healing. The moral of the story is just when you think your body is healing, give it a little extra time, and it will be well worth the wait before you become too actively engaged again.

9. Serving on several regional and national committees resulted in numerous out-of-state trips. While many stories could be told, I will limit myself to three. The first was a memorable trip to San Francisco. My brother-in-law, Ron, accompanied me on the trip. It was a relatively inexpensive trip for him since he could room with me and my room cost was charged to my account. He was an architect by training, and so he loved to travel to other sites for architectural observation. One evening we decided to go to a popular place, Funnochio's. It was a place where one could enjoy drinks in a nightclub setting. The main show was female impersonators. They had small Filipino men dressed as women, with nylon stockings and all, walking around and flirting with the clientele. One of them came by our table, lifted his/her skirt a bit, and said, "Hey!" in a real low voice that just freaked us out. We laughed and laughed and got the biggest kick out of that.

10. Another trip took six colleagues and me to evaluate **IPM** programs in Southern Georgia. These meetings often were a couple of days of state programs to review, and then we would stay on one extra day to do some local activities. On this trip, we went down to the coast in the Gulf of Mexico and learned what a rising tide really meant. We split up into two groups of three and got in small boats, canoe style, and went out to an oyster bar. At low tide, the oyster bars are no longer covered with water but become land and can be explored for oysters. The boat I was in had a bit more sense than the other boat, which had three others and the senior advisor to the group from Washington, D.C. They got out of their boat and climbed up on the oyster bar while their boat was left untied on the oyster bar. Unbeknownst to them, the tide began rising to the point that it reached the boat and freed the boat from its resting state as the boat drifted out to sea. There were three men on the oyster bar without their boat, the tide rising and the oyster bar becoming smaller by the moment. There was one pole on the oyster bar, and the three of us in our boat could envision the three guys climbing the pole like monkeys as the water rose. The three guys on the oyster bar began hollering at us to come and save them, and we pretended we did not hear them and, in fact, turned our boat to go and head for shore. They were frantically waving, trying to get our attention, and the more they waved, the less attention we gave them. Finally, we did turn around, go retrieve their boat, and tow it to them so they could be rescued. To this day, they owe us.

11. I recall a somewhat narrow escape for six to eight of my fellow colleagues who attended their annual meeting of the APS that was held in Knoxville, Tennessee. One evening we went out for a drink to an establishment that was known to have pole dancers. There may have been other things going on there that we were not aware of, but we enjoyed our drinks and the entertainment and left. The next day, in the newspaper, we read that the place we were at was raided by the police, the customers retained, and this all happened within a half hour after we left. Can you imagine the headlines that would've been in the paper had we still been there? "Eight doctors held for potential soliciting at a questionable establishment!"

12. I would be remiss if I did not mention some great eating restaurants in Kentucky. Some favorite eating places on the road were the Moonlight Inn Bar-B-Que in Owensboro, Sue & Charlie's Catfish in the Purchase area, the Steakhouse south of Hopkinsville, the Tavern Inn in Bardstown, and the New Orleans House seafood buffet in Louisville and Lexington.

CHAPTER 10

The Sabbatical Year, 1986-1987

We took one year out of the University of Kentucky years (1986–1987) for a sabbatical leave. One of the great benefits of working at a university is that most have a sabbatical policy where every seven years, a professor can take a sabbatical leave and remain on salary for six months. Most faculty members do not take advantage of this benefit.

Why? I suspect this is because of the change in uprooting the routine established and the extra work involved to arrange for a sabbatical. Most sabbaticals from U.S. universities are taken within the United States. Some are taken abroad. Much work is required to plan and prepare and make arrangements to take a sabbatical. The purpose of a sabbatical is to provide a time for renewal, to pursue an area of research and collaboration without the many distractions of current work, to write or publish a scholarly paper uninterrupted, or other varied reasoned activities. In essence, it has a lot of latitude, and there are few who return who would say it was not worthwhile.

I was primed for a sabbatical because of the many activities that were claiming my time. I had eleven years of employment already at Kentucky. I was chair of the board of directors at the one-thousand-member church I attended. I would need to turn that over to the vice chair a few months early, but I did not have a problem with that because I had taken over several months prior to my predecessor's term ending. I was president of the Association of University of Kentucky Extension Specialists, and again, because of the timing of the sabbatical, I would need to have the vice chair step in a few months early in that appointment. There were numerous committees that I was serving on in the department and the college and externally. Would it not be nice to get off all these committees, drop them, and start anew upon return from the sabbatical?

Clearing all channels within the college and university was easily accomplished and did not require a lot of effort. More effort was required to determine what was available and where one would go. With my having lived overseas for two years on two different occasions previously, an international sabbatical where family could accompany me was highly desired.

Because of the state of research in the United States, Europe, Israel, Australia/New Zealand, or Japan became a likely choice. If I were staying within the States, California would've been a likely choice since my colleague had recently completed a six-month sabbatical ```there.

After I chose Europe as my first choice, it was soon narrowed down to three countries: England, Germany, and the Netherlands. There were research people in the department who had connections with England, having had sabbaticals there. I was offered a six-month sabbatical at the John Innis Institute in England. Professor Hoffman at the Technical Institute of Weihenstephan in the Bavarian area of Germany (about twenty miles outside of Munich, Germany) was appealing, and a six-month offer was received. Professor Hoffman's offer was appealing from another aspect; my predictive systems research for plant disease control in Kentucky was closely aligned with their research efforts. The third offer was from the Agricultural University of Wageningen in the Netherlands, located in the western part of the state near Arnhem. The Netherlands offer had the possibility of a $10,000 fellowship. Doing some math, I reasoned that a paid six-month sabbatical, utilizing another two and a half months of unused annual leave, plus the $10,000 fellowship would leave me an effective salary for ten and a half to eleven months. If I were to root up my family, whom I definitely wanted to take with me, then a year made a lot more sense to me than just six months. Thus, the decision was to go to the Netherlands.

Arrangements were made to begin the sabbatical in August 1986 and conclude in August 1987. This would fit in well with the school year for two kids who, had they stayed in the United States, would've entered the seventh and tenth grades. From another perspective, the older child was moving from junior high to high school and the younger child from elementary to junior high. The stars were aligning well for us. Leaving for a year from the stateside required making many arrangements, from covering the jobs that you were doing to deciding whether to rent out the house or to change the billing and mailing addresses and just a whole host of other things. It also required making arrangements for your new home, primarily finding a place to live while on sabbatical, and the various registrations required for living in a new country. Amazingly, as I recall, this all went off without too much of a hitch. I would really hate to think about even going through all the logistics of this again. We packed our bags, bade farewell, and were off. This was not nearly as difficult for our parents as we were moving to a very civilized country for only one year, with a likelihood that many of them may be able to visit during our year there.

My early knowledge of the Netherlands was that it consisted of Dutch people and their way of life. There were two cities, Amsterdam and Rotterdam. Why so many "dams" in the names of the cities? Well, much of the Netherlands is below sea level. They have recovered much of their land from under the sea. Navel explorations were much of their history. Yes, there were windmills and wooden shoes, keeping up the tradition, especially in the countryside. Swine and dairy were important animal industries. Just as New Zealand has more sheep than people, the Netherlands has more swine than people. Many people know the Netherlands for their flowers and their cheese. These two were fascinating industries. Of course, the museums and many paintings of Rembrandt and van Gogh exist in the country. Venice has nothing on many of these cities, which have canals for streets. Some homes actually extend out onto the canal; a boat is tied up to the back of the house for ready use. It is not a good idea to have a sleepwalking issue when living there. All this is to say that an extremely exciting year awaited us.

The jet lag did affect all of us, and we were quite tired upon arrival. A faculty member greeted us at the airport and took us out to our new home that he had arranged for us to rent while on our sabbatical. You see, the homeowner at 45 Didenveek was a university professor as well and was taking a sabbatical in England at the same time. How convenient! After a short nap, we went down to the bike shop with the advisor's help and purchased four bikes, one for each of us. This was to be a primary form of transportation for us, come rain or shine—and rain, it did. It was not the Midwest downpour of buckets of rain but the continual dripping of rain under overcast skies.

The Department of Phytopathology was in the College of Agriculture and had approximately fifteen to twenty faculty members; that's roughly the same size as the University of Kentucky plant pathology department. There were several internationally well-known professors within the department. Dr. Dekker was the chair and seemed to take a real liking to me and was proud to have me do my sabbatical there. Dr. Zadocs was a well-known epidemiologist, small in stature but with a very active mind and years of experience. Dr. Martin Devard was a bit younger but an up-and-coming host parasite interaction professor with much potential. Dr. Devard was assigned to be our host and help make the arrangements described above.

While my work and interest for the sabbatical were not totally laid out before I came, I had the option of seeing what was there and in what field I wished to work or pursue. It came down to two choices. One was with Dr. Devard, which would be more of a laboratory work environment, more similar to my PhD dissertation. The other was a combined field-and-laboratory effort with Dr. Zadocs and epidemiology studies that fit more closely with my extension research work in Kentucky. After visiting with Dr. Devard, while I think he may have been just a bit disappointed, we both agreed that working with Dr. Zadocs was likely a better fit for my interest. Dr. Zadocs was very structured, wanted meetings by appointment, seemed to have many other activities going on within and outside the department, and was all business. He made the most of every minute, but he always took time for his morning and afternoon coffee with colleagues. He had a couple of other international students and one seasoned field person who was very helpful to me in setting up field plots and arranging travel to various sites in the country for fieldwork. Much of my work would take place out in the polders, land recovered from the sea, and also on the experiment station land close by.

The two boys were enrolled in the French Lyceum school and had their work cut out for them as everything was spoken *in Dutch*. They spent many hours at the language library listening to tapes and trying to get a command of the Dutch language. They were much more successful than their parents, but perhaps the greatest way for them to learn the language was to have both of them play on soccer club teams. JJ was in an advanced math curriculum program at Kentucky, and so he ended up taking a new math book with him to do his studies remotely for his math course. The other studies were taken at the lyceum. Jon took all his courses at the Dutch Lyceum.

They rode their bikes to and from school, about two kilometers away, and also to all their soccer practices, which was closer to five kilometers from our home. It was but a week or two, with frustrated kids coming home and saying, "I couldn't understand a word they were saying." Upon checking it out further, we realized that along with other Dutch students, they were enrolled in second-year French and third-year German language courses. We were able to talk to the administrators and get them out of their advanced language classes. As time went on, with more offsite interaction with Dutch friends as well as soccer games and practices, they began enjoying school more and getting more out of it. By the end of the year, they became very proficient in Dutch.

Europeans are big on outdoor markets, and the Dutch people are no exception. The midweek and Saturday morning markets were frequently visited. Sometimes, on Wednesday, I would leave the university to go for twenty to thirty minutes to the market to pick up some fresh fruit and vegetables. There was music, the monkey grinder, and other festivities to make the marketplace come alive and be a fun place to visit. The consumption of raw sardines with or without onions was something that our family had difficulty accepting. There were grocery stores, such as Albert Heijn, where indoor shopping could occur. Nearly daily trips were made to the grocery or the open market rather than our traditional one or two trips per week in the States. We acquired the Dutch taste for their cheese and pastries.

In addition to the larger cities, there were many small cities and towns throughout the Netherlands, many only two or three miles apart. Travel between towns that were close by was largely by bicycle. There were also trains that served many of the larger-distance segments. For the first six weeks that we lived in the Netherlands, we only had the four bikes; we did not have a car. As fall approached with cooler temperatures and our desire to travel around the country as well as other countries in Europe, a car seemed highly desirable. With the help of our advisor and new friends made within the department, we found a used Mitsubishi Tredia that served us well. The train worked well for some travel and would be great for an individual, but when you had four people and had four tickets, the extra convenience of the car made a lot of sense. We took many day trips around the country in preparation for the onslaught of visitors that we would have in the spring and summer of '87. Some of our favorites included the flower auction in Alsmeer, the cheese factory in Alkmaar, the beach at Svagingen, and Schiphol Airport in miniature near Rotterdam.

Compared to the States, everything seems so close by in the Netherlands. The trips made to Paris, to certain parts of Germany, and to Belgium were day trips. One of our favorite trips that we took several visitors with us to was to Brussels, Belgium, for some chocolates on to yet the old historic city of Ghent with an old cathedral and to the seaside port of Bruges. Other closer sites included Arnhem, the city from the book *A Bridge Too Far*, which was only ten miles away. Amsterdam was less than eighty minutes away, with several cities on the way. Delph, the famous dish named after it, was only an hour away and exhibited many canals within the city. A more spectacular view than the Keukenhof flower gardens in the spring would be hard to find.

There are fields of flowers that look like an artist's paintbrush of different colors, with tremendous landscaping and flowers in a park. Tulips predominate; hyacinths, daffodils, and other bold flowers are prevalent.

The key to maximizing one's time is to accomplish several things with one trip. I was invited to do speaking engagements and tried to combine them with vacation visitations with my family and with visitors. One was when Judy's parents visited us. I had accepted a speaking engagement at Monheim, Germany, for the Bayer Corporation. One of the stateside representatives from Bayer was doing an exchange from his Kansas City location at this German headquarters facility, and it was great to see a familiar face; he was very helpful. We were treated royally, including a very nice dinner for Judy's parents and my family. The hospitality was unending, and my father-in-law was very impressed. You may recall from an earlier section of the book his embarrassment at the Moulin Rouge; this was my returning the favor to him.

Two couples, the Wakefields and the McMurrys—friends from Lexington, Kentucky—traveled over to spend the week in Austria at a timeshare that he had exchanged. I had a speaking engagement in Basel for the Ciba-Geigy Corporation. I went a day or two earlier to do the presentation, and then we all met in Basel. The other trip was to visit and consult with Professor Hoffman at Weihenstephan University. My first of three trips there was by train, the last two by car with the family.

Stories:

1. As I had mentioned earlier, my decision among the three locations was to do my sabbatical in the Netherlands, but I kept in close contact with Professor Hoffman at Weihenstephan. Networking is an excellent way to achieve goals and assist in your success, both then and now. It was soon after my arrival that arrangements were made to visit Professor Hoffman and his program and discuss mutual efforts to collaborate further. Without a car, the train seemed to be the next best option. I could get on a late afternoon train, ride overnight, and arrive in Munich the next morning. The train did not have a private sleeping quarter, or at least, I did not find

one. The unit I was in was for six people, but we had seven, which included a mother and a small child. The mother and small child were the only two who knew each other. We rode along in silence for several hours before it became time to get ready for sleep. There were triple bunks on each side of the car unit. Everyone went to his or her designated location. Much of this was done by hand signals. I was the middle bunk on one side. A man who fit the description of the typical heavyset man made his way to the top bunk. Pretty soon, I saw some wrestling and jostling under the blankets and saw a couple of feet hanging out over the edge; soon, some underwear dropped down below the sheet, were retrieved and held up, and disappeared under the covers. After some more maneuvering, he seemed to be tucked in for the night under the covers. I removed a few clothes but kept enough on so that I would not be totally embarrassed should the covers come off or if I needed to leave the bunk on short notice. Another young lady and a middle-aged lady made arrangements to hunker down for the evening, and the mother with a small child did her duty of nursing the child before the evening sleep, all in the presence of those in the train car. In some ways, I felt that I had a semester crash course all in one night. We arrived, and after a day and a half with Professor Hoffman, I took the day train back to the Netherlands. Professor Hoffman and I hit it off well, and we made arrangements for future visits with the instruction that I would bring my family with me and we would be housed at his home. I did bring the family on the next trip that I made to visit Dr. and Mrs. Hoffman. We had a lovely stay in their home, and the two families bonded such that our two boys considered them as their European grandparents. Dr. Hoffman had actually fought in World War II on the side of the Germans, and he was not proud of that fact. He was shot down, was captured by the Canadians, and served as a cook in their camp until the end of the war. He arranged to sneak his three daughters and wife out of Eastern Germany, stating that he did not want them to grow up in Communist Germany. He said there was a site that our boys must see, even though it hurt him to show it to them. His wife was just too embarrassed to accompany us to Dachau, the experimental prison camp that Hitler used for captured Jews and others during World War II. Professor Hoffman took us on a personal guided tour of the Dachau museum and explained many of the events that took place there. It was truly inhuman and an unforgettable experience. He told our boys that whatever they did in life, they should do all they can to prevent anything like this ever happening again. I believe this is an experience that both boys will remember for the rest of their lives.

2. While not the Alps, the resort area of Villigen had skiable mountains in the winter, and one weekend the family made a trip of the approximately 150 miles to Villigen to ski. We checked into our hotel, a nice large hotel at the slopes, and went out to ski. The slopes in Villigen compared to the Alps like the Appalachian Mountains

compare to the Rockies. We did have a good time skiing, the four of us. After getting back to the hotel, I went in search of a sauna and saw one advertised at the hotel. I opened the door to walk in and was directly faced with the shower area where both genders were showering together. I immediately thought this was a private club and searched further. Not finding an additional sauna area, I inquired and was told this was for all guests. I went back to the room and asked if any other family members wanted to join me to go to the sauna. Both boys accepted. We went to the area and did not find anyone showering and entered the sauna with our towels. There sat a middle-aged woman in the sauna, European style. We sat down and enjoyed the sauna. After a few looks and an attempt at conversation, it became evident that the lady was from the Netherlands, and JJ and she became conversationalists in Dutch. I enjoyed listening to this exchange in a very natural setting for Europeans yet uncomfortable for me. Obviously, JJ was comfortable, and I cannot speak for Jon. It was interesting. The next morning, when again out on the ski slope, I recognized the sauna lady skiing.

3. Parents' reactions and behaviors can have a big impact on their children. This next story illustrates just that. We were on a trip to Amsterdam with the entire family, and walking down the streets of Amsterdam, naturally, we became hungry, so we decided to stop at a restaurant that served pizza. It was a full-order restaurant, and in typical European style, it was designed to be a slow

meal. We did order and receive our food and were ready to be on our way. We had already been at the restaurant for over an hour, had completed our meal, and were waiting for the check to pay. Europeans are in no hurry to give you the check; I guess they want you to sit there and digest your meal fully before getting up and leaving. Repeated requests of the waiter passing by to give us our check seemed to go unheeded. Finally, after what seemed like ten attempts but was more likely about four, I told the family, "Let's go. We're leaving." They got up with me, and we walked through the restaurant and out the front door and proceeded down the sidewalk without paying. As we were walking away from the restaurant, it did get the attention of the waiter, and he came out onto the street and hollered at us to come back. I think the family wanted to turn around and go back, but I instructed them to keep on walking, and we did. The boys will never forget that we walked away from the restaurant without paying. I was simply too upset at that time for being ignored multiple times and requesting the check to make payment. There may be a moral to the story, but I am not sure how to relate it.

4. Languages can be challenging, and certainly, I got an early introduction of how challenging they can be. We went to a late summer visit to Arnhem and the open-air museum. It was an outdoor historical museum that focused on the planes and other events that took place during World War II, a museum that is very worthwhile seeing if one gets over to that area of the country. It

was a warm afternoon, and there were vendors set up to serve food and drinks. Judy and the two boys did not want to stand in line with me to wait to order, so I said I would order for them. We wanted to each get an ice cream cone. I finally made it to the front of the line and thought I had ordered in Dutch "vier iceja," four ice cream cones. What they heard, along with seeing a single person, was "bier en iceja," and they promptly brought me a beer and ice cream cone. I said, "Nay, nay," raised four fingers, and pointed to my ice cream cone. When all else fails, sign language can be most helpful, even better than trying to speak another language.

5. Another story of language difficulty occurred later during my tenure and was more embarrassing than the beer and ice cream story. It occurred after I should've had better command of the language. I did not have the excuse of being a newbie. The cheese in the Netherlands is to die for, especially the gouda. I went into the local Albert Heijn grocery store, went up to the cheese counter, and again said in my less-than-perfect Dutch that I would have "halof kilo de kaas," thinking I was ordering half a kilo of cheese. "Half" and "eleven" are very similar, and what they heard me say was "eleven kilograms of cheese" or the equivalent of twenty-five pounds. They repeated questioningly, "Eleven kilograms?" I said yes, and so puzzled, they started to cut approximately twenty-five pounds of the large wheel of cheese for me, at which point I said, "No, no, no," and

repeated, "Half." They looked puzzled at me and then, using sign communication, indicated a small one-pound wedge in the cheese, and I nodded affirmatively. Thus, I made another awkward but successful transaction and got my one pound of cheese. This transaction will be related in an interesting future story.

6. Our Dutch house was very poorly insulated, and that was fine for the spring, summer, and fall seasons but not for the winter, especially when we were hit with a very cold winter. We shivered through much of those cold days and piled on many extra blankets as frost and ice developed on the inside of our windows. We had a lovely older neighbor, Mrs. Wolda, who loved the kids and was very friendly.

Our backyards joined, and we could visit each other when we sat out in the backyard, a popular event during the nicer weather, to take tea and cookies, all the while viewing the beautiful flowering backyards and watching the birds. She would often invite our boys over for some of her cookies, which they thoroughly enjoyed. When our two boys' cousin and his family, Judy's sister, visited, their cousin was really into rap songs, and the three boys developed a talking rap script and sang and played it for us as well as for Mrs. Wolda. I don't recall seeing a woman so happy, laughing with tears rolling down her eyes, as when she listened to these three young kids rapping it up for her. It is a memory that sticks in my mind to this day.

7. We were loving German music—the band, the oompah, and the vocals that went with it. A favorite spot for us on Sunday afternoon was the neighboring village, and sitting on the shores of the lake/pond with a group performing just offshore on their platform-like boat was a true joy. This was an event we often enjoyed with just our family but also occasionally with other friends and, in particular, a must-stop for visitors. Sitting on long logs in multiple rows, we got some great photos when our friends from Kentucky visited. The women were busy talking, the music playing. Right on cue, one of the large dogs who had just gone for a swim walked behind the women and began shaking himself dry, giving the women a surprise shower. They stood up, shrieked, and

looked in disbelief at one another. My buddies and I, at the other end of the log, rolled in laughter.

8. Sinterklaas occurs each December 5 and, in many respects, is like our Christmas. The history differs in that Santa does not come by sleigh but comes by boat and is traditionally portrayed as a black man. Small cinnamon cookies called *pepernotens* were prevalent and often used, when sneaking up on houses, to throw at the windows of the house, making a small clattering noise, and then after the throw, you would run away. While that activity was fine, I preferred to eat the *pepernotens* as they were quite delicious and addictive. It also signaled the winter season coming on in full force. Some winters are relatively mild, and others can be quite severe with prolonged freezing temperatures and snow. In our year, we hit the severe lottery. It was the first year for twenty years or more that the neighboring Rhine River froze over. This was received warmly or, I should say, coldly by the local people, who loved to get their skates out and skate on the frozen river. It was a scene out of picture books, with people wrapped in scarves and skating. We joined the celebration on multiple occasions and enjoyed this unique aspect of our sabbatical.

9. Visitors abounded during our sabbatical. There were Judy's parents, my brother and his wife, friends from college, and others. I choose to select a visit that coincided with my wife's sister and much of her family concurrently with our Lexington, Kentucky, friends the

McMurrys. This particular visit resulted in so many memories as we traveled from the Netherlands down through Germany and Switzerland and into Austria. There was a caravan of three cars. Keeping in touch with all three cars on the high-speed *autobahn* and in town was a challenge. While the car we had had a top-end speed of ninety miles per hour, there were cars that passed us as though we were sitting still; 120 plus miles per hour was not unusual. It was important that you stayed in the right-hand lanes. Frequently, the rearview mirror may look free of cars, and in the next ten seconds, there would be a car just zooming by you. Drivers, by and large, were good drivers; however, pileups of forty to fifty cars are common in Europe because of high-speed cruising—a chain reaction. We met the Kentucky family in Basel after I had given one of my talks to Ciba-Geigy. Switzerland is truly beautiful but, even in those days, very expensive. The company took me to lunch, and the lunch bill was over $200 for the three of us. I was not used to spending that kind of money. Back to Basel, I thought I knew my way around, having been there for a couple of days, and asked the other two cars to trust me and said we would get on our way. After leading them into Germany and France and back into Switzerland multiple times, I lost their confidence. This became a real joke for many years whenever we seemed to get a bit lost—"What, are we in Basel again?" Here are a few highlights of the trip so you get the gist of the fun that we had. Stopping for a wine-and-cheese lunch along the Rhine River, we leisurely spread our meal out over a blanket, and Lorraine, Judy's sister, pointed to the sky, saw a bird, and explained, "It's a plane! It's a plane!" and everyone laughed. I think the wine had already taken an effect. In Salzburg, we visited the production site of *The Sound of Music*, and once again, the two sisters got into a giggling mood and could not stop laughing. Lorraine pleaded that her sister stop laughing because she was peeing in her pants, and this increased the laughter all the more. In Vienna, on a more serious note, we were able to take in a Sunday afternoon symphony outdoors, which was truly classical music as it was meant to be. Lucerne, Switzerland, is the most memorable and beautiful city in Switzerland. After our Salzburg and Vienna stops, it was on to the higher altitudes of Austria and our week timeshare that the Kentucky friends had managed to obtain. What fun we had! I had my camera in tow all the time and made it a priority to shoot scenes of people walking away; this would be their posterior side. This distressed our Kentucky friend, Mary, who had a slightly larger backside than the two sisters. I can still hear her saying as she turned around and saw that I was filming her, "Oh, stop it." One evening we went to this restaurant that had evening entertainment, and we all perfected our chicken dance routine, with lots of fun and lots of laughter. On the return, we went to the Eagle's Nest, the Hitler site, and saw the commanding view that he had there. On the roadway down, we stopped at the tunnel where Hitler's last days were, and the men in our group went into the tunnel, but I did not since I wasn't feeling

100 percent at that time. Without mishap, we made our way back through Bavaria, enjoyed a German beer or two, and made it safely back to the Netherlands. All persons on that wonderful trip would have memories for the rest of their lives.

10. The schooling there was quite different from what we had experienced in the States. In my day, sex talk was off-limits and only mentioned in private. Europeans seem to be less inhibited by sex. Two events are shared to make my point. JJ went with his friend and the friend's family to the beach, and I recall him coming back and sharing that it was a different experience when his friend's mother came to the lunch picnic and sat at the table topless. When they were going to the beach, most if not all clothes were removed, and evidently, they were not bothered to be put back on for a lunch or small interruption. Both kids had group outdoor overnight living experiences. These were done in groups. In many ways, this did increase socialization and prepare students better for when they would leave the family home and be on their own. The elder son had to secure a part-time job while preparing for one of these excursions. He had to communicate with the employer, negotiate, and work for them while gone. I believe he chose a swimming pool job. They were given a list of employers in the region, and it was their responsibility to get things set up. It was a good example of developing independence. A saying that continues to resonate with my two sons and me to this day is "Ya, ya. Of niet," translated "Yes, yes. Isn't

that right?" or "Isn't that so?" Another phrase that was used by my younger son's teacher was "and dat sorta dinga," translated "and that sort of thing," which was what she repeatedly tacked onto many of her sentences. The boys also learned to like to eat mayonnaise with the popular french fries that so many kids loved. Their mother, on the other hand, never adjusted to this and still prefers ketchup with french fries to this day. In my opinion, all of the above were educational experiences not available in U.S. textbooks.

11. Both boys learned the language quite well in the end. The elder son, two years later, upon entering college, took a Dutch proficiency test and was awarded two years of college credit in Dutch, the foreign language. The younger son learned Dutch and focused a bit more on street talk. One day, when his uncle was visiting, the two of them rode their bikes down to the morning market; they sat along the side of the street for a breather and perhaps a small bite to eat. Several other Dutch boys rode by on their bikes and evidently mentioned in Dutch the two gringos sitting by the wayside in a not-so-complimentary way. My son shouted back at them, "Ha ya bek, clot zak!" and received a startled look back from the boys riding their bikes. His uncle inquired, "What did you say to them?" My son said that he told them to "shut your mouth, asshole." This provided many years of laughter between the two.

12. If the boys are asked, "When was your dad the most angry?" they would likely reply when we went on a bike ride, the three of us, to the nearby town of Nijmegen and also into Germany, a one-hundred-plus-kilometer bike ride. It was planned to take the entire day, included with a lunch packed by their mother. The trip did not get off to a good start and almost did not happen. We were riding down the sidewalk a little less than a mile on our trip, riding past the home of my professor/advisor, when the younger son exclaimed as we were riding by, "Hey, Martin, baby!" Dr. Martin Devard was standing in his backyard as we drove by, and I was certain he heard the slang and what I perceived as derogatory reference. We stopped at the next intersection and had a heart-to-heart talk; I was questioning if we should turn around and cancel the rest the trip or go on, and in no uncertain terms, they knew I was ticked off. We ended up going on and completing our scheduled full-day event, but the remainder of the day had a "chill" in the air because of this comment that was made.

13. I will end this baker's dozen of stories with one of my favorite stories. You now have the impression that during my years, I was the deliverer of many pranks and jokes. To do that, it is important that you are willing to be what one may call the "butt of the joke." Truly, I was in this next instance. My counterpart had a son the age of JJ, the elder son. JJ was one of the taller kids his age and was a star on the basketball team. One day JJ came upon five or six of his friends visiting on the sidewalk

in conversation. My counterpart's son was relaying a story to his friends, saying, "There is an American here in town who thinks he can speak good Dutch," and he relayed the story of the eleven kilos of cheese instead of half a kilo. JJ interrupted the group and said, "Do not laugh. That was my father!" in perfect Dutch. I was my own enemy in that case as I shared that story with my counterpart and he, in turn, with his family. I am glad everyone got a good laugh out of this and it is a story that has been retold many times.

CHAPTER 11

The National Association of Wheat
Growers Foundation, 1989–1992

Arriving back from the sabbatical leave in 1987, we were welcomed by friends and colleagues. It was not quite the same, but it was hard to put a finger on why life seemed different. It did not take long to get reengaged in the work cycle and back on several committees. I was forty-three years of age; perhaps a non-recognized midlife crisis was simmering. I was invited to serve on a writing team for a new classy national wheat pest management publication that would be useful to wheat producers and the wheat industry. I was associate author on a grain storage chapter and lead author on another chapter dealing with wheat diseases. This publication was a slick color photo and narrative publication completed in early 1989. Several of the authors, including myself, were invited to Washington, D.C., to participate in the rollout of the publication before the NAWG in early 1989.

At this time, the popular University of Kentucky extension director, also known as the father of no-till agriculture, was set to retire, and his position was advertised. The dean of the college appointed an eight-person search committee that included four to five of what he considered his top extension specialists. When he asked me to serve on the committee, he said he only wanted me to be on the committee if I was not a candidate for the position. I took this as a sign that he would have liked for me to apply for the position, potentially joining his team of administrators in the College of Agriculture at the University of Kentucky.

In 1987, upon my return from the sabbatical, Ciba-Geigy, a large producer of pesticides, contacted me and wanted to come out to the campus, produce videos of wheat diseases, and interview me. They sent their film crew from New York City to our campus and spent a day and a half shooting video clips and interviews both at the lab and in the field. These clips became known as "Stuckey from Kentucky," a short descriptor created several years earlier. The descriptor origin occurred at an annual meeting of our profession where extension specialists in plant pathology gathered for a breakfast. There were close to a hundred in attendance, and as was common, after the breakfast, they would go around the room, and we would introduce ourselves. This took a while, generally accomplished in fifteen to twenty minutes. One year I decided to keep it short, so when I stood up, I said two words—"Stuckey, Kentucky"—and sat down. People got a kick out of that, and it stuck. A moral to the story is that when you can say something/communicate in few words, the better it is for retention by others.

I am not sure how best to describe what took place in early 1989, but whatever it was had been brewing ever since I returned from the sabbatical. My annual evaluations and raises remained at the top of the scale, but somehow I did not feel as fulfilled as I had felt in my earlier years. I looked around and saw some of my older colleagues living life on Easy Street. They too were tenured, and they were approaching retirement years. While they may have been very efficient in their work and search for knowledge, they did not exhibit the energy and enthusiasm that younger faculty members striving to become fully tenured did.

There was a term known as "dying on the vine" used for faculty members who seemed to glide into retirement. I did not want to be one of them. I seemed to lose just a little bit of an edge for my job. If this were happening at age forty-five, what would it be like at fifty-five? These questions haunted me. With age, other employment becomes harder to obtain.

Who wants to hire an older person who has limited years of employment left at a higher salary than someone younger and with more years of employment left? However, what better life could I have, a fully tenured professor with job guarantee, living in a great part of the country with many friends and family?

Nonetheless, the presentation of the wheat handbook went well, and after that presentation, the senior vice president of the NAWG came back into the meeting and asked if he could see me outside for a moment. While I did not know it at the time, this would become another seminal life-changing event. Jerry Reese informed me that they had a position open for director of the foundation in the organization and inquired if I would be interested in that position. He encouraged me to think about it and said they would love to have me, it would be a very stimulating and rewarding position, etc. It did give me a lot to think about and one that I would consider strongly, more so than some other offers I had received over the past couple of years, especially one with Merck & Company, located in New Jersey. I had several friends who were employees of Merck, and I slightly envied the unlimited budget they had for supporting professionals with whom they worked. We were showered with gifts and free trips, but I can truly say that never once was my honesty compromised and my recommendations altered as a result of such treatment. With the Wheat Growers position, there would not be gifts and free trips given, but I would have substantial funds for travel at my discretion.

Perhaps I should expound a bit on some of the free trips received while I was a professor at the University of Kentucky. Merck salespeople enjoyed hosting a group of specialists, one from each university, in the Southern region for a long weekend at Fort Myers, Florida, or Fort Walton Beach, Florida. During the winter, short meetings were held to spend more time going deep-sea fishing. Just a few years ago, I parted with my personalized fishing rod and reel given to me. We went out on these deep-sea fishing trips irrespective of the weather once we were there. One year it was quite rough, and over half of the fishing participants became seasick. Anyone who has become seasick knows that terrible feeling. Continued vomiting until there is nothing left to bring up creates a condition known as the dry heaves. Finally, getting back on shore and taking a shower made one feel like they were out rocking on the water again. I remember one guy who did not get sick coming around and offering a drink or a sandwich to us, which was the last thing that we wanted, and he laughed. Another guy was fishing out over the edge of the boat, pitching his cookies, and commented, "I might as well fish even if I am sick." He was a true diehard. Most of the rest of us had our heads buried in a garbage can. Generally, we had grouper and red snapper available to take home in dried ice to enjoy long after our fishing expedition.

Another company, Mobay, took a multidisciplinary team of eight to ten faculty members north during the summer to a lake in Canada to do walleye fishing. We flew into Northern Michigan and, from there, had a car ride of four to five hours until we got to the small flight area, where we boarded a seaplane that flew us to the lake where we would be for the next five days, secluded, with very few on the lake. There were two dorm facilities and a couple of cooks to serve our meals. Talk about getting away from it all—this was it. I can still taste the fresh lake walleye that we caught and had fixed on a small island for lunch at noon repeatedly. They tasted so good. Sorry, I got distracted a bit. Back to my story.

Jerry Reese kept calling and inquiring and encouraging me to accept the position offered at the Wheat Growers office. I decided that I would be giving up too much and declined the offer. A week later, he contacted me again and wondered if I changed my mind or if he could change my mind. Once again, I said no but must have been a little less definitive as he noticed a crack. It was at this time that the administration became aware that I was seriously considering another position and leaving the University of Kentucky. The dean of the college said he would go to the president to get an adjustment in my salary; he also wondered what position I would like within the college and said that he would be open to making that happen. He also offered to contact the president and visit with him when he felt that he was not being persuasive in keeping me at Kentucky.

My salary was adjusted from $54,000 to $60,000 with the annual increase scheduled for July 1. Suddenly, the $65,000 job offer that was $11,000 above my current salary did not seem like such an increase, especially living in the Washington, D.C., area compared to Lexington. I had several phone conversations with the president of the university, who had a math discipline, and he assured me that he would be staying at the University of Kentucky despite the rumors that were floating around in relation to a basketball scandal.

Jerry Reese wanted to fly my wife and me out to D.C. to look at the area if I was giving the job serious consideration. As I recall, Judy was not really excited about me changing jobs, but as they say, it would not hurt to take a look. That, we did, and given the fact that I could not get this position with great potential out of my mind, we—or I should say I, with the consent of Judy—decided to make the move. This move was to open even more doors for the future. Our parents in their wisdom had reservations about this move.

We looked in Virginia and in Maryland in the suburbs surrounding D.C. where many D.C. workers lived. Virginia was a bit more Southern, but there were many bridges to cross if one were driving into D.C. There was the corridor from D.C. out to Dulles Airport, and then there was Alexandria, south and west of D.C.; both areas were well connected with the metro mass transit system for travel into and out of the city. Maryland did not have bridges to cross to get to D.C., and they did have metro mass transit as well as a MARC train that had service.

We settled on Maryland, in the town of Gaithersburg, just north of Rockville, which had metro service from the Shady Grove stop and also had a MARC train service from Gaithersburg, both direct routes to Union Station. My office would be a block and a half from the Senate buildings at the capital and a block and a half from Union Station. Both the Red Line metro and the train went into Union Station. It was quite convenient for the commute of forty-five minutes each way. We rented an apartment close to the site where we were having a home built in the small community of Hampton Estates. After about three months, our new home was completed, and we were able to move. We made good friends there, and the fifty-five new homes were near a park, only a mile from the train stop, and six miles from the end of the Red Line metro transit. Again, the timing of the move seemed a good fit from the prospects of our kids; the older one had graduated from high school and was now going to enter college in the fall, and the younger one was moving from the ninth grade to high school.

Time to begin work. What exactly was the foundation director of the national lobby group, the NAWG? In essence, it was the research and education arm of the lobby group. It was a 501(c)(3) unit, and the office building was listed as a foundation property for tax purposes. The staff at Wheat Growers consisted of eight employees in the association and myself and a secretary in the foundation. You have heard "the tail wagging the dog"; well, the foundation was the tail, and it was not yet wagging the dog.

There were eighteen wheat-growing states in the United States that were members of the NAWG. These were the major wheat-growing areas of the United States. Following my appointment, two other states joined, Kentucky and Virginia. There were only three states east of the Mississippi that were members. Those were North Carolina, Virginia, and Kentucky. Minnesota, the two Dakotas, Montana, Idaho, Washington, Oregon, Colorado, Wyoming, Nebraska, Kansas, Oklahoma, Texas, Arizona, New Mexico, Arkansas, and California made up the remaining states.

The primary purpose of these states to join the association was to have collective representation in Washington, D.C., for programs that would benefit wheat producers in their states. The wisdom of the farmers of the association was to create a side branch known as "the foundation" to provide research and education programs apart from the lobby effort and also to have a legitimate partition of the organization to benefit from tax assessments in building ownership and contributions that could be received that would benefit the organization through the foundation.

The foundation had one previous director prior to my arrival. There was a sister organization known as Wheat Associates that comprised most of the same states but with the purpose of promoting wheat marketing and trade. From the beginning, the foundation seemed to be better aligned with Wheat Associates than Wheat Growers. As director of the foundation, I reported directly to the CEO of the NAWG, a very political position. Interestingly, my advocate, Jerry Reese, had the title of senior vice president after having been the CEO but was demoted because of a comment he had made about a senator's wife during a cocktail reception prior to my arrival. Jerry was much more reasonable; he appreciated the research and education, whereas the CEO did not. This was sure to become a future storm. Within a year after I was hired, Jerry retired, and I got the distinct impression that it was his job to hire a foundation director, get the director on his feet, and then leave. Jerry was very well connected in D.C. and introduced me to many valuable contacts before he left, especially within the USDA and industry. The CEO did none of that!

The wheat lobby group was a powerful commodity group for its constituents but not as strong as the corn, soybean, cotton, and sugar industries. These groups had strong affiliation with senators in the agricultural states where their crop was represented. The groups would work together in certain cases but again, on many occasions, would work against one another for their own specific purposes. One of the new initiatives when I arrived on the scene was to push for additional agricultural research funding. The state universities were among those strongly supporting this and invited the commodity groups and industry to join their efforts. The industry did a lot of agricultural research, but it was viewed as slightly tainted since they had an ulterior motive to promote their products with the research they were doing. The state universities, on the other hand, were viewed as more independent with unbiased research results.

It was not long, with some of my previous connections within the USDA, that I was appointed the coordinator of the grains research team to support increased funding through what was known as the National Research Initiative (NRI). This team consisted of representatives from corn, barley, oats, sorghum, and wheat. Those organizations that did not have foundations often had university grain breeders participate in the group. One in particular was the oat breeder from the University of Minnesota who became instrumental in my next job, but that is three years away.

Another friend whom I had met back in graduate school at Michigan State when he came as a student guest lecturer was Dr. Arthur Kelman. Our paths crossed numerous times, and our relationship would only become stronger. He was an advocate who encouraged me to apply at the University of

Wisconsin prior to my going to the University of Kentucky. After being dean at the University of Wisconsin, he returned to North Carolina State University, where he finished his career. He was appointed the chief scientist at the USDA and in charge of the NRI. Working together, we gained additional mutual respect for each other. My coordination of the grain commodities and eventually testifying before Congress on the need for additional funding for agriculture research increased my stature with him. Much of this discourse is to demonstrate the tremendous importance of networking and having a broad base of communication, not knowing what your future will hold.

Jerry Reese was introducing me not only to organizations and persons that I could see direct relationships with and benefit from knowing but also to others that I thought were a far reach, such as the American Petroleum Institute and Toyota trucks and cars. The introductions generally occurred over lunches or at early evening receptions. My point is that he had good insight into expanding the circle of supporters for our organization. I could readily see the connection through the government and private industry as the chemical industry, farm equipment industry, and other agricultural entities that did business with wheat producers.

A development committee of agricultural businesses was formed, to be affiliated with the foundation. This was a very strong and powerful group of which I was appreciative; I worked hard to create programs they were interested in and that would benefit the research and education aspect for wheat producers. Members of this committee, some of which joined after I became director, included Monsanto, DuPont, Dow Elanco, Zeneca, Ciba-Geigy, Mobay/Bayer, John Deere, Case IH, Burlington Northern Railroad, etc.

Each of these companies was very supportive, contributing annual fees of $5,000 or more plus much more additional funds for programs that they sponsored. There was the wheat yield contest sponsored by Ciba-Geigy that became a very big project across all five classes of wheat, with the top three yields in each of the classes being recognized widely and promoted. This was the same company that sent out the film crews when I was at the University of Kentucky to do wheat videos. Another was a farm safety program sponsored by John Deere and Dow Elanco. Yet another was a Monsanto program to recognize new leading young producers in various states. DuPont had a leadership program that brought people in to see their plant and some educational talks on an annual basis. Burlington Northern Railroad funded a transportation study routed through the foundation and contracted to a team led by scientists at North Dakota State University to identify some of the issues related to car shortage and the transportation of wheat. There were other programs that were industry sponsored and supported, but as you can see, my plate was becoming full administering all these new programs.

In addition, I worked closely with other wheat-related industries such as the Millers' Federation and some studies with U.S. Wheat Associates dealing with quality issues for export. The Wheat Industry Resource Committee was a group of scientists at universities doing work in wheat research that I became close to, along with wheat breeders across the country. Many meetings and committees sought my participation and attendance. These efforts would frequently lead to special workshops, video-recorded meetings, and publications of such meetings, which also required some time, although others did much of this work in these organizations. It seemed like the blessing of the foundation and the wheat growers was important to these groups. I had no problem getting cooperation and collaboration.

Yet another significant initiative of the foundation was to encourage a pooling of some of the funding from individual states to go to a competitive grants program, defined as research of common interest among states. This had the advantage of providing a larger pot of funds to do significant research and to limit the amount of duplication of research that was occurring in multiple states. As a start, the first funded research was to Dr. Whistler at Purdue University, a renowned carbohydrate research scientist. His project was to look at the separation of small and large granules of starch in wheat for the purpose of developing facial cosmetics. There was no question that this laboratory was highly qualified. Furthermore, if the small starch granules could be used to develop facial creams, this would increase the market for wheat. The rub was that these funds were coming from state associations. and the state of Indiana was not a state member. We did survive this minor conflict, and most people agreed that the concept of pooling some money together to make a bigger pot to do a larger project was worth pursuing.

One additional program that must be mentioned and given some detail is the collaboration with the economics group within the USDA. Together, we developed a program known as "The Importance of Developing Economies of Developing Countries for the Wheat Export Market." We recruited up to three spokespersons per state who would take the information provided and share that with people in their communities, be it church groups, service organizations, or others. Many of the states the first year started with single representatives; some that were more gung ho with the program had three. This program grew each year. The wheat producers were trained as spokespersons for the program, stating that foreign aid to developing countries was important for their economies to improve so they would become traders and purchasers of U.S. agricultural products. Just so, the programs did not teach foreign countries to become producers in the crops that we wanted to export to them. For example, the soybean production techniques given to the Brazilians came back to haunt the U.S. farmer as the Brazilians began to grow large acreages of soybeans that competed with the United States for other export markets. This program was the first commodity-funded program by a Biden Pell Grant from Congress, certainly a feather in the foundation and my hat.

The first year, the group was brought into D.C. for three days of training and listening to some of the top experts in the field. Speakers included Carol Brookins, president of World Perspectives, Congressman Beuriter from Nebraska, Dennis Avery from the Hudson Institute, John Costello from Citizens Network, and many others. We also created a training session for speaking on camera on news programs. This program was highly successful and visible. The second year, the group met at Winrock International on Petit Jean Mountain, Arkansas, home of Winrock International. Winrock also had an office in Virginia, just outside D.C. The second year, the spokespersons received training in international development and had a good session in economics. Speakers were brought in from around the country to address thirty or so wheat producers. One year, we made arrangements to visit Heifer International, which was en route from Little Rock to the Winrock headquarters. Several years into the program, the second group to visit Winrock were having a great meeting.

While the foundation had invited Winrock to be a partner in this program, assisting in providing additional education to wheat producers, Winrock began their own program, successfully obtaining grant funds to begin a new program called the Farmer-to-Farmer Program in the newly independent states of the Soviet Union. Winrock invited Wheat Growers to be a partner and to assist in identifying farmers who would become exchange persons to provide training and also to host farmers from the newly independent states to learn the techniques that the United

States was using. This was a rather large grant, and the foundation was going to receive a good piece of that to administer the program.

Many of the development committee members, especially farm equipment and international chemical companies, were excited about the program, much more than my officemates at the NAWG and Wheat Associates. To accommodate these programs required an increase in staffing, so the foundation grew from two persons to four full-time persons and also included partial salaries for several who were working in the NAWG for their limited support. I was providing as much support for the rest of the office, personnel and services that I felt were legitimate. The CEO wanted me to put more people on salary without their work supporting our work. He even reasoned that I should put over 100 percent of one of my employee's salary on the grant. We already had office overhead and other expenses that are legitimate tied to the grant. A real conflict was brewing, plus uneasiness with some of the export people in states that were affiliated with Wheat Associates.

The chair of my development committee from Case IH inquired of my salary and was astonished that it was not more than what it was. From my starting salary of $65,000, I had received a couple of increases, one based on Jerry Reese going to bat for me, to $73,600, which the CEO was clearly not happy with because it brought me very close to the highest salaried person in the office other than him, who had more work experience but did not have a terminal degree. When the chairman of the development committee, against my knowledge, went to the CEO and president of the foundation and made the case that I was greatly underpaid and that they needed to increase my pay, they viewed it as meddling and perhaps erroneously assumed that I was behind the request for an increase. I was not.

Back to the Winrock meeting. There was a conference call among my CEO, the grower president of the foundation, and me regarding continued participation in the Farmer-to-Farmer Program. The CEO of Winrock, Bob Havener, had just spoken to our group and applauded us for the insight that we had in partnering with them when I had to inform them that an executive decision had been made to discontinue our involvement in their program. I was heartbroken, as were the wheat growers that were involved in the program. They asked me who had made that decision, and I told them it was an executive decision. They inquired who the executives were; I told them the CEO of NAWG, the president of the foundation, and me and that the vote was two to one. I was the lone person voting for the program. They were very upset and initiated calls to their fellow wheat grower, who was president of the foundation. He did not react kindly to those calls and, of course, blamed me for inciting them to make the calls. From that day forward, there were numerous roadblocks put up in front of me. It was obvious that many saw the foundation becoming the body of the dog and no longer the tail, and they were uncomfortable with losing power.

My staff revised and improved the monthly *Wheat Technology* publication produced within our foundation, sharing research and new developments among the various sectors of the wheat community. The artistry of the young gal in charge of putting it together became very popular. The foundation had just underwritten the cost of upgrading all the computers in the office and networking them for a cost of over $60,000, forwarded from foundation funds to be repaid, and accounting trickery books showed that the foundation was losing money. This was used as a reason to discontinue publishing *Wheat Technology*, which cost about $1,100 per issue. One of the development committee members was so impressed with the publication that they offered to make a contribution to totally offset the cost of *Wheat Technology*. The CEO and president of the foundation declined this. Others put more roadblocks in my way through the lack of cooperation in the NAWG office.

Seeing and forecasting a rocky road ahead, it was no wonder I applied when I was invited to apply for the chairman position of plant pathology at North Carolina State University. I loved my job where I was, but it was difficult to operate successfully. So I thought I would apply when encouraged. There were twenty-three professionals who applied; some were previous department heads, so it was a good job and one that was well sought after. They narrowed the search down to three candidates, and I was one of those three. One of the final three was a former president of the APS and the current department chair at the neighboring state university of Clemson. The third was a biotechnology professor at Virginia Polytech institute and State University. We were each invited to interview on campus. I knew at least half of the faculty before going for the interview. The problem was the stature of the senior candidate from Clemson, who knew the entire faculty.

After the interviews, the dean called me and told me there were two candidates that the faculty agreed could lead their department: the person from Clemson and me. The faculty did vote for the person from Clemson as their first choice and me as their second choice. Either of us would be acceptable, but if neither one of us was available, they would then continue the search. This was an honor, but what fun is it coming in second? I had taken several days of personal leave to go and interview.

The president of the foundation learned of my application and told the CEO, and they were very disappointed that I was looking at other positions. It did not matter that I was asked to apply; I was out looking. This occurred in February 1992. In March, I learned that the person from Clemson had accepted the offer. The chief scientist for agricultural research in the USDA is now at North Carolina State University. I was disappointed I did not get the job. He felt my Washington, D.C., experience, savvy, and working across so many lines would've been a big asset to their department, whereas a senior fellow would retain the department pretty much as status quo.

Fast-forward to Friday, May 8, 1992. We were taking our secretary out for lunch since it was going to be her last day as she had obtained another higher-paying job. It was that morning before going to lunch that the CEO came into my office and, for the second or third time, began berating and swearing at me, wondering what was wrong with my blankity-blank mind etc., and said I would need to leave, i.e., I was fired. I could come in over the weekend and pick up my things, but I was not to come in on Monday or thereafter. I knew my situation was bad, but what a shock! The accountant told me he certainly did not understand why they were doing what they were doing with the way the foundation was performing so well. Both of our parents were very upset with my dismissal and the way it was handled.

Politics can be a very nasty business. I learned the hard way. A short press release was put out that I had left the foundation. Calls came in inquiring, and the response was that I had left and they did not know where I was. I had some friends who had mailed some correspondence to me at the office. Nothing was forwarded to me. My two colleagues in the foundation were in shock and disbelief when I told them that the lunch for the secretary was a double farewell, that I would be leaving, and that this was my last day. On Monday, they went into the CEO's office and demanded to know what was going on and what their future was. One quit within a month, and the other one hung on for some time as a replacement for me was brought in, a lady who did not have the qualifications that I had, and the saying among growers and professionals was that she was a joke. She did not last long.

The foundation no longer flourished. After a year or so, a capable person was hired, but it was not the same, and the statement was made that we would not let what happened to me happen to him. My departure created a real stir, several states threatening to resign from the association. I was issued a decree that I was not to contact any person, group, or affiliation with which I had contacts because of Wheat Growers and that if I violated that, my accumulated savings would not be granted me. I was given six weeks of annual leave payment and promised several months after that I would be receiving my retirement funds if I did not violate the contract. I really felt very mistreated and considered getting a lawyer and exposing the CEO and others who were so unprofessional and had violated the nonprofit status of the foundation on several occasions. I did not do that for the benefit of many of the wheat growers whom I had become friends with and cared for deeply.

Now I was without a job and had one son going back for his senior year in college in the fall, the other son beginning college in the fall. What an untimely time to be out of work! I used my network of friends. One was at the Agriculture Research Institute, where I served on their board, and the potential of a position was there, but this organization was struggling and did not have a bright future. There was a possibility of taking a position with the USDA, but they currently were not hiring, although I did have a commitment that I would be highly considered when they began rehiring.

Another friend in the USDA with the Agricultural Research Service advised me with caution about a job posting at the Council for Agricultural Science and Technology (CAST). The position looked good to me, but she cautioned that she had heard there were some problems within the office and that the organization was facing some tough times. Nonetheless, in late June or early July, I put in my application for the position. The chair of the search committee happened to be an oat breeder who had worked with me on the Agricultural Research Initiative when I chaired the grain commodity committee on behalf of agriculture research support. What a useful connection! He was excited about my application and kept in touch with me.

In August, after vacationing in Colorado and trying to keep up with any news regarding the position, I was informed that I was one of two candidates they planned to interview. In mid-August, I traveled to Ames, Iowa, the headquarters for CAST, to interview with the oat breeder from the University of Minnesota, the administrator from the University of Georgia and the current president of CAST, and a local agronomist from the industry who was also on the search committee. These three interviewed me in person and connected to a conference call with other search committee members. One was the vice president of General Mills, another was the president of the Foundation for Agronomic Research, a subsidiary of the Potassium and

Potash Institute, and yet another was the associate dean of the college at Ohio State University. The associate dean had applied for the college dean position at the University of Kentucky when I was a faculty member there, so I did have some connection with him. All in all, it was a good interview but again with some highly placed individuals in the agricultural community. Of course, we had dinner at the famous Hickory Park restaurant, known for its barbecue and a favorite dining place for many who came to Ames.

Within three or four days, I received a call offering the position to me. I told them I would like to go over the offer with them, think about it for several days, and get back to them. I did not want to wait too long as I had no other good leads for a job in the near future. In my mind, this was not as difficult a decision as some of the others I had faced earlier in my career. I was now forty-eight years old, and if everything worked out well, this could be my capstone job. Pleasantly, the job offer came in at $90,000, a significant raise from what I was getting at Wheat Growers, plus the cost of living in Ames was much less than that in Washington, D.C. My start date was September 1, 1992.

Before I move to the next job, there will be a few stories told and a listing of some of the accomplishments included in less than three years, which, to this day, amazes me.

Richard Stuckey

Stories:

1. Each summer, there was a meeting for state association officials and other interested farmers to conduct business and enjoy the summer weather. Colorado and Idaho were two popular areas for summer meetings. The first one was held at Steamboat Springs in Colorado. I recall two events at that meeting. The first was a live auction where different growers and businesses donated articles of value to be auctioned off to growers and agribusinesses in the audience. This was a fundraiser for the foundation organized by Jerry Reese, my advisor at the foundation. It was fast and furious, and I was one of the callers who recognized bids from the audience. There were paintings that were bid off, and then we were responsible for getting them packaged and sent to the address of the person buying them since they were too large to carry with them on the return trip. I do not recall how much was raised, but it was a nice substantial sum and provided discretionary income for the foundation. This was at a time when the foundation had very limited resources and prior to the full establishment of the development committee and the programs they supported plus the grants that we were soon able to receive to help support our program. I recall one of the gals in our office who was in charge of fundraising for the grower associations stating that my efforts in fundraising had sex appeal, whereas hers did not. She was a bit jealous of the support I was receiving from the development committee for the research/educational aspect and that such contributions

were eligible for tax deductions. The other memory was playing a beautiful golf course, freezing up, and having difficulty hitting the ball with any regularity. Although I had played the game before, I did absolutely terribly and was an embarrassment to my advisor.

2. Many wheat growers were also barley growers. The barley group did not have an organized presence in Washington, D.C., and they petitioned the wheat growers to contract with them to represent their interest in regulatory and legislative affairs in D.C. A contract was drawn up and approved by both parties, which included a point person within the wheat growers to represent the barley group. Guess who was assigned to be the point person? Yes, the CEO asked me if I would take on that responsibility; of course, I had no choice but to say yes. So this added workload to my schedule in addition to trying to advance the foundation program. Much of the barley-growing region was in Minnesota, the Dakotas, and Montana, and the meetings were generally held in North Dakota. I was familiar with the barley crop, not nearly as much as the wheat crop, but it is a relative. I was very inexperienced with the regulatory and legislative issues and did not have the appropriate contacts there. So after a year or so, I think all parties realized this was not the appropriate fit. This is something the CEO should have known from the beginning, but he was interested in gaining the dollar and not expending any of his staff to get that dollar.

One could also argue a conflict of interest for research and education in the regulatory and legislative arenas.

3. My first testimony before Congress was interesting and something I realized I would be doing many times in the future, but at that time, it was totally new and a somewhat intimidating experience. The testimony was prepared, reviewed by my legislative affairs counterparts in the NAWG part of our organization. A few suggestions were made, but the major reason for asking for the review was to make sure that it was approved by the organization so I would not take flack for the testimony given. I got through it fine, and it bolstered my confidence that I should not fear conversing with anyone no matter his or her rank or viewed prestige. This boldness would help me in the future.

4. Two enjoyable international trips were taken during my time with the foundation. One was a trip to Europe, Germany in particular, to view the wheat-growing areas and practices. Accompanying me were Del Wiedemann, the current NAWG president, a farmer from Kansas, and Dr. Steve Amosson, an agricultural economist from Texas who was president of the Wheat Industry Resource Committee. Meetings were arranged with researchers and influential leaders in Germany, and one of the very memorable events was attending Oktoberfest in Munich, the second of three times I experienced Oktoberfest. The second international experience was with Winrock International on an exploratory trip for

the Farmer-to-Farmer Program that the foundation was to participate in with Winrock. I traveled with their program director to Prague, Czechoslovakia, and to Poland, where we visited many sites and locations. What a difference between Prague and Warsaw! This travel took place in February, just months before I was relieved of my job. Two other meetings that I was denied attending were one to South Africa to see wheat reproduction there and the other to a golf tournament in North Carolina. A young colleague on the NAWG's staff was given the opportunity to go to those two meetings even though the agenda clearly was more in my purview. This was so much more evidence of illogical reasoning by the CEO.

5. Two specific activities were viewed as very helpful to the organization. One was a study in the use of soft red winter wheat that was published. The NAWG had established a priority of attracting states that grew this class of wheat since state membership was low in this area, where there was potential growth. With this report, we gained favor with Virginia and Kentucky, and also, North Carolina thought we were doing something for them. Another team member and I went to Georgia to encourage their joining the association. The other activity for which I received praise from our CEO, one of the very few times, was through my connections at program leader levels in the USDA that a dreaded disease of wheat had entered the United States. There was a disease known as Karnal bunt known to exist in Mexico for many years

but was successfully kept out of the United States. The CEO of Wheat Associates nicknamed the disease "the AIDS of wheat." The disease belongs to the smut group of diseases and, in addition to being black and sooty looking, had a detectible fishy odor. I alerted people in my organization and they, in turn, other affiliate organizations. Immediately, a meeting was convened in our foundation board meeting room. Reactions to this news were strong and varied. Everyone appreciated the advanced notice; there were different recommendations for handling the problem. Several wanted to deny the fact; others wanted to downplay it and say it would all be controlled. Yet others wanted to set up quarantines. The disease was currently confined to a cargo ship in the port of Houston. From this meeting, a hastily called meeting with the secretary of agriculture was arranged, and I was invited to participate in the meeting. The CEO told me that this information that I had obtained was very useful. The extent of politics and information massaging was becoming clear to me.

6. For many reasons, I used the MARC train to commute from my Gaithersburg home into Washington, D.C. A monthly pass was much cheaper than taking the metro. I could park my car for free in a large parking lot just a mile from my home compared to the six-mile commute to the end of the metro line plus a parking fee each day. Another advantage was that you could eat on the train but not on the metro, and it was easier to do work or read the paper on the train because of less

commotion and stops. The disadvantage was that there were only five runs in the morning, which was not really a problem, but only five runs in the afternoon, which oftentimes created a problem. Trains, like planes, do not wait. Either you're there on time or you miss the boat. I met a fellow and two gals who rode the train each day. As much as possible, we tried to coordinate our schedules to be on the same train going home in the afternoon so that we could play cards and visit to make that forty-five-minute commute go faster.

7. My brother-in-law, Ron, an architect, who designed our back patio

had some work in Maryland and would occasionally stay with us when he came out to review the work that was progressing. The first three months of my job, before my family moved out with me, I rented an apartment in

Virginia, and Ron visited during that time. We went to see a movie one evening, *When Harry Met Sally*, and both thoroughly enjoyed the movie and the famous scene when the older lady sitting next to the table where Harry and Sally were dining exclaimed that she would have what Sally was having. Sally was faking her excitement to prove to Harry that girls could fake it. I was running a bit late as usual, so I had to speed and take shortcuts to get to the movie on time. Ron said he learned the art of city driving from me during that trip. We so enjoyed the movie and the famous scene that I got a tape and recorded that portion for later use. The use was only months away as that summer, we had planned a great trip on Lake Powell in Utah for four of our very good Kentucky friends as well as Judy's sister and brother-in-law. Six couples rented a houseboat for a week on Lake Powell. Judy and I flew to Denver, Colorado, where her sister and Ron lived. From there, we carpooled to Lake Powell to meet the other four couples. We stayed overnight in Western Colorado and shared a double bedroom to cut down on expenses. I brought the tape recorder and the recorded scene and placed the tape recorder on the floor next to me after both couples retired. Ron was in on the secret, but neither of our wives was. All was quiet because of the ten-minute lag I had placed at the beginning of the tape when suddenly, a slow moan sounded. Increasing moans followed this! The sisters did not know what to think at first and then started laughing and realized the joke that was being played. They enthusiastically endorsed playing the same prank on the houseboat. We did, and it was a success, with small snickers and giggles occurring until finally, one party said, "Stuckey, is that you again?"

8. You may recall my sabbatical leave in collaboration with Professor Hoffman in Germany. My consulting work with Professor Hoffman using predictive systems of fungicide applications for disease control on wheat was an impetus for him and his colleague to plan a trip to the United States to visit wheat production, in particular Kentucky, and to visit me in Washington, D.C. It was great to see him and his colleague again and welcome them to the foundation that I was directing. I explained to them the workings of the association and foundation on behalf of the wheat producers. They were very impressed and stated frequently that they wished they had such an organization in Germany. They stayed overnight with us in our home, and one extremely embarrassing situation developed for Professor Hoffman. We had a nice meal and good conversation, and everything was going smoothly, whereupon after retiring for a short period, he very sheepishly came down to inform me that the bathroom had plugged up. He was so embarrassed; I felt truly sorry for him. I told him it was not uncommon that the toilet did not flush well and it was not made in Germany.

9. My firing from my position as director of the NAWG was traumatic for me. It was unjust. It was poor timing. The silent muzzle placed on me was nearly unbearable.

The lies being told about me were tough to swallow—I was a problem in the office, I was difficult to get along with, etc. Several of the growers figured it out and stated that they viewed me as the sacrificial lamb and that the real problem was not me. This came from some growers whom I had only known occasionally for less than three years, but evidently, they had seen enough to know the type of person I was trying to be. It was not surprising that Kentucky growers who had known me for a much longer period stated that what was being said did not fit at all with the person whom they knew. The Kentucky growers wanted to see me back at Kentucky, and one suggested that if I was interested, they would set up a position within the college where I would go to the state capitol to lobby for funds coming to the University of Kentucky. While going back to Kentucky would have been an option, going back into the department would have several detriments. I had been gone for three years, had a much higher-level position, and knew I would not be content there. I was really not sure that I wanted to get into the lobby business, although I had learned enough in three years that I could have been successful in that arena. While I kept this option in the back of my mind, I wanted to pursue other positions that might become available, and one just did, so onto the next chapter.

***

Major Successes and New Programs Developed during My Three Years as Director of the NAWG Foundation

- Started the National Wheat Yield Contest (sponsored by Ciba-Geigy).
- Pooled state research funding for national wheat utilization research.
- Oversaw large field research plots demonstrating no-till and various input practices on wheat production near Memphis, Tennessee (sponsored by Zeneca).
- Started a farm safety program in collaboration with Farm Safety for Just Kids (sponsored by John Deere and Dow Elanco).
- Funded research on wheat transportation by rail issues (sponsored by Burlington Northern Railroad, with additional support from several other railroads).
- Developed and made major improvements in the appearance and content of the monthly *Wheat Technology* publication.
- Reinvigorated the Wheat Industry Research Committee Group.
- Worked with and became a member of the Wheat Breeders Group.
- Developed an extensive program with the help of an agricultural economist in the USDA on developing the economies of developing countries for the benefit of U.S. wheat exports.
- Hosted a seminar and workshop on the milling, baking, and cooking qualities of soft red winter wheat at the Virginia Polytech Institute.

- Testified before Congress and acted as the commodity grains leader for research support.
- Established programs for development committee members.
- Invited participant/consultant to USDA programs.
- And many other activities

CHAPTER 12

The Years, 1992–2001

CAST was a broad-based organization with minimal staffing and maximum volunteering. When I arrived in early September 1992

in addition to my position as executive vice president, I had a secretary, a scientific editor, a vice president for development, an information technology person, and two part-time order and mailing persons—a total of six persons plus myself.

The strength of the organization was the twenty-eight scientific societies and their representatives who served on the board of directors. The societies contributed annual membership dues, and their representatives provided governance for the organization. There were a host of scientists who were invited to serve on task forces to prepare a wide variety of publications that related to food, agricultural, and environmental issues of importance to the nation and to others that interacted with our nation.

These were volunteers and were not paid for their services but had expenses covered when requested. The staff did the work. The board identified the projects undertaken and assisted the executive vice president in identifying the appropriate scientists to serve on the task force. Invitations were extended from the executive vice president, and then they worked closely with the scientific editor.

When problems arose, which were infrequent, it was the executive vice president who stepped in. The vice president for development was responsible for raising the funds to run the organization. When I arrived, these funds came primarily from individuals and organizations that supported our mission of making the science available on issues of national concern to the legislators, the regulators, and the public through the media. As with any organization, funders wanted to meet and hear from the top staff person, and that required much travel and visitation on my part to secure some of the larger donations. There was a cap of $25,000 per year/company in contributions to our organization; this was put in place to prevent a single entity from dictating or directing our research.

When I arrived, there had been some turmoil within the office and organization. The founder of the organization in 1972 was still an active part of the organization and involved in 1986–1987, but it was time to move on to new leadership. A former dean at Auburn University was hired to stabilize the ship from 1987 to 1989; then he retired, and his retirement opened the position for the one that I accepted. This is what

I was warned about by a good friend in the USDA when she stated that she thought the organization was a good organization but that there were troubles there. It did not take long for me to learn more about these troubles. There were four key staff people still there who lived through the 1986–1987 turmoil and subsequent years. I heard different versions from different staff people, but the common thread was that it was not a pleasant time.

My predecessor was a senior person, lacked the energy of a younger person, and seemed to have been content reading the paper, keeping up with the issues that came up, and pacifying ruffled feathers. It was no wonder then that my vice president for development commented on many occasions, "I have never seen anyone in your position with so much energy and passion for the job, working endless hours for the organization." I am and always have been a proponent of "lead by example," and I wanted my staff to do the same because without the full team working and pulling together, our challenge would be much greater. I asked my staff to put their family first and the organization second. We could not have the organization as fourth or fifth priority. A second request was to ask the question "What is best for the organization?" rather than "What is best for me?"

Let me backtrack just a bit regarding the physical move from Maryland to Iowa. Judy had a job of director of the YWCA preschool program in Gaithersburg. We had a house in Gaithersburg to sell. I was set to begin work on September 1, 1992. It was important that I be at the staff office in Ames, Iowa. I moved there and rented an apartment, and for the next year, we had two residences. Judy could retire from her job and would do so if the house sold. Since much of my work was in Washington, D.C., even though the office was in Iowa, about every other weekend, I would go back to Maryland for a long weekend to do work to establish relationships in Washington, D.C., either late in the week or early the following week.

To many members of the board, it was surprising that only two weeks after my employment,

Richard E. Stuckey Named Executive Vice President

Richard E. Stuckey has been named executive vice president of the Council for Agricultural Science and Technology (CAST), effective September 1, 1992, as announced by Gale A. Buchanan, president. CAST, a nonprofit consortium of 29 professional scientific societies in food and agriculture, compiles and publishes reports on public issues related to food and agricultural science, and provides educational material for high school science teachers.

Dr. Stuckey, an Ohio native, received his B.A. degree in biology education from Goshen College, Goshen, Indiana and his M.S. and Ph.D. degrees in plant pathology from Michigan State University. Between his undergraduate and graduate studies, he taught two years at a teacher training school in Laos, Southeast Asia with International Voluntary Services, Inc. Upon receiving his Ph.D., Dr. Stuckey accepted a two-year, tri-university consortium assignment as the plant pathology advisor to the Uruguayan Ministry of Agriculture in Montevideo, Uruguay. Dr. Stuckey continued his professional career at the University of Kentucky from 1975 to 1989 where he was promoted to Extension Professor of Plant Pathology. In 1986 he was awarded a fellowship from the Agricultural University of Wageningen, The Netherlands, where he spent a year sabbatical leave to pursue his knowledge of disease predictive systems.

From 1989 to 1992, Dr. Stuckey was director of the National Association of Wheat Growers Foundation, Washington, D.C. The foundation flourished under his leadership. The

I had arranged a scientist from the University of Minnesota to testify before Congress on the pending North American Free Trade Agreement (NAFTA). One of my answers that impressed the search committee was when I was asked, "How do you get things done with the legislature?" I replied, "You work through the staff of the elected official," which impressed several on the committee who had experience dealing in legislative affairs. I knew the lead staff person of Kika de la Garza, then the chair of the agricultural committee in the house, through which I used my connections to arrange for testimony to be given by a highly respected scientist. This relationship came about through my previous job, getting back to the importance of networking and capitalizing on past relationships.

Fast-forward to a long year of trying to sell our house and questioning the statement of the realtor in 1989 when we looked for housing on our move to D.C. He told us that whatever you do, put everything you can into the purchase of a home, then add at least 25 percent, because home prices have soared in the last four to five years, and Washington, D.C., is recession proof. In 1989, there was a decline in the housing market in certain areas of the country and even in the area of Massachusetts, which should've been a clue for us that this could be possible for D.C.

Finally, in the fall of 1993, we decided to have Judy move with me to Iowa even though the house had not sold. I came back for the weekend and business. We packed up what we could into our large used Pontiac sedan after a thorough cleaning of the house and headed to Greenbrier, a swank area next to White Sulphur Springs, West Virginia, where the National Agricultural Chemical Association was holding their annual meeting. Imagine the looks on the faces of the attendants who waited on us to check in, having just checked in a number of executives, when they opened our trunk to retrieve our luggage and saw mops and cleaning materials! Were these people real? Did they belong here?

From that meeting, we traveled further by car until we reached our destinations in Ames. We rented an apartment for six to nine months while our house was being built. Judy's brother-in-law, Ron Birkey, an architect, designed our home.

This new arrangement seemed like heaven to me as I had progressed several steps from traveling by car, essentially sleeping in my car/hotel parking lot for a few days, and was finally able to rent a small apartment for myself for the first year. Things were looking up.

There are many interesting aspects to life. It seemed like mine were coming full circle from a broad liberal arts background to specializing in one small aspect for a PhD thesis on to work on many crops to a position focusing back on wheat and, from there, to a multidisciplinary position of not only plants but also animals, social, economic, nutrition, food, toxicology, and legal aspects, to name a few. This truly was going to be a challenging job; while I had energy, was I up to the challenge? There would be supporters, and there would be detractors in my path ahead. There would be political aspects in this job as well, but one major difference was that I was at the top of the organization and not subject to a less informed CEO who had little backbone for doing what was right and seeing the big picture.

Over the next few years, as the organization progressed, there were many requests for our organization to participate with other groups and for me personally to become involved with and serve on various boards, committees, and special meetings. I soon wished there were forty hours in the day to accomplish and participate in all that I would've loved to do. A compromise was made to expand my workday and be selective in what I chose to do. My laptop computer was a blessing and a curse at the same time. The office was in Ames, Iowa, but much of the work was in Washington, D.C. There were meetings in D.C. that were impossible for me to attend on short notice because of the distance, but those scheduled in advance, I could include in my schedule.

On average, I made twenty-plus trips a year to Washington, D.C., where it soon became evident that we needed to have representation in D.C. to represent CAST when I was not able to be there. This was very helpful to keep a pulse on the situation. Why was the office in Ames instead of D.C.? Because the founder was a faculty member at Iowa State, and the first office was in his personal office, expanded to a room in Memorial Hall at Iowa State University and, from there, to a rental facility across the street, which was the place that I inherited. In negotiation with the landlord and my insistence that interior remodeling of the office space be accomplished at his expense for our continued rental, he insisted that our organization pay for the renovation (not a good practice to put money into a building that you do not own).

Thus, we pursued other property and eventually purchased land, a prior Quick Trip gas station. We remodeled it into a building with offices for our use that became the home of the organization in 1993, which exists to this day. It was again designed by my brother-in-law, Ron, the architect, and refinished by a local construction group to make a very useful office. It was ultra-modern inside, even though it possessed an exterior that resembled a former Quick Trip gas station. It was located a couple of miles from campus. With the exception of the enclosed executive vice president and scientific editor offices, the other offices were open with five-foot wall separations, giving the office an open, inviting atmosphere. For the rest of the staff, it took some getting used to because conversations could be heard when visiting with one another or overhearing phone conversations; for some not minding their own business, this became a distraction and something for me to try and resolve.

The organization was coming of age. It was twenty-plus years old, known in various circles but not to the extent that it would become known over the next ten years. Over the next nine years and succeeding my tenure, the organization continued to evolve. It was becoming apparent to some researchers that doing research in the lab was not enough for that research to be supported by the public. We needed to have communicators of that research to the various elements of society that science and *not* misperceptions often disseminated by other interest groups be supported. CAST was uniquely positioned to accomplish this endeavor. CAST was like another organization that will be discussed in my retirement years, known to many of its supporters as the best-kept secret. How do you remove that label and become known and valued in wide circles?

In the early years of my administration, we contracted to do a marketing study, and part of that study was to create a stronger, bolder logo and become more visible in Washington, D.C. Discussion centered on whether we should move our headquarters to Washington, D.C., or retain them in Iowa. The lower cost of doing business and operations in Iowa as well as the perceived integrity of being located outside of the political arena in the heartland of the country won the argument. However, it was recognized that we needed more presence in D.C. There were a number of organizations that provided services for organizations in D.C. My previous job was working for one with the wheat producers. The difficulty for CAST was that it represented a wide variety of scientific societies and that just one specific organization would not work.

Finally, an organization headed by a former congressional science fellow working for one of the congressmen and now having the universities as a major client seemed the best fit. A contract was drawn up; there would be an office desk within the organization located close to Capitol Hill for me when I came into town and also, later on, a part-time staff person dedicated to CAST interests. The person hired was also a formal congressional science fellow. Congressional science fellows were supported by the scientific society for a year of work in a congressional office. These young scientists, recently having achieved their PhDs, became valuable assets to their respective sciences, to the workings of Washington, D.C., and to the overall attempt to make the science more relevant to the legislative process of making laws. This approach worked well for the first several years, at which time the cost of doing business increased significantly, and it seemed to me that more and more of the time of the CAST representative was being devoted to other causes. This caused some heartburn and, in the end, led to changing representation in D.C. to another organization that also had a wide reach in D.C.

Both political sides of the aisle were represented in the office. The organization also represented several universities as well as the peanut and sheep industries. The offices were conveniently located close to the Capitol and had an office for me as well as a nice large boardroom that was available for me to meet and hold briefings with congressional science fellows and the media when we would do our briefings in D.C. This group had significant contact and impact in many congressional agricultural offices and, to a lesser extent, in the regulatory branch of government. At one point in time, the two leads in the office inquired of me whether I would be interested in a very high-level position within the USDA because they felt confident they could secure that position for me. Wisely, I declined because those positions are highly political, and you may have a job today but not one tomorrow, especially if the executive branch of government changes power. The representation of Meyers & Associates continued through my employment, although there was a shift in needed services as CAST developed; we ended up hiring a full-time person to be located in Washington, D.C., working solely for CAST. By doing this, we negotiated less time required and less expense from our previous representative office.

Back in the office at Ames, there was a good retention of staff with the exception of the executive secretary. It must've been stressful working for me, although I preferred the use of the term working with me. The person in the position when I was hired lasted a couple of years, her replacement also a couple of years, and then my third hire remained through my retirement for my last five to six years. All three were good employees and loyal to the organization while I was there. Beyond the executive secretary, there were three long-term top leadership staff members and two lower-salaried staff members with lesser positions, yet all positions are important to the working of the organization. The two lower staff persons were often disgruntled, complained, and, at times, were disruptive to the rest of the staff. One of the two had bulimia and also a suspected narcotics abuse problem. The mood changed significantly from one day to the next. She thought she was capable of walking on water and often told me that if I put her in charge of being the executive secretary, our organization would really fly.

The other staff person who was in charge of the distribution of publications produced dated back to the early days of CAST and had a total allegiance to the founding father who was a significant part of the turmoil in 1986–1987 and resided in the community. Prior to my arrival, it had become so bad that like an older parent, the keys to the building were taken away from him. I am sure this was very difficult for him to accept when he had invested so much in founding the organization. He was a hardcore scientist and had little interest in getting along with organizations that espoused different views. His approach had labeled the organization being very right of center. While this appealed to some of our supporters, it did create problems of credibility in the circles where we wished to be valued and our services used. There is a saying that at times, there is a need to walk a fine line, and this was certainly true for my position.

The second employee who became disgruntled had, previous to my arrival, declined to have a portion of her salary put into a retirement program that would be matched two dollars for each dollar the employee put in the account. She did not look to the future and, when she decided to retire, was very upset that she did not have a retirement fund to draw upon. She was not a happy camper and went to the founding father, who was sympathetic to her, and they enlisted the other disgruntled employee to join their cause. The second employee, with the grievance of not having a retirement fund to draw upon, also had an alcohol problem after work hours.

It became necessary to hire a lawyer to defend our case. This was done, and we were on solid ground with the exception that the founding father began soliciting members of the board and writing directly to the board. If what he was writing was the truth, that would've been fine, but fueled by accusations made by the two disgruntled employees, it became a liability. Finally, the president of the board at that time and also the vice president of General Mills convinced me to settle and make a payment of the $10,000 requested to the employee just to get rid of the case because it was taking way too much of our time and a big distraction. He was correct, and this is what is often done in today's world but was very difficult for me to do based on my ethics. It was done, and within a few months, the distraction was gone, and we could focus all our time back on the organization.

Leadership training for staff as well as board and member societies was viewed as important. Special sessions with consultants could easily be arranged for the on-site training of staff and an hour or two carved out annually at one of our two board meetings held each year. What about the health of our scientific societies? A major program was developed with the support of the W. K. Kellogg Foundation and a consultant group who had connections with the foundation. A large grant was obtained to hold a major conference inviting one to five representatives from each member society to a three-day leadership conference. Over 150 scientists and leaders attended the conference in St. Louis, Missouri. It was a key mark event that put CAST front and foremost among our scientific societies. Many of these societies were facing issues of finance and membership. In addition to getting challenging presentations from international speakers and creating a new form of communication using the medium of art

these members were given sufficient time to meet and gather in groups and learn from one another. It was just a start of add-on programs that many of the societies would come to value.

This program was scrutinized by some believing we were moving away from our original mission of providing and interpreting the science behind issues of national concern that related to the food agriculture environment for the legislature, the regulators, the executive branch, and the public through the media—point considered well taken. However, my argument remains that the health of CAST was due in large part to the health of its member scientific societies, and many of them were in trouble at this particular time. This argument sold, yet the encouragement was not to go too far adrift and remember the reason for the creation of the organization.

Subsequent funding was achieved, and smaller groups of thirty to forty from among our member societies became engaged in additional follow-up training and awareness that included retreats to Callaway Gardens in Georgia to Tuskegee University in Alabama and other interesting sites. The idea was to get away to a somewhat remote place distant from the workplace yet where new knowledge and new perspectives could be realized. Another twist to this program was inviting the executive directors and the executive vice president of the scientific societies to meet concurrently at the same meeting but with a separate contract of training as those that were enrolled in the program from their society. The gathering of executive directors/executive vice presidents was very beneficial to many of those who managed their societies. We often learn from one another.

Richard Stuckey

The Council for Engineering and Scientific Society Executives (CESSE) was an organization that I belonged to. Several of our member society executives were also members. CESSE had two meetings each year, one for the executives and their staff and the other for executives only. The model and experiencing CESSE was a big help in structuring the Kellogg Foundation–supported programming. As they say, rank has its privileges. This was particularly true of the executive-only meetings. We met at extremely nice places, received deep discounts on lodging, and were provided more meals and food than we ever wanted. The superb wining and dining by our city hosts was an attempt to get our business and bring our annual individual society meetings to that city.

Some of our larger organizations could have fifteen to twenty thousand people attending an annual meeting. We met at many convention centers in Hawaii, Palm Springs, California, Coronado Island, Dallas, Texas, Park City, Utah, the Cleveland Rock 'n' Roll Hall of Fame, McCormick Place in Chicago, etc. What made these events even more special was our spouses could accompany us and have programs of their own while we were in meetings, and we could enjoy the social events together. It was at the Rock 'n' Roll Hall of Fame that Judy did the twist with Chubby Checker, live and in person!

As mentioned earlier, connections are very important. One connection I had was with the USDA experiment station administrator and also with the executive director of the American Veterinary Medical Association, who later became FDA administrator. These two individuals nominated me for membership in the Cosmos Club, a prestigious club that had a hotel and restaurant residence on Massachusetts Avenue near DuPont Circle. I was accepted and admitted into the organization. The $1,000-per-year fee was soon realized in nightly fee savings. The room rate was under $100 per night where comparable hotels were in the $250-per-night range. The meals were great and reasonable. I could hold meetings there for individuals or groups. One of those groups was the Congressional Science Fellows. These were held one to two times per year to bring them up to date on task activities and encourage their promotions of CAST in their offices on the Hill. There was a large library there, and I was able to include CAST publications in the library.

There were also cultural events held there. Classical music performances in the auditorium and a dinner and lecture with Supreme Court justice Sandra Day O'Connor were two that remain as memories. Many visitors who were taken to lunch there or met me there were very impressed to know of the organization and the prestige that it held. I used that not as an elevation of myself but of the organization I represented. The facilities were used as a forum for discussing alternate views from scientists with opposing perspectives. It was amazing to me, with the assistance of the connections I had, to be able to attract well-known national persons to debate at such a forum. I guess each person felt they could convince the other in the audience to agree with their viewpoint.

From the start of my employment, I continually fought the perception that the organization was right-wing as well as funded by and the voice of industry. Granted, that industry does have an agenda to promote its business and make profit for its shareholders. On the other hand, there are organizations that claim to be pure science that have other agendas from which they try and draw funds and support for their cause. Oftentimes, there are holes in their science. Walk the fine line. It seems like getting the groups together would be beneficial for better understanding.

The Farm Bill was often a point of contention where many different groups were lobbying inclusion and priority on certain parts of the budget and funding. To that end, in late 1993, an invitation was extended to eight to ten diverse organizations to have up to two persons per organization attend a CAST forum in Minneapolis, Minnesota. Surprisingly to me, we did get good participation representing the fringes of both sides. The fact that CAST was a driver to provide discussion and understanding was a feather in our cap and made many suspect organizations take notice of the new leadership in CAST. In the end, there was more understanding; however, many organizations remained entrenched in their positions.

Another major effort was a conference that we hosted in preparation for the 1995 Farm Bill. Our Washington representatives were very helpful and spent much time in developing this well-thought-out conference, which was well attended by all those interested in the outcome of the Farm Bill. Why? It was because they all had a part in the conference. The conference was structured such that there would be a major speaker and then a panel, very diverse in nature, to discuss the speaker's presentation and dialogue among themselves. There would also be some time allotted for questions from the audience to individual panelists. Everyone was involved. Again, with the conference being held in D.C., we had access to many top-notch presenters. One of those was Sen. Richard Lugar, a Republican who was chair of the agricultural Senate committee. Another was Democratic congressman Charlie Stenholm from Texas. One of our major supporters from an agricultural industry who questioned the effectiveness of CAST came away from the conference and said that CAST was a can-do organization and had his support.

Another major event was held in 1997, the twenty-fifth anniversary of the organization. An international symposium was held, entitled "Food Production and Security: Domestic and International Dimensions." Again, with the help of others, international speakers were secured to make major presentations at the conference. Catherine Bertini, head of the World Food Program located in Europe, was one of the many international speakers. At this event, we also recognized the past twenty-five presidents of CAST and honored them. Through my cultivation of the Chicago Board of Trade, we were able to hold a reception late one afternoon down on the trading floor with high-end hors d'oeuvres provided by their restaurant as well as a presentation by the president of the Chicago Board of Trade down in the pit. This was a neat experience for those attending the conference. All this is to say that this was another first-class event held and conducted by CAST.

There is no question that CAST evolved during my tenure. Frequently, there was a challenge of finances that required some new thinking while staying true to the mission. Many of the approaches that we undertook were successful, while others were not. The key to the overall success was to identify those ideas and efforts that were not workable and discontinue them at an early stage rather than continuing to follow those approaches down a rat hole. Certainly, the marketing effort, along with a new CAST logo, and revisiting the mission and strategic plan were worth the effort spent. Our increased involvement with other organizations, the networking, the representation of CAST in Washington, D.C., and the seminal workshops and events were also useful to put CAST on the map.

In an increasing time of wanting information now and not later, this required speeding up our publications as well as reviewing the types of publications prepared and the dissemination of the publications. At times, it seemed like we were on a treadmill that kept speeding up, but what was experienced in the 1990s was nothing compared to what was to come in the 2020s. We did have a website, modified its utility and accessibility, and began making a number of publications free to our members and, to some extent, to nonmembers to have the publications gain accessibility and use. This impacted our revenue source but was overcome by the increased success in obtaining grants for support.

What were some of the things we tried that did not work? One major one was the hiring of an outside source to do our fundraising. This group was recommended by an influential board member who had used the group successfully at one of the major land grant universities. Also, another board member was in the process of hiring this group for the nonprofit organization that he was heavily involved with, albeit in the very early stages. The concept was cost sharing when they went into major markets for multiple organizations. It was expensive for us to make personal visits to cities where many companies and nonprofits had their headquarters. The personal visits were necessary to be successful in fundraising. For example, there were many such companies in the Chicago area. I would try to schedule multiple visits in a single trip to Chicago, but this could be difficult and time-consuming. Our travel budget was limited. The hired group could go into Chicago and visit three or four of our members and, at the same time, visit members of other organizations that they represented. Thus, we may be charged for 30 percent of their travel expenses on a given trip based on how many members they visited on our behalf. The other argument was that they could meet with people higher up within the organization and thus have access to more funding. This all sounds good but, in reality, did not work. They claimed they would greatly increase our revenue multifold. Some erroneous thinking was that while this approach might be successful for a university that has graduates with a strong allegiance to the university, it was not the same for a nonprofit. Also, the idea that they would get higher up into the organization was not true because I was already operating at the vice president level in most organizations and, even in some cases, the CEO level, so there was no room to go higher.

The final breakup came after two seasons when the increased revenue did not meet the benchmarks that had been established and their accounting was questioned. For example, we may have increased marginally some contributions from certain members, but we lost several members, and they did not count the loss of members in their final tally. My argument that it was the bottom line that mattered to us and losing a few members greatly diminished their effectiveness. In the end, we had marginally greater income, if any at all, after we paid their expenses. Another false promise was that they would computerize all of our memberships as well as provide tracking and other useful information. This too was a work in progress that was not as developed as our own system. Fortunately, this arrangement was terminated after two years and none too soon. In the meantime, my vice president for development saw the writing on the wall by losing all of his major accounts and, having to focus on individual members, resigned to accept another position closer to where he lived. This left me in a lurch with no outside contract for fundraising, losing a staff member who had been on board three to four years before

I arrived. Yes, board members can be influential and assist, but these members had other jobs, and the effort landed solely on my lap. There were two or three board members, usually those in the president's role, who would go with me to solicit funds, putting a good word in for the organization but having me do the work.

The final straw was a recommendation made by the outside consulting firm that, after losing my top staff funding person, I fire my scientific editor because she was drawing a good salary and that that was necessary until the organization got back on its feet. This was not a recommendation that was given a second thought as the scientific editor was responsible for working with our task forces and getting top-notch publications out, which was the life blood of our organization in terms of attracting members and support. It's what we did. This was an expensive experiment, but much was learned, and that is key to when things don't work out—that one learns from the experience.

A new development staff person was hired—a very conscientious, supportive team member—but she just didn't have the experience and appeal of the staff person who had left to many of our members. In the end, I was, in essence, ordered to fire the staff person by the board member treasurer, who was highly influential and a former president of a major university. It was perhaps the hardest thing I had to do. She was a very nice person, but the person had been given several challenges to improve, and while attempted, the results simply were not there. At the corporate level, the firing and severance of staff is an event that goes on all the time. In a small staff where everyone is treated like family, it is a much more difficult task.

Another event that was tried several times but only had marginal success was an individual membership drive across many states within the United States. We identified four leading member advocates to be the state leader for a membership drive. This required a fair amount of effort on CAST staff, but we were only moderately successful. We needed a person who had the name recognition within the state, and they, in turn, would recruit additional members for their committee. This effort, both times tried, did not yield results that were desired.

A somewhat different effort targeting businesses and universities within the state was to have multiple memberships for a given level of support. In the university, graduate students were targeted as receiving free publications and membership. At the corporate level, having the corporation contribute a fivefold individual membership would allow them to place ten of their employees on a free subscription list. Likewise, we developed a stratified-level membership, giving recognition to higher annual membership contributions and also a lifetime membership. A push for lifetime membership was made and was quite successful, and these lifetime members are still identified in the annual reports. The purpose of sharing this information is that many things were tried to increase membership; some were unsuccessful, others marginally successful, and yet others viewed as quite successful.

To summarize the evolutionary process without going into great detail, the publications were revised to include short one-to-four-page issue papers that could be published in much less time than the one-hundred-plus-page reports. We included international authors on our reports as subject matter permitted, and we began doing congressional briefings once our reports were published for Congress, the regulatory agency to which the topic pertained (EPA, FDA, USDA, etc.), and included White House briefings with the Office of Science and Technology for a number of our reports. While in D.C., we would also hold separate meetings for various coalitions that had interest in the subject material. Food safety and biotechnology were two topics that could be counted on to draw a crowd and also get media attention. With increased visibility and popularity, the detractors also became more evident. The use of our reports and activities gained attention, and we were on a roll, so to speak.

Because of the now thirty-eight member societies and the increasing number of board members, board restructuring was needed. The board structure developed for CAST, when only a few societies were members, allowed larger societies to have up to three representatives on the board; the smaller societies would have one person on the board. Societies that had three members on the board paid a little over $5,000 in annual dues, while those with single members on the board paid $1,500 per year. As new society members joined CAST, it resulted in nearly sixty members on the board, an unwieldy number to conduct effective meetings. What is a fair and equitable way to reduce the size of the board? To reduce the size of the board, could larger societies have single representatives and multiple smaller societies share one representative? There was an executive committee of eight persons who could be decision makers between the two full board meetings each year. The members serving on the executive committee did not count as one of the Scientific Society representatives on the board; they were additional. We soon found that the sharing of a representative by multiple societies was not a viable solution; everyone wanted their own representative. The best we could accomplish was a single representative per society and to reduce the annual fee of the larger societies. We still had too large of a board, although this procedure reduced the board from fifty-eight to thirty-eight members plus the eight-member executive committee.

Over the years, many board members expressed concern that I would burn out. I was young and energetic, believed in the mission, and worked extremely hard to make the organization successful. I thought they were wrong, but they were right. The extensive travel to D.C. to make our mission and information known, the many trips for fundraising across the country, the organization hosting many special events, and my participation and collaboration with other organizations began to take a toll. When I was not on travel and at the home office, stacks of mail other than first-class letters were taken home to read and review in the evenings.

The laptop computer was taken with me on trips, plugged in, and worked on while I was on the plane and at layovers in airports and correspondence replied to in the evenings while I was on travel because of the meetings and visits during the day. Over the years, this did have a wearing effect.

When my financial advisor advised me, if I enjoyed working for the government, to continue working but that, if not, I had sufficient funds to retire, it was an appealing comment. With the increasing months, this became more and more appealing, and in light of several coworkers in other organizations who had succumbed to heart attacks and other fatal illnesses, this had a chilling effect. Finally, after much deliberation at the age of fifty-six, I thought retirement was an avenue I wished to pursue and a new occupation where I could remain active. When I shared this with my executive committee, they were astounded. I told them in May 2000 that I would continue working until September 2001 if they wanted me to, or I could leave within two weeks if they preferred. They stated that they wanted me to continue working and did not take immediate action, I think because they hoped I would change my mind. When the fall of 2000 arrived and I was still insistent that I would retire, they took me seriously and began quietly looking for my successor. They did not want to announce the search process before they were ready to go because of what it would do to financial support when the top staff person was in flux. That process and transition will be discussed in the prelude to the retirement years, the next chapter.

The networking with other organizations and the request to serve on their boards and participate in mutual efforts were truly amazing and very rewarding yet time-consuming. Organizations whose boards I served on or that I had very close affiliations with included Food, Land, and People, the Farm Foundation, the Institute for Science in Society, the Agricultural Research Institute, the International Food Information Council, the Washington Policy Group (with Drabenstott, Armbruster, and Cargill as representatives and myself on the executive committee, headed by Jim Auerbach), the National Association of Conservation Districts, the National Association of State Departments of Agriculture, FFA, the World Food Prize, the Biotechnology Industry Organization, Diane's Organization, and many others. Organizations that we got along well with but were not necessarily affiliated with were the Rodale Institute and Alternative Agriculture. Those organizations that had high visibility in D.C. and whose testimonies were often in conflict with ours were the Agricultural Working Group, the Center for Science in the Public Interest, and the Union of Concerned Scientists.

To give the reader an idea of my total submersion upon entering a new job, my first month of employment as well as my report to the board of directors and the executive directors of the member scientific societies are provided below. It was indeed a busy month and one of many busy months to follow. My October 12, 1992 communication to the board and executive directors after one month of employment is presented below.

COUNCIL FOR AGRICULTURAL SCIENCE AND TECHNOLOGY

137 LYNN AVENUE
AMES, IOWA 50010-7197
(515) 292-2125
FAX (515) 292-4512

AMERICAN ACADEMY OF VETERINARY
AND COMPARATIVE TOXICOLOGY

AMERICAN ASSOCIATION
OF CEREAL CHEMISTS

AMERICAN DAIRY SCIENCE
ASSOCIATION

AMERICAN FORAGE
AND GRASSLAND COUNCIL

AMERICAN MEAT
SCIENCE ASSOCIATION

AMERICAN
METEOROLOGICAL SOCIETY

AMERICAN PEANUT RESEARCH
AND EDUCATION SOCIETY

AMERICAN
PHYTOPATHOLOGICAL SOCIETY

AMERICAN SOCIETY FOR
HORTICULTURAL SCIENCE

AMERICAN SOCIETY OF
AGRICULTURAL ENGINEERS

AMERICAN SOCIETY OF AGRONOMY

AMERICAN SOCIETY OF
ANIMAL SCIENCE

AMERICAN VETERINARY
MEDICAL ASSOCIATION

AQUATIC PLANT
MANAGEMENT SOCIETY

ASSOCIATION OF
OFFICIAL SEED ANALYSTS

COUNCIL ON SOIL TESTING
AND PLANT ANALYSIS

CROP SCIENCE
SOCIETY OF AMERICA

INSTITUTE OF FOOD TECHNOLOGISTS

INTERNATIONAL SOCIETY OF
REGULATORY TOXICOLOGY AND
PHARMACOLOGY

NORTH CENTRAL WEED
SCIENCE SOCIETY

NORTHEASTERN WEED
SCIENCE SOCIETY

PLANT GROWTH REGULATOR
SOCIETY OF AMERICA

POULTRY SCIENCE ASSOCIATION

RURAL SOCIOLOGICAL SOCIETY

SOCIETY OF NEMATOLOGISTS

SOIL SCIENCE
SOCIETY OF AMERICA

SOUTHERN WEED SCIENCE SOCIETY

WEED SCIENCE SOCIETY
OF AMERICA

WESTERN SOCIETY
OF WEED SCIENCE

INTERNET:
B1CAST@EXNET.IASTATE.EDU

DATE: October 12, 1992

TO: CAST Board of Directors

FROM: Dick Stuckey, CAST Executive Vice President

RE: Report on First Month Activities

I thought I would take the opportunity to share with you some of my activities during my first month since the next board meeting at which I will make a full report is not until late February. The first three weeks were spent in the Washington, DC area making contacts and attending a couple of conferences. During this time I was in contact with the Ames office, both by phone and by fax.

A series of visits were arranged for Sept. 3 and 4. The first visit was with Dr. Stan Cath, Executive Director, Agricultural Research Institute (ARI). Stan has a very full agenda the next two months with responsibility for six major meetings and conferences. Among those are the 1) ARI's International Conference of Agricultural Research Administrators, the ARI annual meeting and a Symposium on the Dynamics of the U.S. Agricultural Research System, McLean, VA, Sept. 13–19; 2) Biobased Fuels Expo, St. Louis, MO, Oct. 6–9; 3) Safeguarding the Food Supply through Irradiation Processing Techniques International Conference, Orlando, FL, Oct. 25–31; and 4) The First International Congress for Program Implementation of the International Organization for Resistant Pest Management (IORPM), McLean, VA, Nov. 1–3. Stan invited me to attend any or all of the administrators meeting next week including their board meeting.

Dr. Luise Light, Executive Director, Eileen Kugler, Deputy Director, and Ellen Cooper, Communications Director all from the Institute for Science in Society (ISIS) met with me. The major purpose of this meeting was to discuss the offer CAST had received to cosponsor a biotechnology conference on food and agriculture. ISIS is a new organization that received its 501 (c)3 status in Sept. 1990. The ISIS mission is to provide clear and objective information to the public on the important scientific and technical issues that may affect their lives. ISIS is active in the areas of human health, food and the environment. While visiting the office, Luise expressed interest in CAST cosponsorship of not only the biotechnology conference but also a conference on FIFRA (Federal Insecticide, Fungicide and Rodenticide Act).

Dr. Robert Watkins and Amy Melnick, Manager, Public Affairs for the American Society for Microbiology (ASM) recommended that the key Congressional staff that they work with are mostly in the House on the House Agricultural and House Appropriations Committees but also have frequent contact with Senate Agricultural Committee staffers. Pat Donnelly was mentioned as an excellent contact who was just recently transferred to permanent staff status on Senator Lugar's staff. When asked about membership

327

Richard Stuckey

CAST Board of Directors
October 12, 1992
Page 2

in CAST, Robert responded that some time ago it was discussed by the board and it may be time to revisit the issue. Robert said ASM is a member of COFARM as is many of CAST's society members. Dr. Rudy Wodzinski (407) 823-7298 of Univ. of Central Florida is Chair, Committee on Agriculture, Food and Industrial Microbiology for ASM and is the person we need to contact. ASM has 39,000 members and Robert said he would alert Rudy of my call within the next three weeks. A call from any CAST board members who may know Rudy could be helpful.

During our visit we discussed how effective a job we do in communicating with the public. Articles in *The New York Times*, *The Washington Post* are not read by the public, while *The Des Moines Register*, *Kansas City Star*, and other smaller local papers are much more likely to reach the public. Robert suggested a PR committee, perhaps our board, contact local area newspapers to share with them CAST reports to get more local exposure. (This approach could be magnified by challenging our company and cooperative sustaining members to do the same). Robert suggested CAST articles are more likely to be published and read in magazines such as *Cosmopolitan*, *Food Science*, *Food and Nutrition*, and *Woman's Day* than in many other magazines. Robert and Amy as well as the staff at ISIS felt a Congressional representative within the D.C. beltway was very important to maintain legislative contacts.

Dr. Al Lazen, Acting Director of the Commission on Life Sciences, National Research Council, National Academy of Sciences shared with me the 1992 report by NRC, "Plant Biology Research and Training for the 21st Century" which had 3 recommendations: 1) A National Institute of Plant Biology (NIPB) be established in the USDA under the direct oversight of the assistant secretary for science and education. NIPB be responsible for leading a coordinated federal plant–biology program that intimately involves other federal agencies that support research and training in plant biology; 2) All agencies that currently support plant–biology research and training maintain and increase their commitment in cooperation with NIPB and USDA; and 3) An independent group of nongovernment scientists be formed to provide continuing advice to the USDA assistant secretary for science and education and to the officials of cooperating agencies concerning NIPB's operation and goals, and to oversee the parallel efforts by other agencies.

Al explained to me the various boards (animal, irradiation effects, biology, and environmental studies and toxicology) within the commission on life sciences. When asked about the progress on the impending NAS report on pesticides in baby foods and diets, he responded that further delays had occurred due to some question with some of the data they were using and the difficulty to encounter other reliable data such that he thought the report would not be issued before early next year.

Skip McAfee, Executive Director of the American Association of Horticultural Science, attempts to put something about CAST in each Horticulture Newsletter. He expressed the need for CAST to continually promote itself to justify society membership expenditures each year, especially in years when budget deficits occur. Skip also mentioned that James Denny from California would be their new Congressional Fellow. Skip was interested in how task force committee members are chosen for reports.

Dr. Catherine Adams, Director of Scientific Affairs, Grocery Manufacturers of America, has a keen interest in food issues. Cathy is concerned about the impact the National Academy of Science report concerning pesticides in children's diets will have on the public. She also has an interest in the CAST report on pathogenic organisms and volunteered to be a peer reviewer if asked. Cathy recommended that I contact Tom Stenzel, Executive Director of International Food Information Council (IFIS).

CAST Board of Directors
October 12, 1992
Page 3

According to Cathy, IFIS is narrowly focused but when they tackle an issue they do so with gusto and will take on "60 Minutes," "20/20," etc. and prepare a hard counterattack. Cathy seemed receptive to receiving an invitation for affiliate membership in CAST.

The first visit of Sept. 4 was to Dick Hallgren, Executive Director of American Meteorological Society Committee on Agriculture and Forest Meteorology. Dick stated he would like to be more familiar with CAST and that as a result of my visit he would spend some time the next 4 or 5 months to become better acquainted. Dick prefers that material be screened for him such that when items of particular interest to AMS occur they can readily be called to his attention. He also mentioned that in his organization there were a number of members approaching retirement and there may be a benefit of knowledgeable resources with time, energy and expertise available to CAST.

Rick Kirchhoff, Executive Director of National Association of State Departments of Agriculture (NASDA), has been in his position 3 months and has an office move scheduled late September. Rick was familiar with CAST having served as a legislative aide some four or five years ago. He stated that they receive so many materials that there are large stacks of reports to review and not all were read or scanned, thus a champion for CAST cause in D.C. would be very helpful. (While we mail reports to all Congressional offices, hand delivery to key offices would likely be efforts well spent). At Dan Larson's suggestion I approached Rick on the potential of enlisting all 50 state Department of Agriculture through one invoicing to NASDA. Rick was hired to streamline the NASDA operation, does not have the $5,000 in the budget, and has reservations with each state running $100. through his office. Rick promised to keep us updated with the frequent changes that occur in mailing lists and addresses for each state Department of Agriculture. Rick agreed that networking and coalition building were important, and he would like to have budgeted funds to accomplish that goal, and if accomplished, NASDA representing the 50 states would consider CAST membership. Rick was enthusiastic about the recent and future reports of CAST.

Louise Salmon, AIBS Meetings Manager, extended an invitation to CAST to co-sponsor the American Institute of Biological Sciences (AIBS) meeting in Ames, IA, August 1–5, 1993. There will be a program planning committee meeting in Ames, Oct. 22–23 which CAST is invited to participate. In talking with Louise, I sensed the involvement of CAST could be largely that of our choosing, ranging from an integral part of the program — welcome, representation in plenary sessions, development (and secure funding) for a symposium, and conduct separate sessions. An idea would be to have a task force committee chair of a pertinent report address an open session or to develop a session where the chair and external resources address the topic. In addition to the above, I believe that CAST would want to take advantage of occupying a table along side other societies, to display publications and recruit memberships. An exhibit booth would also be available to CAST for 1/2 price.

Dr. Neill Schaller, Associate Director, Institute for Alternative Agriculture, Inc. discussed the history of *Alternative Agriculture* and the common resources which each of our organizations share. He, like many others in the two days of visits, offered to extend a helping hand whenever possible.

September 9, I attended the Food Safety Conference in DC. Among the many people I met were Patrick Donnelly (Lugar staff) and Curt Mann (Stenholm staff), James Chambers (Purdue), waste management task force committee, board member Jack Francis, and Dennis Heldman. Congressman Stenholm spoke at the banquet with a strong message that science has to get their message to the public as public perception dictates policy. As scientists we have the facts as evidence but if we can not influence public perception we lose.

After the meeting I visited with Stenholm, he immediately recognized CAST -- said he was about to write to us, "We do a beautiful job on preparing reports but we need to get public interest groups involved." Stenholm believes there is a need for a "blue ribbon commission" representing a cross section of interest groups -- credibility -- would CAST consider initiating this? Stenholm would encourage other groups to endorse our reports. Stenholm said (like Carol Brookins) it is very important for CAST to have someone immediately available to respond to "60 Minutes"...... "but here is the other side of the issue."

During the afternoon I left the conference to meet with Elaine Auld at International Food Information Council (IFIC). IFIC has been around since 1985 and they have been broadening their scope into pesticide effects/presence on food, biotechnology, etc. IFIC is also very interested in the National Academy of Sciences report on pesticides in children's diets – a report Elaine heard could be released in Jan 93 but more likely in Jan 94. IFIC appears to have a close working relationship with GMA and a number of other organizations.

Carol Brookins, President of World Perspectives, and a participant at three of our programs when I was with the Wheat Growers suggested CAST should position themselves to be able to immediately respond to nonscientific hype media reports. The question is how to do this and be timely. Carol is very widely known and respected. She indicated her desire for us to keep in touch.

September 10, I attended the Food Safety Conference in the AM and in the afternoon visited Xavier Equihua (staff aide to de la Garza) to get schedules arranged for Schuh testimony. I also stopped by National Association of Conservation District office and visited with Ernie Shea, Exec. Dir. Ernie suggested we contact Doug Kline, at Soil and Water Conservation Society in Ankeny, IA for interest in CAST. I also called Arthur Kelman in the evening to visit and get his perspective on the Senator Daschle hearing.

September 11, I again attended Food Safety conference in AM and spoke with Donnelly briefly after the meeting. At meeting, Congressional staff responded to reports presented by work groups. In Donnelly's comments he said that in the near future they will be putting out system/approach of how to access important Congressional events and resources. This information will be provided to societies, etc. so that individuals will be able to access info. Pat also said there are 25–30 Science Fellows on the Hill sponsored by individuals and societies but all fall under the umbrella of AAAS. We can call Claudia Sturgis, AAAS (202) 326-6600, for names, addresses, and location, of all the science fellows. Pat commented before the audience, "Go through professional societies, there are people here from CAST, CAST is a great organization that has done a lot of work through our office." During the course of the conference, several speakers referenced the recent CAST publication, *Food Safety, The Interpretation of Risk* and Jack Francis.

I had lunch with *Feed Stuffs* columnist, Carol James, who also heads a public affairs, marketing, issue management communications agency. In the afternoon, I visited Joe Antognini, WSSA President in his office in Beltsville and also used the opportunity to briefly visit with ARS National Program Staff leaders, Charles Murphy and Wilda Martinez.

During these first two weeks, scheduling appointments, arranging schedules for the testimony of Dean Ed Schuh for the house Agriculture Committee hearings on the NAFTA, and the preparation of written testimony for Sen. Daschle's hearing on the National Research Initiative and Sustainable Agriculture consumed the remainder of my time.

CAST Board of Directors
October 12, 1992
Page 5

September 14th, I attended the Agricultural Research Institute's International Conference of Agricultural Research Administrators in McLean, VA. Dr. Duane Acker, USDA Assistant Secretary for Science an Education emphasized research is to be used. Four ways to measure research are: input, activity, output, and impact. At the international conference, Dr. Acker also stressed the importance of public/private relationships and international collaboration that benefits both countries, i.e., the U.S. dependence for exports and genetic resources and other country dependence on food.

The CAST Executive Committee had an AM conference call to discuss the written testimony for the Daschle hearing and the ISIS invitation to cosponsor two conferences. Several committee members had not yet received the testimony draft that was prepared the previous weekend, members agreed the testimony should be submitted, and due to the urgency to submit the report, all members were asked to return any editorial comments to the CAST office by noon on Tuesday. Discussion on the ISIS invitations centered on the need to know more about the organization and on which, the agricultural biotechnology conference or the Delaney Clause workshop, if any, CAST should accept. More information on ISIS and the conferences were requested and a follow up conference call was scheduled for Friday, Sept. 18.

In the afternoon I visited the offices of George Anthan, Ag writer for the Des Moines Register located in Washington, DC, and John Thomas, previous affiliated with the American Veterinary Medical Association and the Animal Health Institute.

Meetings continued on Tuesday as well as a visit to Mike Peden, Executive Director of American Society of Agricultural Consultants. September 15 was the beginning of the ARI Annual Meeting. As an ex-officio member of the ARI board, I attended their directors meeting that evening. While all sessions of the program were interesting, I found the legislative and budget issues of particular interest.

Terry Nipp, AESOP, began by stating there are 13 bills that need to be passed, one is passed (agriculture), one delayed and 11 to receive action in next 30 days. Five or 6 bills are expected to be vetoed. Changes are occurring; Whitten, Chr. House Appropriations Comm. is in poor health and reluctantly releasing power; Whitten's influence is diminishing but he still carries a big stick; in past, in debate things have been added to agriculture, now bills are taken from ag which is what Whitten would have prohibited. Senate side: Burdick died; Ag committee likely to go to Bumpers (Ark), and Environment committee to Moynihan (NY).

Walls Are Coming Down such that budgets are no longer categorized as **domestic, international, and defense.** Now ag can compete for other funds but the reverse is true also, others can compete for ag funds, the total pie will be the same. Congressional side: Great turnover expected, more than 150 new faces which would be unprecedented; danger is new people will have less understanding of ag — be totally consumer oriented; food safety, prices for consumer down, etc.; perception is ag is the only industry that is not regulated on pollution.

Senate: Leahy and Daschle will likely stay in place. House: Rose may leave DORFA (Department Operations, Research and Foreign Agriculture) position, de la Garza likely stay in place unless he is offered and accepts Sec. of Ag if Dems win.

What is role of agriculture research, education and extension? Prefer voluntary action be taken, but if we move into a more regulatory role, then research role is to come forward with the data, or we do not have data, or data is evident that no regulation is needed. **Need to become more**

Richard Stuckey

progressively involved in assisting legislative process.

Definite possible reorganization of USDA. Madigan wants to streamline, Lugar will pursue streamlining regardless of who is in the White House. Merger of ARS/CSRS/ES is in discussion, regardless of budget; however, budget constraints may be so forced to reorganize. The question is there is just so much money available and who will get what is the question — commodity association already have figured it is a zero sum game and they are preparing to carve out their section. Another big Question??? Are we going to address the changes that are coming or are we going to be changed?

John Conrad (professional staff, House Ag Committee), spoke next. He agreed with Nipp but he said there could be 170 new faces and there would be less understanding of agriculture. John thought Stenholm may replace Rose as chair of DORFA.

Budget is tight, dollars scarce. Ag and ag research are vulnerable for knife cut, not protected like social security; Congress is looking for relevance in science research.

Basic and applied science pressure to work together and force consideration of social science as well. Lots of pressure on basic science to show economic benefits. Peer review competitive grants are favored because best science is done. Although special grants are derided because of pork barrel allegations, they continue and someone who did not get competitive funding goes through the back door. John Conrad feels there is a place and need for both but favors a majority in competitive grants. There is a need for special grants, especially for schools that were not wealthy in the 1950s and 1960s.

There are two important bills in research: (1) NRI is a very important attempt to give significance to basic research: (2) AARC is new and is coming directly from the Secretary's office, not from Science and Education. AARC received $4 million in 1992 and $7.5 million in 1993, these funds will be more applied commercialization and more commodity oriented.

Final comments: Legislature can become more involved in science or as scientists we can become more active in the legislative process. John prefers the later for our benefit.

Comments from Stephen Dewhurst (Budget and Program), USDA. USDA is the 4th largest spending agency in government. The breakdown of the $66 billion budget is $52 billion in mandatory spending that includes $25 billion for food stamps, other food assistance and school lunch programs. $1.6 billion is for international programs such as the P.L. 480 program; $2.9 billion for women's and children's program; $3.0 billion for accommodations programs for forests, parks, meat and poultry inspection. The money that is left goes into 3 pots; $1.6 for research (ARS/CSRS/ES); $1.8 for ASCS, Conservation and $3.+ into Farmer's Home Administration, Credit, etc.

The scenario for new budget appropriations is: New programs are difficult to implement, old programs are difficult to sunset, and the end result is a budget trimming process that has been done for many years. Research and education budgets are risky business; we could see proposals with 15% reductions; structural changes are likely in USDA. The opportunities are in the areas of reaching out to broader constituencies where research can offer new knowledge to nontraditional foci.

September 17 was a travel day in my move to Iowa. On September 18 another Executive Committee conference call resulted in the decision to pursue both of the cosponsorship invitations received from ISIS and encouragement for CAST to be represented on the steering committee.

332

September 21 marked my first day in the office. A call from Pat Donnelly informing us that the approval of poultry irradiation by the Food Safety & Inspection Service the past Friday had resulted in a flood of protest calls to USDA. CAST responded to his inquiry with correspondence to seven society members of CAST and the Executive Committee. An excellent response was received and a list of 17 food irradiation experts were contacted who gave their approval to be listed as resource persons to the media. This list was shared with 60 selected media and with the seven societies in the event they receive inquiries. (Vindicator has indicated they will irradiate poultry soon after the approval goes into effect Oct. 21 and will have it in the grocery stores the following day. Demonstrations and news coverage are likely). If news stories are created, the news media will have the scientific perspective available to them.

During my first week at Ames, correspondence, contacts with several of the task force committees, a seminar at Iowa State University and follow-up on the NAFTA hearings were on the agenda. Saturday, September 26, I flew to Indianapolis and met again with Rick Kirchhoff, NASDA, and individually met with a number of the state agriculture officials. At the reception and during the course of the meetings on Sunday and Monday, I was able to visit with Pat Nichols, Executive Director of Agricultural Council of America, who, along with several others, requested membership invoices. Monday AM, I visited DowElanco at their headquarters.

To complete the week, on Thursday and Friday, President Gale Buchanan and I made a number of visits in Washington, DC. Our first was a breakfast visit with Terry Nipp (AESOP consultant). Terry supports coalition building among agricultural interests. He also recognizes and wants to promote rapid response teams and to have people in place via data bases who can comment on the science of issues. Terry said they need to enlarge their physical facilities and would offer a desk and office space for CAST representatives coming to DC for a few days. It was suggested that Chip Morgan, Terry, and I get together for a conference call sometime, if we are not able to meet again soon.

Our next visit was with Bruce Stillings, assistant to Duane Acker, Assistant Secretary for Science and Education, USDA. As past president of AACC, Bruce was very familiar with and had complimentary comments for CAST. Gale and I next visited with Kendall Keith, president and Randy Grogan of National Grain and Feed Association. They were appreciative of our work and from their standpoint everything was now going well after failing to receive all publications a few years ago. We plan to follow up with a letter and encouragement to do an article in their newsletter to recruit membership both state and individual.

We had lunch with Essex Finney, Deputy Administrator to Dean Plowman, Administrator of ARS. Essex was also complimentary of CAST and we acknowledged our gratitude for all the ARS employees who have served on our task forces.

We then visited Susan Offutt, Executive Director, Board on Agriculture, National Research Council (NRC), and Carla Carlson, Director of Communications. Discussions centered around public perceptions, the need for scientific research, immediate response teams, the NRI, and the budget process. Susan hand delivered a letter and text of recent NRC activity.

The last two stops for the day were Mark Dungan, assistant to Agricultural Secretary Madigan and Dr. John Lee, ERS Administrator. Mark was scurrying around as our visit coincided with President Bush's ethanol announcement. Mark's interest is in new uses and alternative crops. He is committed to this area of investment to ensure production utilization. John was quite interested in CAST and offered the expertise of ERS in support of the valuable reports produced by CAST.

Richard Stuckey

CAST Board of Directors
October 12, 1992
Page 8

Breakfast with Dr. Arthur Kelman, Chief Scientist, USDA Competitive Grants Program began our day. Arthur was enthused about his recent participation in a leadership development conference that coincidentally Gale had a large role in developing. Conversation moved to the Daschle hearings. The NRI staff will be meeting with Daschle's staff in the near future. Dr. Kelman is very interested in CAST and desires to keep in close communication.

Robert Melond, APHIS administrator, appreciated our visit and said he wanted to know more about CAST. Robert is supportive of an international approach to treat the source pests such as the screw worm and medfly rather than pointless efforts to restrict entry. Science is the common denominator and could be used to develop international political stability. He would like to see CAST expand their international approach.

Gale and I then participated in a 2.5 hour steering committee meeting with ISIS and others in the initial planning of the agricultural biotechnology conference. The likely dates will be June 10 and 11, 1993. The Conference is designed to be different from previous biotech meetings in that it will strive to be an educational forum for the media and Congress and to bring the science of biotech to the public. What science knows about food and ag biotechnology issues will be emphasized. The meeting will strive to be inclusive demonstrating the spectrum of views — trade, science, public interest, etc. but not attempt to be consensus building nor polarizing its views. In essence, the meeting should create a rational approach to discussion of an issue, to permit the media to hear all sides of an issue.

Our last stop for the day was at the Citizen's Network where we visited with President John Costello. John knew very little of CAST and was especially interested in the international aspects and the reports of global climate warming and free trade. Costello is also supportive of increasing international focus and policy decisions based on science. Citizen's Network has an agribusiness advisory group and a Washington Agricultural Council. Their focus is on the impacts of international events and public policy effects on domestic agriculture. Nearly all former secretaries of agriculture, trade associations, agricultural government agencies, and former ambassadors are members of their association. In addition to their Washington activities, they host roundtables around the country, often times with Congressmen in that region. CAST could be a scientific resource for their roundtables that could dramatically increase our visibility. John requested membership information be sent to him.

If you have read all of this in one setting, the end is very near. As you can surmise, it has been a busy and very enjoyable month for me. The staff has been very busy translating and preparing the minutes of the past board meeting, working on task force reports, publications, memberships, mailing requests, and correspondence. I hope all is going well for you.

---

cc: CAST Society Member Executive Directors

Stories:

1. During my administration, there was a great deal of controversy between programs called **LISA**, which stands for low-input sustainable agriculture, and conventional agriculture. Both sides had merits to their arguments. Reducing the amount of inputs would have benefits to reducing costs and providing added benefits to soil and water quality. The converse argument was that to produce sufficient food, using low-input methods would require more land to be put into production, and this land would be highly erodible and not as well suited for yield production. Why not choose the best-suited land and maximize input and production so that less highly erodible and ill-suited soils would be needed for production? The competition for federal dollars for both approaches was high and the debate vigorous. Can one be supportive of both philosophies? I believe only if you walk a fine line.

2. The same can be said about increased animal production as well as the use of antibiotics and steroids to promote animal health and faster yield. One very controversial issue was the use of bovine somatotropin (bST) in milk production. This is done by administering cows additional doses of bovine growth hormone (BGH), which is naturally produced in cows, as giving them an extra dose will increase their milk production. It will also make the cow work harder, require more management to prevent mastitis, and, in the end, shorten the life of the

cow. Monsanto was the manufacturer of recombinant bST (rbST) and became public enemy number one for those against its use. It was easy to see which side of the argument people were on by the terms they used for the supplement. Those against its use would refer to it as BGH. Those in support of it would use the term rbST. I well remember one in-depth conversation I had at a conference with a person very opposed to its use. He was full bore on natural livestock production—no hormones, no confinement, free land grazing, etc. For discussion purposes, I took the opposing side and, in a very rational, non-heated approach, asked him some questions. "Do you wish to decrease methane production? If you are able to reduce the number of cows to produce an equal amount of milk, you will decrease the methane released into the air. Would this not be beneficial? For livestock confinement, yes, big spills are possible and infrequently do occur. However, having a cow or pig wade through a small stream and defecate in it, does that add to water quality and food safety?" Without belaboring the point, most issues cut both ways, and in this particular discussion, simply because I tried to lower the heat and be reasonable, I recognized that he had some valuable points but asked him to consider the other side of the issue, and when we did, it did not become quite as clear-cut. We departed as mutual friends and had a bit more respect for the other point of view.

3. One of the reports well underway when I had arrived at CAST was the controversial "Water Quality:

Agriculture's Role." This report was published within three months after my arrival. It essentially stated that agriculture is partially to blame for reduced water quality because of some practices, but it also had a role in reducing the impact. Agriculture is necessary to supply food for our country as well as some developing countries. Can we do that in a more benign way and with a less detrimental impact? Fertilizers and pesticides applied to agricultural crops can result in runoff into our water streams. There was considerable pushback, especially by one chemical company that asked to meet in person with the president and me. They were not happy with the blame being put on agriculture. Another such publication that drew the ire especially of the fertilizer industry was the report "Hypoxia in the Gulf of Mexico," which had much of the same pushback. Our objective was to acknowledge not only the issue and role that agriculture contributed but also that much of the solutions to the problems existed through agriculture. Food safety issues, irradiation, mad cow disease, and Asian influenza were all among the highly debated issues but none more so than introducing genetically modified organisms (GMOs) into our food production. The GMO issue was front and foremost for many of my years at CAST. It was indeed difficult to have a civil discussion. Crop breeders would argue that it was a more precise way of developing new crops by knowing what genes were being inserted compared to the cross-breeding and selection process. These crops were used for feed to animals as well as food for humans. Several GMO-related stories ensue.

4. Europe was a hotbed of anti-GMO use in food. I was invited to travel to Austria to hold a briefing at the U.S. Embassy in Vienna, Austria, with invited scientists from universities in attendance, to discuss the GMO issue and the safety of it. Those scientists in attendance were primarily supportive of the technology but had negative feedback from the public and their country. I was asked to do an interview on the Bluegrass Network and so went to the studios and went into the interview room. I had never had an interview quite like this one. I sat down and started making a bit of small talk as an introduction and then inquired as to what questions I might expect to be asked when we started the interview. She said, "Oh, we are rolling right now, and I will do the editing, so don't worry about it." I did worry about it, and that evening, when I listened to the radio broadcast of our interview, the lead statement was "Could three million Austrians be wrong? Today we have Dr. Richard Stuckey with us, and he will respond to the use and safety of GMOs." I know that leadoffs are important and that they try to hook the audience but thought this was a bit of a misleading intro to our interview. That interview helped me be a bit more prepared for future interviews.

5. When articles came out in print, there were, at times, letters of support and others that were quite the opposite.

There was a university in Eastern Iowa that often offered rebuttals to CAST quotes, and near the end of my tenure, I received a personal letter in 2000. It was personal, offensive, and attacking. In my opinion, there's no place for this type of behavior. For a time, I was concerned that direct action would be taken against my home or my office, but thankfully, it was not. One saw that strong emotions and hate existed twenty years ago as they unfortunately do today.

6. CAST did very few individual author reports, mostly, if there were, comments or responses to something already published. One exception was when a well-known and respected author offered his publication to CAST for publication. My scientific editor strongly recommended that CAST publish it because it was a scholarly work. We did, and I paid dearly for the repercussions. The title of the publication was "How Much Land Can Ten Billion People Spare for Nature?" The publication was well written and interesting reading. The publication proposed that using grain for animal production was very inefficient and that cattle in particular should be grass fed. Likewise, soybean meal and products would be better going directly into human consumption than being run through animals. I had learned early in life, in FFA, that the conversion of pounds of grain was the most efficient in poultry, followed by swine, followed by ruminant animals. To say the animal science community did not like this report would be an understatement. For

the next number of years, I would be reminded of our publication of this report.

7. Another report that was highly influential was entitled "Grazing on Public Lands." This was written by a task force of authors and was much more accepted by the animal science community, and it focused on using public lands as a free source of animal protein production for the benefit of society. Congress used this report in large part to develop legislation on the controversial topic of public land use. Because the report was based on science, we were pleased that the report could be used to write legislation.

8. In the late 1990s, I had an umbilical hernia and had it repaired. A week later, I boarded a flight from Des Moines to Washington, D.C. I was in my normal white shirt and sports coat for airline travel into the capital. Our flight was delayed, and much to my dismay, there was a rupture, and blood spewed forth all over my shirt. I was frightened and thankful for the delay, got off the plane like the rest of the passengers, and immediately went to the phone to call my physician to see what I should do before continuing travel. I discreetly closed my sports coat because the appearance with the totally blood-soaked shirt was that I was likely shot. Upon conferring with my doctor's office, I learned that this was natural a week to ten days following surgery and was told not to be concerned and to proceed with my trip. I pulled another shirt from my carry-on, went into

the restroom, changed shirts, cleaned up, and went on my way. Had this happened en route, I likely would have frantically called the flight attendant over and created a panic on the plane.

9. My vice president for development, in charge of raising funds for the organization, was always searching for new gimmicks to raise funds. He recognized that the best way was for him to schedule appointments for me to visit our sustaining members, but what he could do in addition was to be creative and try to raise additional funds. With my approval, he purchased a thousand or so Louisville Slugger mini bats and had the CAST logo stamped on them; these were handed out to various members and at meetings, encouraging them to go to bat for CAST. This was rather clever, and since we had a number of extras, I did give one to my parents, which returned to my possession after their final days here on earth. However, the main story is "What is the appeal to walk for CAST?" For this, the vice president agreed to walk from his home to the office one day, a walk of some thirty miles, and get members to pledge so much per mile. Knowing the distance and believing he had not sufficiently trained for such an exercise, we did not over-encourage him. He did follow through and completed the walk, starting very early in the morning and finishing in the dark with blisters and very sore feet. If I recall correctly, I think it required him to miss the next couple of days of work to let his body rest and heal.

He did raise some funds doing this, but one well-placed call would have achieved more.

10. One story that sold very well to our supporters regarding the effectiveness of CAST was that of a report by a known young reporter at that time. Bob Arnot of CBS National News reported that he had planned a story to present on the evening news, but in contacting CAST, he realized that his story was not a story, and he was not going forward with that on the news. This is precisely the preemptive desire that we wished to have—when science is known and used, it can prevent misleading information from being given.

11. Another effective tool was when one of our members agreed to have their media team do an extensive interview with me on how food is grown and used as well as the safety factors that go into that. This was an all-day shoot with a prepared script done in Chicago. We were able to show this at multiple events and meetings, and this was well received by many.

12. One of my greatest honors was presenting the only agricultural Nobel Peace Prize winner, Dr. Norman Borlaug, with a nice trophy and recognition at a major agricultural annual meeting event.

Dr. Borlaug is known as the father of the Green Revolution. With the use of genetics, he and his team were able to develop high-yielding varieties with significant disease resistance. Since his early training was in plant pathology, as was mine, and he later moved into the crop-breeding program, we had something in common. An award is now awarded annually from CAST known as the Dr. Borlaug Communication Award, given for top scientists who communicate effectively the science of food, agriculture, and environment. The past 12 years the award has been awarded in conjunction with the World Food Prize/Borlaug dialogue program.

13. A quote that remained with me when I was with the NAWG was when a vice president for DuPont stated, "What people are in on, they are not against." This resonated with me, and I remain a believer of this to this day. Another quote while I was at CAST that remains

engrained was given by a futurist, Canadian Robert Theobald, when he said, "We often look across the river at the grass on the other side thinking it is greener. It should not be our objective to get to the other side. What we really need to do is to get in the stream and navigate that stream through calm and rapids because if we simply go to the other side, we will be passed by, just as we are on this side."

14. My vice president for development arranged for special clearance for me to visit scientists at Cape Canaveral, NASA. Security was tight, and it was extremely interesting to see the greenhouses and their production of food for space travel for their astronauts. There were many security checkpoints and validation required, which was quite amazing. This visit was scheduled in conjunction with several other visits to the state of Florida.

15. Iowa is known as the land of pork, where there are more hogs than people in the state. The Iowa pork chop is a delicacy if prepared properly. The one-and-a-quarter-to-one-and-a-half-inch-thick center-cut pork chops are delicious. One summer, on our weeklong vacation to Little Eden Camp

in Onekama, Michigan, I made arrangements to purchase and deliver on ice over two hundred chops to grill for the campers. My parents and my two brothers were also at camp, and my two brothers helped me grill the pork chops, which received rave reviews. The $400 or so cost plus the transporting of nearly six hundred miles was well worth the investment for the great feeling of giving. Do kindness and be generous when you can, and your rewards will be substantial.

CHAPTER 13

Early Retirement Years, 2001–2007

Our Home on Cherry Creek Drive

Following my decision to retire and a timeline, there were more forks in the road. The transition process became a work in progress. Once this was announced to my executive committee in May 1999, attention was given to the location of our retirement. It was not going to be Iowa. We both wanted to leave winter weather. Possible choices included the Carolinas, Arizona, Nevada, and California. We planned to visit many of those communities between the time of my announcement and prior to September 2001. Florida was given some consideration, but the bugs and humidity put that on the second tier at best for year-round living. The Carolinas were also suspect because of the humidity and heat in the summer but were viewed as more tolerable than Florida. Our eyes moved west as the highest probability. A former executive committee member had a summer home in Palm Desert, California, certainly an option. Another former president of CAST had a winter home in Mesquite, Nevada, another possibility. Both of these gentlemen soon made their major residences from Michigan to Palm Desert and from Minnesota to Mesquite after experiencing some time in the Southern climes.

In the fall of 1999, the CAST board of directors fall meeting was held in Phoenix, Arizona. We decided this would be an excellent time to do a little scouting of some potential Arizona locations. We took a weeklong vacation in advance of the meeting in September and visited the two locales that we considered. One was a Robson community near Tucson, and the other was a Del Webb community in Surprise, a suburb of Phoenix. We originally thought the smaller university town of Tucson could be more to our liking and spent three days there. We enjoyed our time there. We then spent four days at Sun City Grand, a new Del Webb facility in Surprise. We immediately fell in love with Sun City Grand. It had beauty, it had facilities, it had organized activities, it had plans for four golf courses (two of which were already completed and open for play), it had a beautiful softball field that had just been dedicated by All-Star Yankee pitcher Whitey Ford, it was close enough to the airport (forty minutes away), and the fact that we planned to travel and receive guests made it a logical choice. The marketing of Sun City Grand sold itself. A realtor gave us her card, a packet of information, the keys to a villa, and a golf cart and told us to enjoy ourselves. What more could we want? I wanted to stay there and not go to my meetings. While I was at my meetings, Judy went back out to do some additional research and work with a realtor. On Sunday, before we flew back to Iowa, I went back out, and we made an offer on a resale property that was not accepted. We went back to Iowa with our minds still on Arizona.

As we were working from a distance with our realtor, another resale became available. In November, we made an offer and ended up closing in December 1999. Now all I had to do was retire. It was a modest home of just under two thousand square feet, all on one floor. We decided we would see what the summer was like and what the phrase "but it's a dry heat" really meant by spending a week in the middle of the summer in Arizona. I took a week's vacation, and Judy extended for a week in July 2000; we thought it was doable that we could make this our year-round home. Thus, with retirement looming much closer in March 2001, we purchased another larger home of nearly 2,800 square feet, with a large patio, a swimming pool, and a hot tub overlooking the golf course. Heaven had arrived!

The scientific editor announced her retirement in late 2000, effective January 1, 2001. Although my retirement was known and kept a very close secret from the board, my retirement was officially announced in early January 2001. It was quite a shake-up for a small staff. I did proceed to hire a very qualified scientific editor who was a friend of my wife and whose husband was on the faculty at Iowa State University. I shared with her that I would be retiring but that this would provide a good opportunity for her; if she did not care for the position, she could easily resign because of my retirement if things didn't work out in the future. She accepted the position, eventually moved up to the position of executive vice president in 2012, and retired in 2015.

The search process for my replacement began in earnest in January 2001. A selection was made without my input, but on paper, the choice looked excellent, with a PhD in crop genetics, a legislative aide on Sen. Bob Kerrey's (NE-D) staff, and a law degree on her résumé. She would begin work in late March, and we would have a three-month overlap, so my retirement would be the end of June 2001. This was fine with me. The two of us decided that she would begin running the office and directing the programs, and I would try to clean up and recruit as much of the finances as I could to make them current for her. Since her location was in Washington, D.C., she would work from there and commute on occasion to the office in Ames, a reversal of what I had. Still, it seemed to make good sense in that we would have someone within minutes of meetings in Washington, and the remainder of the staff would stay in Ames, a much more economical location from which to operate. Things went pretty smoothly, but there was one incident that created much concern to me as well as others.

There was a farewell party for me and an introduction to the new executive vice president in Ames, Iowa, in May 2001.

It was held at Iowa State University and attended by several deans and many professors from Iowa State as well as several from surrounding state universities. The meeting was to start with a program, tributes to my tenure, acknowledgment on my part, and introduction and comments by my replacement. She was late for the meeting—not a good start. The meeting was held up for a few minutes but then started without her in attendance. That could have been known as strike one. Then I sat in horror when she got up and stated that she got her PhD from the University of Minnesota; although she was offered an assistantship for a PhD at Iowa State, Iowa State was not good enough, and she got her degree from the superior University of Minnesota program. Can you believe such a statement in front of an 80 percent Iowa State University attendance? She may have claimed to say that in jest, but it did not come across that way, and I certainly didn't take it that way. We had a special dinner for about thirty of the board members in attendance, deans of the university, and a few selected others that evening. Our next-door neighbor and dean of the College of Education was at the dinner and shared with me that he was not impressed with the new hire, especially after hearing her remarks.

In May, my younger brother Ron inquired of coming down to Arizona to spend a long weekend to see our place with his new wife. It was a difficult time for me to get away, and I thought we would have plenty of time to do that later, so I told him it would not work out. The last week of June, he invited us to travel from Ames, Iowa, to Chicago to join him, my dad, my other brother, and my younger son, who lived there, for a Chicago White Sox baseball game. This was the weekend after Friday, my last day at work. Unfortunately, we had already made plans to spend the weekend with two other couples from Ames at one of their lake homes in Wisconsin. Again, I declined, much to my regret because a month later, he would not be able to issue any more invitations to me.

The physical move to Sun City Grand was made July 13. We were bade a fond farewell, with neighbors spaced throughout our neighborhood waving as we departed in our car for the trip to Arizona. We had closed on the new property—18052 Cherry Creek Drive, Surprise, AZ—in March 2001, so that was the home that we moved into. We were barely unpacked but making good progress the first two weeks of living in Arizona when we received the terrible news, on July 28, that my younger brother Ron was killed in a tractor accident. This devastated our family as he was a caregiver to my aging parents. A book could be written on his life. A great guy, he would give the shirt off his back for anyone, tried to please in any way he could, and was very generous. Our sons have many fond experiences of being on the farm and spending time with him. On the night before his death, he had stayed up late and just bought tickets for my parents, my brother and his wife, and his family to come and spend Christmas with us in 2001. The other tickets were used, but it was a semi-sad Christmas because of the fact that one ticket was not used.

I had already become emerged in activities in Grand, having been signed up to a softball team, when we received the dreaded news of my brother's death. I remember to this day, very distinctly, the situation when I received the dreaded call from my mother. We were out on our patio with some new friends who were moving to Grand— admiring the pool, the golf course view, etc.—when the phone rang and my mom informed me that my brother Ron had been killed in a tractor accident. What a shock! What disbelief! *Tell me it's not true.* I was so looking forward to retirement and being able to spend more time with my brothers and parents. We had set up a farming operation called Stuckey Brothers, where my brother Ron was the primary manager of the operation; my second brother, Larry, was still working as an anesthetist, and I had been working full-time. I had planned to spend nearly a month in the spring planting the crops and another month in the fall harvesting the crops.

The death of my brother was a game changer for our family. In many ways, he was the glue, there with my aging parents day in and day out, assisting them with their new life in an independent living community. He had just retired from teaching vocational agriculture at his local high school yet retained a bus-driving route for special education students.

In fact, he had already purchased a gift for each of his dozen or more special education students for Christmas that year, a full five months off. Compare that to his elder brother, who frequently does his Christmas shopping the week of Christmas or the day before Christmas!

Going back for the services was very difficult. I still remember walking into my parents' house and seeing the devastated looks on their faces as they realized that their caregiver was no longer there to look after them and to share their later years of retirement. I was convinced that one of the toughest things for any parent is to have one of their children pass away before they do. It is just not supposed to happen that way, although it is a frequent occurrence with wars, accidents, and diseases. We were all scheduled to go to a camp in Northern Michigan, Little Eden Camp, in the middle of August, which we did, but this too was very difficult because we did this frequently each year, but there was a special person missing this year. I did go home as planned to help harvest crops in September and October, but it was extremely difficult to harvest the crops that my brother had planted, and we realized that he would not be planting any more crops on this earth. Then the week of Christmas holidays that he had booked for the entire family in Arizona did take place, but one ticket was not used, and that too was very painful. This one event put a major damper on the beginning of my retirement. My life would go on. I'd be with sorrow, but what about my parents? They lived another seven years before passing away, and I know the news of July 28, 2001, was remembered every day.

It did not take long to get immersed in the many activities that Sun City Grand offered. Judy immediately became involved in the many music activities and actually became a founding member of the fifties and sixties rock 'n' roll groups the Retro-Rock and the Beach Bums, playing many venues—at restaurants, at private parties, and on stage for music events and many other special events. They were very good and harmonized extremely well. She soon joined up with a girls golf group that expanded from a dozen members to over twenty, and once a month, they celebrated a wine/whiners get-together. Several of the ladies in this group also became a part of the couples Sunday golf group that we were members of. We would play late morning or early afternoon and then get together for dinner at one of our houses—wonderful memories.

My activities in addition to golf were softball and playing cards. Softball took precedence, and in addition to playing twice a week at Sun City Grand,

I joined a travel team that played competitive softball on weekends in Arizona and surrounding states.

We both joined a walkers group, where most mornings, we would walk the two to three miles and end up at the café for coffee and fellowship. In 2003, I was elected president of the softball club, which had a membership of over three hundred softball players and has since expanded to nearly five hundred. I served in that capacity for two years, and many new programs were initiated, including an advertising program where businesses could place signs on our outfield fence and we could gain revenue for our club as well as our community. This program exists to this day and is very popular. I was invited to throw out the first pitch at the Spring Training of a major league baseball game.

Judy also became president of the Grand Singers, the major group within the music club. She did this for two years as well.

And people worried that I would become bored in retirement! This was fun, but it seemed like all play, and I did miss some of the work and interaction that had been so much a part of my life for so many years. I was a rather hot commodity for continued involvement in the work that I had put so much effort into because now I was retired and had plenty of time—at least, that was the thinking. I continued to serve on several boards for a few more years, accepted the invitation to serve on the public policy board of the APS, and accepted the position of chair of a new publication endeavor known as the Plant Management Network (PMN). A bit more will be told about each of these as they would become a part of my work life for the next four to five years.

The public policy board of the APS was well suited for me. I had spent much of the last twelve years in and around Washington, D.C., where public policy had its home. While this was not overly time-consuming, it did consist of several (three to four) trips to Washington, D.C., each year. We met with many of the people whom I had interacted with before, so I had instant recognition and felt I could contribute to the goals of the board. The APS had a consultant who did much of their politicking for the society members and headed up this effort. This reduced the amount of work considerably in planning for the visits and position statements that were required by board members.

The other major effort was, again, working with the APS to chair the effort to establish the multidisciplinary PMN publication series. Chairing a committee is much different from being a member of the committee, as anyone who has been in that position knows. It is much easier to recruit a member than it is to obtain a chair. I agreed to chair the multidisciplinary team of committee members to create a suite of publications that included plant production and plant protection articles and provided a home for such applied publications. If you go way back to the Kentucky years, you will find mention of the *Fungicide and Nematicide Test Results*, which I was business manager of for many years; well, these publications could now be a part of the PMN. Ever heard of the saying "What comes around goes around"? This is another validation of that statement.

The PMN committee met twice a year, once in Arizona during the winter, convenient for me, and generally once during the summer, in a more temperate zone. Being chair did require additional meetings for me with the headquarters staff in Minneapolis, Minnesota. It was these two major efforts that were largely responsible for me receiving the Volunteer of the Year award in 2007 from the APS. During this time, I did attend nearly all the annual meetings of the APS. Terming off the public policy board after six years and stepping down as chair of the PMN committee served as a transition from early retirement to mid-retirement years.

One other significant event during this time that should be mentioned is that my successor at CAST, as predicted by some, was having difficulty and was removed from her position. I was invited to return to my old position but declined, but their persistence convinced me to be involved during the search for a successor. I did not accept the interim title of executive vice president, but having invested so much time in the organization, I did want CAST to succeed and agreed to work part-time with the title of senior advisor while the search was being conducted.

In essence, I did end up running the organization from a staff position and did not relocate from Arizona but spent much time traveling back to Washington, D.C., and to the Iowa offices while encouraging the search committee to proceed with haste to identify a new leader. This time, I was involved in the search process, and we did hire a capable replacement after my serving seven months as a senior advisor. I enjoyed reengaging with the organization and with many other people who were in their same positions three years earlier when I was still employed by the organization. Working with task force authors, administrators in Washington, D.C., congressional staff, briefings, and regulatory agencies was fun but time-consuming, and I was officially retired. This was not what I had signed up for, but I was glad to do it and also glad to have it come to an end.

It was at this juncture that I decided the national level of activity was a part of my history, something enjoyable for the most part. However, it was time to turn more locally, reduce the amount of travel, and try to contribute to society while, at the same time, having more free and discretionary time to do leisurely travel and enjoy the retirement life where I was living.

Stories:

1. The weddings of our two sons during this period were highlight stories for us. They both waited until they were of age, thirty-plus, and married one year apart, one on the West Coast and the other near the East Coast, both beautiful yet contrasting weddings. My parents and brother as well as Judy's sister and her husband were able to attend both weddings. JJ and Amanda were married in an outdoor wedding in a park overlooking Washington Lake. The wedding event was a weekend affair with their fun-time bachelor-type party, which included both sexes, in a restaurant-reserved venue the night before the wedding. The post-wedding event included a rented facility where JJ's band could perform and guests were decked out in tie-dye shirts. It was an eye-opener for my parents but lots of fun. Jon and Jessica were married a year later in Philadelphia at a historic site. It was an outdoor wedding with many attendees seated on the lawn with a lovely backdrop. A large party—complete with a terrific buffet, a toast, and a roast—and a lively, fun evening preceded the wedding. A full dinner following the wedding ceremony ensued with the announced entrance of special guests as they were seated at their tables. Dancing, food, and libations were not in short supply. Both sons have wedding photos for those who wish for a more robust recap of the two treasured events.

2. Joining a travel softball team necessitated, on average, one weekend each month to travel to a tournament. There are many stories that could be told. One I distinctly remember was traveling late in the afternoon up to Pinetop, Arizona, a high-elevation location nice for summer softball tournaments and normally a three-and-a-half-hour drive. Getting through Phoenix, I missed the turn to go up I-87 and realized that once I had gone to Globe, about twenty miles beyond where I should have turned off. To me, this was too late to turn around and go back, so why not take another route that we had not taken, that looked rather scenic? Again, if my memory is correct, Judy suggested that we add the twenty miles, go back, and get on the road that we knew would take us to our destination. I was driving; I won out. Men can be stubborn! We got over to the eastern part of the state and prepared to take the road north up to Pinetop. It appeared to be a well-marked road. I knew we were in trouble when, after a short distance up the road, a sign read Next Rest Stop 45 Miles. The road was curvy, it became dark, and travel at points needed to be fifteen to twenty miles an hour for safe passage. The three-and-a-half-hour trip became an eight-hour trip, and we ended up missing the team dinner that evening. Much to my dismay, upon arrival, I learned that the missing item that I had not packed for that trip happened to be my undershorts. This translated into much ribbing for many trips to come. "Stuckey, what did you forget this trip?"

3. Another softball memory, I would prefer to forget, but it sticks in my mind. While law officers often get rapped for bad behavior after they leave the force because of their belief of invincibility, one teammate did fit the mold. This teammate was a good player but had a very short fuse, as evidenced by a brawl that he got into in the golf clubhouse when he tried to cut the line. A charge was filed, and he had to appear before a judge, and when the judge announced a small fine and three weeks of anger management courses, he went berserk and told the judge that he did not need any blankity-blank anger management courses. The length of time and anger management courses were doubled. This individual was also kicked out of league games for fighting as well as abuse directed at umpires, so it was not unusual that in the competitive tournament games, he would become unglued. I was coaching third base when the short-tempered player was on second base and a hit went to the outfield; the ball was quickly thrown into the cutoff man, where it was bobbled and moved away from the player, but I had already put up the hold sign at third base. He turned and saw the ball was not even in the hands of the cutoff man as it was scooted away and said he could've easily made it home. He was correct, but at the time, I didn't know the ball would be bobbled and wanted to play it safe. He started screaming at me, a teammate, and then yelled across to the first-base dugout and told the coach to get someone over here at third base who knew how to coach. It was a very unprofessional display of disarray on the same

team. Perhaps it was justice that on his next bat, he went high into second base with spikes in the air, and thus, an intense scuffle with a second baseman ensued, upon which punches were thrown and he was expelled from the game. The ironic thing is that in most of these episodes, he ended up on the bottom and on the short end of the deal. He had a lovely wife, and I truly felt sorry for the embarrassment that he caused her on many occasions.

4. Most softball players reviewed my presidency of the softball club as very successful. Many improvements were achieved, membership grew, and while there were occasional arguments on the field, they were treated with suspensions and punishment equivalent to the offense. We had many male and female fans in the stands, and thus, language and actions often displayed by the guys were not appropriate. I recall one incident where a verbal and hand gesture exchange was made in full view of all at the field. The two were summoned for an appearance before the board. The one superior player who thought the other had instigated the altercation thought he was being exonerated, which was not the case. We remain friends to this day and occasionally have breakfast together.

5. Two years after my presidency, there was a dispute regarding players being able to choose which league they wished to play in. In essence, the president and vice president were blindsided at a club meeting where one

of their friends got up and made the motion that players could play wherever they wanted so they could be bigger fish in a small pond. The president and vice president immediately resigned and left only three members of the five-member board in place. I was recruited heavily to come and assume the presidency for the remaining eight months of the year until a new election would be held. I did so and gained many fans for stepping in and helping out in a time of need, but it was a reminder that I had been there, done that, and I was anxious to complete this additional service. The same can be said for many other jobs; once you have done it, it is less exciting and invigorating to return and do the same thing.

6. A couple of Wild Hare editions are included in Appendix A for your reading enjoyment. Many of these were written in jest and exaggerated beyond reality the abilities of the Wild Hare on the softball field. These were disseminated to only a couple of friends and close family for their amusement. I was worried that they would get out to the broader softball community, and some may take it that I had a tremendously elevated opinion of my softball abilities and myself. In short, they were very exaggerated accounts.

7. Another controversy that occurred during this period involved the church of which we had become members in late 2002. There was a change of pastors, and many in the church believed that the incoming pastor had not been truly vetted. A huge turmoil ensued, and an

entire book could be written and was considered for the benefit of future congregations to avert such a problem. I had become the chair of the Truth in Love Committee to try to work out the differences, meet with the pastor and his supporters, and resolve the conflict. This did not make new friends for me, but it was viewed as another example of a call to leadership.

8. The use of emails is a great way to communicate with a selected group. Just be careful that you know who is in your group and that you screen those whom you do not wish to receive that information. The president of the church council was a voice for the current pastor, and he and I met on a number of occasions, had developed a relatively good relationship considering we were on opposite sides of the issue, and had met for lunch and other small group meetings when I was communicating with a group of twelve or fifteen persons on our side of the argument. One of those questioned why I would be meeting with the church council president and some of the appeasement I had made to him. I responded that in part, it was to appease his ego, hit the Send button, and, unfortunately, immediately upon sending, realized that his address was among those receiving this communication. I wanted so badly to retrieve that email or, in some way, prevent it from reaching his desk. There was no way to do that, and while I heard from him on that email, I'm sure it was shared with many others who were on his side of the issue, including the pastor. The end result is that nearly 40 percent of the congregation

left, most to other churches, some not attending church
to this day, which is truly sad. Some twelve-plus years
later, there is an effort where we live for members of the
two primary congregations to meet jointly for monthly
communion services in the COVID year of 2020.

9. Moving from state and national voluntary services to
more local levels was a big shift for me. This would
only grow over time and become a focus for my future
retirement years. One of the organizations that I became
deeply involved in was Benevilla, at that time known as
Interfaith Community Care. It was founded in 1981 to
be able to provide services to aging people who do not
have family and friends nearby to assist them with their
aging. I was invited to join the development committee
by a pastor at the church and another friend at the
church who was a generous donor. I was also invited to
serve on the board of directors, and you will learn more
in the next chapter.

10. When I retired at an early age, I always felt that I
would not feel cheated if I received three years of a fun
retirement life. One of the ways that we enjoyed life was
to take trips, many of them cruises.

This was done mostly with friends, who ranged from new friends we made in Arizona to our Kentucky friends from years ago and, in particular, a renewed friendship of college days. We discovered two former classmates who were residing in the Phoenix area. We also cruised by ourselves, including one in honor of our fortieth anniversary, which was to the fjords of Norway on the Crystal cruise lines.

A listing of the cruises taken (Appendix C), are most of them—numbering twenty or more, I hope to recall. For most people, this would be an inordinate amount of cruises taken; however, for those who cruise, there are many who will surpass this number.

11. There were numerous parties, from holidays such as New Year's, Halloween, Valentine's, and Christmas to many others that were scheduled and occasionally spontaneous in nature. We had a fun group of people who liked to have fun and were willing to dress up and become a bit crazy, which added to the fun and enjoyment.

12. We also became members of the Sunday couples' golf group, which originated out of the ladies' Thursday golf group. This fun group started with six to eight couples,

and in addition to playing on Sunday afternoons and then going to one of the couple's homes for dinner later that afternoon, there were outings to other Arizona cities for weekend golf. One that became a fixture was to Laughlin, Nevada, where there was also gaming to go along with the golf getaway. These memories will remain forever. The important point here is to do fun things with people you enjoy being with while you can. Twelve years later, there are at least four who are no longer with us.

13. Celebrating Judy's major birthdays on the fives and zeroes became a tradition. For her sixtieth birthday, her sister and a friend, Mim, joined us for a lovely dinner at Tapatia, overlooking the city of Phoenix. Very special was the *surprise* appearance of both of our boys at the restaurant.

CHAPTER 14

Mid-Retirement Years, 2008–2014

These years, by and large, were good years, from my mid-sixties to seventy years of age. Although I was physically active, I didn't notice the aging process taking place. I was still active in sports; in fact, it was during this period that the travel team I played on won the world senior softball championship in 2010. I proudly wear the large Super Bowl imitation ring to this day. Major leadership roles were assumed in my two favorite service nonprofit organizations. Those were Benevilla and Rotary.

In many ways, it seems as though this is the age where you can simulate all your life experiences and still have the energy to be an effective leader. This is not to say that one cannot be younger and be an effective leader or older and also be an effective leader; however, for me, everything just seemed to come together. Perhaps it was that I had been roughly ten years into my new environment, was safely retired, and was not threatened by the lack of work or income such that I could now focus on philanthropy efforts.

As touched on in earlier chapters, what are the keys to effective leadership? First, leading by example is so important. The people you are trying to convince to support your vision need to see that you truly believe in the mission and are an active participant. This is true in nearly every area of service. Take, for example, the generals and military leaders. Who are the successful ones? They are the ones who lead their service members into battle. How often have we been disenchanted with political leaders who demonstrate the principle of "Do as I say, not as I do"? No one likes a hypocrite.

Second, having credibility is also important. Do you know your subject matter? Do you truly believe in what you are trying to promote or sell? This is the mark of a good salesman, whether it is a car, a home, or an investment or simply supporting the organization that you are trying to lead.

Third is knowing your audience and trying to relate to them. For example, are you trying to lead an organization of senior citizens, which was the case in my Rotary Club, located in a senior retirement community with mostly aging white males? What triggers them? How can we get the members involved when many have already been there and done that and a good number of others are more interested in social events with friends? As a leader, you can challenge and demonstrate what can happen when many people get behind an issue. There will be more on this topic later—selecting challenging speakers and challenging, productive projects, important for success.

Fourth, be inclusive; make every member feel important and that they have something to contribute. The organization will not be made whole unless everyone contributes and does their part.

Fifth, encourage ideas and discussion. The old saying that "two heads are better than one" also applies to forty heads or more being better than one. Once everyone feels comfortable contributing ideas, the challenge is to merge and narrow those ideas into achievable projects. Thorough, open, and honest discussions are needed before prioritizing the ideas into a manageable number of projects. Those ideas not accepted are saved for a time to revisit them when the agreed-upon ideas are put in place and the organization can advance additional ideas. Each member, even if their idea was not popular at the time, must be led to feel that they have contributed to expanding the thought process of other members. So often, an idea that has not received the necessary level of popularity has led another individual to think of an idea that has.

Sixth, as a leader, be realistic about your expectations and don't be discouraged if you do not exceed your goals. Set realistic goals. Is the group you are trying to lead young, energetic people or older, more established people? Is it a combination of both or something in between? Typically, younger people will have more energy, be under more time constraints, and have less resources or at least more places where their resources need to be distributed. The older folks will typically have more resources and be able to contribute dollars over physical efforts. This, in many ways, gets back to knowing your audience or your members.

Seventh, make it fun, not work. Yes, it is work, but work can be fun. When fun encompasses the work, everyone benefits.

Eighth, celebrate your successes. Create a party, large or small, to recognize and celebrate what has been accomplished. Thank and re-thank many times all those involved and who have contributed to making it a success. This will go a long way to gaining enthusiasm for moving on to the next project.

To illustrate some of the above, I will focus on detailing a bit of my two favorite, most rewarding organizations that were served during this time frame. In addition, I will identify several other activities that consumed considerable amounts of time yet served to make one whole.

Benevilla, an organization founded in 1981 to serve the elderly in the northwest valley of Phoenix, has evolved into a major human services organization over the years. I joined the board in 2009 and was privileged to be chair of the board in 2011.

A capital campaign was begun in 2004 to prepare for a move to a new headquarters office. This was intended to be a $5.4 million project. Over several years, nearly $5 million were raised, but the project now had a $7.4 million cost. The facilities were completed, but a loan of $2.9 million was secured, and the monthly interest payment was $19,000, a significant blow to the budget and operation of the organization. The 2007–2008 recession had hit, and fundraising was challenging. In 2010, it was recognized that we simply had to get the debt paid down, and thus, a second capital campaign was organized for the purpose of eliminating the debt. When asking donors to contribute to a capital campaign, what effect would that have on their annual giving? It was determined to combine the two, the capital campaign and the annual giving, into one effort and begin a $4 million campaign, $3 million for debt elimination and $1 million for operations. I became the chair for this effort. The president and CEO, Michelle Dionisio, and I recruited two well-connected leaders in the community to work with us on this campaign, along with a consulting group to advise us on the process. With much work and effort and ingenuity, we proceeded.

One contributor suggested that in addition to the commitments, we solicit loans from generous donors at no interest, to be paid back at a later date. The idea was that those donors might forgive these loans. We had three such donors, two for $200,000 each and one for $100,000. This meant that we had $500,000 that we could pay down on the debt, but in actuality, it was still a return payment that may need to be made. As it turned out, one of the $200,000 gifts was forgiven, the other one was requested back over a period of five years and some of that returned was used for their annual contributions, and the other $100,000 was requested back because of some hardships that had occurred within the family. Our lead gift was $500,000 and came somewhat of a surprise from a person who had volunteered and given much smaller amounts over the prior years.

We did allow three- to five-year commitments to make payments, which, again, did not immediately reduce the debt, and we needed more to totally eliminate the debt. Single-year commitments paid upfront are the safest way to go. However, more money can be raised if you allow people to pay out over a longer time. The danger of accepting three- to five-year commitments is that life can change, where later-year commitments may be broken. While 95 percent of the long-term commitments were honored, we had one donor who had committed $100,000 over four years and passed away during the first year; thus, we lost $75,000 in committed contributions. The other difficulty in multi-year commitments is that in this case only 25% of the money received in the first year could go to operations. This created a short fall in needed operational funding. We got by but found it necessary to go back to our donors the second year to support our annual operations. Most of those who made single year contributions were willing to do so, and we were able to use 25% of second year capital campaign contributions to supplement the shortfall. The process was challenging but we did get by and survive. The end result over the next three to four years was that we reduced our debt from $2.9 million down to $200,000, and that made a tremendous difference on the amount of interest that we had to pay.

The consultants also advised that I stay on as chair of the board through the conclusion of this project, which took until May, four to five months into the year 2012. The short story is that I was deeply committed to Benevilla and gained a lot of experience in this area, kind of like a baptism by water because capital campaigns were nothing that I had ever done or experienced before. If your heart is there, you can succeed, and you will learn and grow with the new experience.

Benevilla is often referred to as the best-kept secret in the northwest valley of Phoenix. We wanted to change that and increase exposure. One way was to change the name from Interfaith Community Care services to Benevilla. A full study was done with the help of Arizona State University students that included contacting many of our members and asking what the organization meant to them; the theme of home, family, etc. resonated, and that's what the name Benevilla means—"good home." We were also increasing our level of support through foundations and businesses, and the policy for some was not to donate to religious organizations. We were not a religious organization but oftentimes confused with one in Arizona, so a new name was deemed as important. Changing a name that had been held for nearly thirty years was also a challenge for some of our donors and members. We survived.

Benevilla grew from a daycare center for adults suffering from dementia and physical restrictions to multiple life enrichment centers, a child development program, an intergenerational center, and a program for disabled adults. My two favorite programs included the intergenerational center, where preschool children and adults with early stages of dementia were able to get together to do arts, projects, exercises, and other activities, which created a grandparent–child relationship in many cases. This program was unique for the state of Arizona when it was founded.

The other program was the helping partners program. The group of thirty-plus in this program consisted of persons between ages eighteen and sixty. Disabled persons are cared for while they are in school, but what happens to them when they leave high school? Many times, their parents are still working and need a place to care for their loved one. Through the innovativeness of the organization, many activities and service projects were made available for this group. This gave them a real sense of worth and had them looking forward to coming and socializing each day with others. One very gratifying event to me was my involvement in having this group, who had a choir, perform at an Arizona State University basketball game by singing the national anthem at halftime. To do so required that we purchase a number of tickets for the game, and the amount came to $840. I agreed to contribute half that amount, $420, and challenged the rest of the board of directors to fund the other half, which they did. I will never forget the performance that this choir gave with their hearts more so than their voices, singing the national anthem, and the hush that came over the crowd that witnessed this event— good marketing, good warm feelings, and good memories that exist to this day. The recognition for this and my involvement in the program still exists with members of this group. The other big event that happened with the helping partners that I did not have a lot to do with but others with foresight did was to train them and certify them to be food handlers; therefore, they could be paid by the organization to help prepare and package food for the other centers and for a meals-on-wheels program. The photos of the recipients who received their very first ever paychecks were priceless.

Because I believed in the organization, it was easy for me to donate time and effort as well as resources. Time and effort could include chairing an annual golf tournament as a fundraiser and also serving on a committee many years for a gala, another fundraiser. There were other projects spearheaded by an energetic young board member for an event called the Festival of Cheer. This was held at the Peoria baseball spring training complex for the Seattle Mariners and the San Diego Padres and brought in talent representing many countries, actual snow trucked down from Flagstaff, and many other special events to make it a truly family event. I actually was coerced (volunteered) to be Santa for several years. One year, it was especially challenging as I had just completed a surgery and had a black and bruised eye that I thought was covered up quite well; however, several kids were more observant, noticed it, and were somewhat alarmed. It's just one more example of "Where your heart is, there will be your time and talents."

Our eldest grandson, Jacob, began spending several weeks each summer with us at the age of two in 2009. We fondly called it Camp Arizona. At age four to five, he became involved with me at Benevilla and in Rotary. He would attend events with me at Benevilla and also at the weekly Rotary meeting. What Papa was involved in, he wanted to be involved in. What an example we can create for those who look up to us—and at such an early age!

Rotary became my other love for involvement, another service organization that does well not only in the local community but also in the nation and internationally. Their one well-known international program is the eradication of polio in the world through the use of vaccines. Soon after my tenure as chair of the board at Benevilla, I became president elect and then president of our local Rotary Club of Sun City West. I had served on the board of the Rotary Club for several years and was chair of several committees; however, the presidency of a club raises the time and commitment to an entirely new level. It can be very rewarding but can become almost a full-time job. If you do not want a volunteer job to overwhelm you, you need to get other members involved and doing their part to assist you. A successful tenure is not pulling the wagon by yourself but leading the way, again with many "horses" pulling the wagon with you. A few popular annual events were the annual Rotary golf tournament that raised about $30,000 per year and distributing dictionaries to over two thousand third-graders. Both of these programs were programs that I was involved in and led for several years. We tried to add something to the programs each year to increase their attractiveness for participation and support. As an example for the golf tournament, one year, we had a trick shot artist pro demonstrate his skills with the golf ball and golf clubs; another year, we had four senior LPGA golfers join us, and each played at least one hole with all golfers who registered for the golf tournament. For several years, we had items donated for an auction that evening at our dinner and recognition program. What I am stressing here is to add something to make it interesting for events that are held on a regular basis. Rotary—along with the Lions, Kiwanis, and many other service organizations—is a wonderful way to contribute your time and talent, and I would encourage those interested to learn more about those organizations to see which are best suited to your interests.

Apart from Benevilla and Rotary, I found the church to be a segue for me going from service to social activity. Although encouraged to serve on the church council, I declined because of the two other organizations I was so heavily involved in. I did agree to serve on a number of committees or, as I like to call them, task forces. What is the difference between a committee and a task force? My definition is that a committee can continue on ad infinitum year after year, whereas a task force is assigned a specific job, and once that is completed, the task force is disbanded. Certainly, the task force had far more appeal to me, and thus, I served on the search committee for a new pastor, which was a very rewarding experience. We had a chair and a chaplain who were very important to the process. There were also six or seven members on the committee who had many common and some diverse views and approaches that made the whole exercise very worthwhile, and friendships were created through this process. The church also had many social get-togethers for the members of the church. Christmas parties, monthly Sunday night dinners with entertainment, service projects (Feed My Starving Children), and adopting a different nonprofit in the local community on a monthly basis for extra giving/donation opportunities, along with additional small group and Bible studies, gave members plenty of opportunities to become involved.

Softball was recreational as well as social. The nearly five-hundred-member club was a good way to meet and play with other members of a similar interest. From this group, some travel opportunities like a week to Branson, Missouri, and a monthly spades card group were formed. Softball was played year round, and teams were drafted three to four times a year, so you had the opportunity to play and learn to know many different players who moved here from all over the country.

Continuing on the social side, both Judy and I played golf. Judy helped form a ladies group that played once a week, and also, from this ladies' Thursday golf group, they invited their husbands to be part of a couples' golf group that played on Sunday afternoons, followed by dinner at one of the couples' homes. This group became very close and also traveled several weekends a year to golf destinations within the state. Joining a walking group to walk two to three miles every morning followed by coffee was another social outlet for many years. Cruises with other couples, family gatherings, and get-togethers as well as playing cards either in the evening or during the day as time permitted were other venues for socialization. My preference for card games moved to the mind-challenging game of bridge, which I thoroughly enjoy.

I often have to think back on the CAST board members who were concerned that I would become bored in retirement. From what has been described in the first two chapters of retirement life, I believe their concerns are no longer valid.

Stories:

1. For me, it all starts with family.

I was a part of a family from my birth on. Then I got married and began a family of my own, and in the end, it will all come back to family. It is a journey along the way that provides additional enrichment to one's life in addition to the family always being there. My first story is about a surprise visit to my parents for their sixty-fifth anniversary back in Ohio. My brother and his wife were going to lunch at a favorite Chinese restaurant with my parents in our hometown of Archbold, Ohio. My first cousin and her husband, both very close to my parents, were also going to be there to celebrate a sixty-fifth anniversary lunch. Unbeknownst to my parents, I had made arrangements to fly back from Arizona and surprise them at lunch. In Arizona, we had grapefruit, orange, and lemon trees. The lemon tree produced exceedingly large lemons of the kind that you cannot buy in stores. My mother made lots and lots of lemonade over the years, and she admired the lemons she had seen when she visited and also took photos of the abundance and size of the lemons. So I packed eight large lemons in my suitcase for my trip back. I flew into Detroit, rented a car, and drove to the restaurant. Excitement was building. I love surprises. As I parked the car, carried the lemons with me, and approached the restaurant, I looked inside, and sure enough, there were the six of them, having just begun eating at the table. I walked behind them, placed three or four of the large lemons on the table in front of them, and said, "Here. You wanted lemons, so I thought I would just deliver them in person." The next ten seconds were scary. I thought my parents were going to have a heart attack. The surprise was totally complete and, after their hearts stopped racing, much appreciated but gave me some cause for concern. We had a wonderful weekend. Little did I know at that time that neither of my parents would be alive the next April to celebrate a sixty-sixth wedding anniversary. My dad passed away on August 1 from multiple health issues and my mother of a large aneurysm near her heart on November 28, both in 2008.

2. In the two years prior to the retirement of our popular senior pastor, he proposed the purchase of and fundraising for a large million-dollar church organ. I had mixed emotions on spending so much money for a state-of-the-art church organ. My concern was that there were many other local and national needs where our money could better be spent. It seemed to me that spending that much money was spending it on us, for our own enjoyment, and not for the needs of the community and world at large. The other side of the issue presented was that it would enhance our worship service; many special events could be held featuring the organ, and this would be a recruitment tool for new members to join the church. This argument also had merit, but in some way, it appeared to me that there was not a full open discussion; in many ways, the information provided was coercion, although this is overstated. What I did not like was to see division within the church, which I had experienced ten years ago at another church. Finally, a vote was held, and it passed go by a two-thirds vote of only 20 percent of the congregation. It was certainly not

a mandate. To make it more palatable, in the fundraising drive, there was an opportunity to commit funds for purposes other than the organ, which made people feel better about giving, but in the end, a higher percentage of the other part of the contribution would go to the organ. Another issue that developed several years later when the senior pastor retired was the council action to force the two assistant pastors into retirement so the new senior pastor would have free reign to identify and have congregational approval of an associate pastor(s). Some members questioned the need for this action to be taken, while others felt it was merited; once again, it was a process that could've been handled better. These two issues led some families to leave, joining other churches, and some of them to return three or four years later. It was nothing the scale of the previous church split ten years ago, but it did bring back painful memories.

3. Time for a more positive story. The year was 2010. After competing and having high hopes of a world softball senior championship the previous two years and having that elude our team, 2010 was the year that our goal was achieved. There were twenty or so teams competing, most from the United States, with some from Mexico and Europe in our division. In the seeding round, we ended up a fourth seed, which allowed us one bye when the double elimination tournament began. The number one seed went undefeated in the seeding round and was a team from Arkansas, known as the Arkansas Cracker Barrel. After winning several games, we met

the Cracker Barrel team and were trailing by a couple of runs, going into the final inning. We burst out with seventeen runs in the top of the open inning. They were not able to match that output in the bottom of the inning, and this sent them to the loser's bracket, from which they emerged to challenge us for the championship. We could win the championship by giving them their second defeat, or if they beat us, we would have to go to the third and final playoff game. They beat us nine to five and set up the stage for the final game. We were ahead most of the way and entered the final inning with a small lead that had us leading twenty-two to sixteen, going into the last half with them at bat. They scored four runs and had one out and runners on the corners. Their leading player, who had gone sixteen for sixteen in the tournament, was on deck. The batter hit a sharp ground ball fielded by our first baseman, who tagged the runner from first going to second and stepped on first base for the double play and the end of the game. We won the national championship. Their star player said that they would've won the game if he had come to bat based on his hitting during the tournament. I told him that I thought we would have walked him. "How do you know you would have gotten up to bat?" The ironic twist to the game was that I sat out the last inning and almost went in to play first base for that last inning; however, the normal first baseman, who was excellent at fielding and making double plays, went in instead. I missed the opportunity to be the hero but also missed the opportunity to become the GOAT. (Recall the GOAT I played in my senior high school baseball game.) I happily settled for the outcome that occurred.

4. We ordered our championship rings. I proudly displayed and was wearing mine when we attended a Las Vegas show, the Terry Fator puppet and impersonator show. We were seated in the third or fourth row with two other couples, and I sat next to a couple of older ladies. I was holding the program up and reading it when the lady next to me nudged me and said, "Who are you? I know I should know you," and pointed to my Super Bowl–like ring. I asked her if she remembered Roger Staubach of the Dallas Cowboys. She said, "Oh, sure," and I responded that I was a lineman for the Dallas Cowboys and Roger Staubach. She seemed very satisfied with that answer, and so moments later, I had to tell her that that was just a story and that the ring was an old man's senior softball championship ring.

5. Two dinner parties stand out in my mind of the time that I was chair of the board of Benevilla. A personal friend who had encouraged me to become involved in Benevilla hosted one, and he was extremely proud that I was the incoming chairman of the board. He arranged and paid for a private dinner of seventy-five people at a popular restaurant. I was humbled that he was so generous and certainly did not want to disappoint him; it caused me to work harder at times than I may have, kind of like wanting to make your parents feel proud of you.

6. A second dinner party encouraged by the same donor was held at a larger venue, open and encouraged by all those affiliated with Benevilla to attend; it was a roasting dinner party of the president and CEO, Michelle Dionisio. You might want to say this donor loved dinner parties. Yes, he did. Michelle had reservations about a roasting party. She seemed unfamiliar with them and feared the outcome. I had a difficult time convincing her to go along with the idea. My main selling point was that sometimes, for the benefit of the organization, we need to do things that make us uncomfortable. Her parents, many former leaders, and current and former staff participated in the fun evening. I do know that she enjoyed the event more after it was all over than before and during. If you make a good selling point, you can get reluctant people to become involved and participate.

7. Grandkids visiting grandparents are rewards of all the work that you have done before you reach that age. I like to quote my father, who stated that if he knew grandkids were so much fun, he would've had them first. We enjoyed our grandkids visiting with and without their parents. Our eldest grandchild, Jacob, was seven or eight at the time and has been following my participation at Benevilla and in Rotary. He approached me and told me in preparation for his next visit that summer that he would like to volunteer at Benevilla. He said there were two things he could do. One, he could work in the library and organize books because he knew that you separate books by fiction and nonfiction and further by

the Dewey decimal system. The other volunteer position that appealed to him was to deliver meals on wheels to seniors in the community. He rightly stated that to do this, he would need my involvement because he was not old enough to drive a car. This latter offer resonated with me, and so I signed up to deliver meals as a volunteer for the organization so that he could accompany me with that when he visited. That, we did; we had a great time, and that has been expanded to his brother as well as our other son and his kids when they came down to visit. The seniors seem to love seeing the children as much as or more than the meals. Many continually ask about my grandchildren who visited them, giving them meals, after they had returned home.

8. Jacob had become very familiar with Benevilla and had a full tour of the facilities along with experience in the meal delivery program. Our Rotary Club met at sites of organizations that we supported through our donations. One of those organizations was Benevilla, and it so happened that the Rotary meeting on the campus of Benevilla coincided with one of Jacob's weeks in Arizona. Naturally, Jacob wanted to attend this meeting and did. He was very attentive, as he always was, and when a group of Rotarians stayed after the meeting to take a tour of Benevilla, Jacob and I joined them. It was here that Jacob shared his knowledge of Benevilla on the tour, such that many suggested that he be the tour guide. It is amazing how much young minds can absorb and retain. It was not overly surprising that

Jacob had some of his $25 spending money given to him for his time in Arizona and that he would buy his grandparents an ice cream cone on occasion and had nearly $18 left over. He expressed to me that he wanted to donate what he had left to Benevilla. This presented an excellent opportunity for me to share the concept of tithing with him, giving 10 percent of what he had to a church or charitable organization. He insisted that he wanted to give the entire amount to Benevilla, so that was what he did. That donation got him on the computerized mailing list for solicitations, and the next year, he wanted to contribute $100 from his savings account. This was discussed with his parents, and the decision was made to allow him to do so. On his next visit, I made arrangements for a meeting with the CEO and the vice president for donor relations to meet with the two of us and for him to make that presentation. If only we had more donors like him! What a statement for a young person to make such a contribution from his own personal account! Then his younger brother, wanting to be like his elder brother, insisted on also giving $100 from his personal account.

9. Some special friends dating back to a year or two together in college were living in Scottsdale, Arizona. They had a beautiful yacht called *Lexi Lu*, which was docked in Sidney, Canada. Each year, for many years, we were invited to cruise on their yacht with them to either the Gulf Islands or the San Juan Islands. What a fun time, cruising from port to port, visiting many

islands in our beautiful Pacific Northwest! Some islands had numerous good restaurants; others had relatively few, as few as a single restaurant or two. Since this event occurred annually in mid- to late summer, the blackberries growing wild on the islands were ripe for picking. The men did the picking, dodging the many blackberry thorns, and the women made the desserts of blackberry cobbler a la mode! Yum, yum! This annual trip also has the advantage of coupling with a visit to our families living in the northwest.

10. In 2014, there was the opportunity to return to the country of Laos, where Judy and I had worked and lived forty-six to forty-eight years ago. Our former employer, IVS, was organizing the two-week trip. Judy was not excited about going, and so I invited a close friend, Frank Joyce, to join me. He accepted. My problem was that we had planned a Disney visit and cruise with our two families just prior to the scheduled departure of the Laos trip. Our one family from Oregon was able to join us to Florida and the Disney experience. The other family needed to decline as they were expecting a child within six weeks and felt that it would be too dangerous to be on travel during that time. We were scheduled to return on Saturday, January 4, from Florida back to Phoenix, Arizona. We did. My trip to Laos left early on Monday morning, January 6. These were much too close connections for Judy but not for me. At least, that was what I thought. Was I packed? Certainly not. I had returned from nearly a two-week vacation trip with

quite different clothes than what would be needed for the next trip. Arriving late afternoon on Saturday, I did get unpacked but saved the packing for Sunday for the next trip. Early Sunday afternoon, I began searching for my passport. It was not to be found. I had it on the ship when disembarking. Finally, in mid-afternoon, I began frantically making calls to friends who had worked with the airlines, including our pilot friend, Scott, based out of Houston, Texas. I was able to ascertain by calls to the airport that my passport had been located and was in the lost-and-found section at the airport. Evidently, it dropped out of my shirt pocket when I bent over at a very crowded Orlando airport. The lost-and-found box where my passport resided was closed until the morning. My flight from Phoenix was supposed to leave at 8:00 a.m., with a close connection in San Francisco prior to departing for Tokyo and Bangkok. Was there a way to get the passport on a plane to have it delivered to Phoenix? No flights were due in Phoenix from United, the carrier I was taking, until after ten in the morning. What about flying the passport to San Francisco? There was a flight from Orlando to San Francisco on Monday morning, arriving at around 10:00 a.m. Now could I get my passport on that plane and hand-delivered to San Francisco so that I could retrieve it there? Through the personal pilot friend in Houston and his connection to another pilot he knew who was in Orlando, arrangements were made for him to stop by the lost-and-found section, provide needed identification, retrieve the passport, and take it to the flight attendants on the Orlando–San

Francisco flight to hand-carry it to San Francisco. Wow! It was a long shot but the only possibility that we could make the trip. That finalized, I called to see if there was an earlier flight from Phoenix to San Francisco, and there was one leaving at 6:30 a.m. on Monday but was already two seats oversold. It was still worth the effort to go down and try to get on that flight so I would have a little more time before the scheduled 12:30 p.m. departure from San Francisco. I went down early, leaving at around 4:00 a.m. for the airport. Going standby, one is not able to check luggage, so downsizing my two-week travel luggage to hand-carried luggage was a necessity. I got to the counter in Phoenix and learned there was a spot on the plane; however, they asked me for my passport to check in. I had my driver's license, which should've been sufficient to travel to San Francisco; however, since this was the beginning of an international flight, they said I needed my passport to check in. I tried to tell my story, but they were not buying it and said I would not be able to get on the plane without my passport. I checked for other flights and did find one on Southwest that was leaving in about forty-five minutes, going from Phoenix to San Francisco and arriving at around 9:30 a.m.—perfect. I bought the ticket, got on the plane, and, while on the plane, had some additional thoughts. Maybe, just maybe, all the stars were going to align for me, and this long shot may come through; however, more obstacles were ahead. There are several terminals in San Francisco. I was arriving at a non-United terminal. How would I get from one terminal to the next without going through security and needing a passport? Could I have someone pick up my passport, deliver it to the front desk, and hold it there for me to pick up so that I could get through security? It seemed like a long shot. A second problem: since I was not arriving until after the departure of the initial United flight from Phoenix, if I were a no-show there, would they bump me off the rest of my flight itinerary? It was a real concern. These were just two of the additional concerns as I sat helplessly on the flight to San Francisco. I did arrive in San Francisco and, after searching around, found that there was a shuttle between terminals and was greatly relieved because this meant that I could enter the United terminal without going through security with my passport in hand. Yes, I did and immediately went to the check-in desk for the San Francisco–Tokyo flight to assure them I was there but would be unable to check in until I received my passport. I was still listed on the full flight. The next stop was to the desk where the Orlando flight was scheduled to land. I went through a full explanation with the desk attendant, who I could tell was having a difficult time believing such a story and who informed me that the flight was a bit late but was scheduled to arrive by ten forty-five. I anxiously waited and was relieved when the plane landed and people were getting off the plane, but no passport was delivered to the desk as was promised. After I waited for what seemed like hours and the desk attendant assured me that flight attendants were the last to leave the plane, finally, a flight attendant arrived and handed the desk attendant an envelope. The desk attendant took a passport out of the envelope. What great relief to see a passport out of the envelope—until the desk attendant looked at the passport and then looked at me and said, "John Campbell?" My heart sank, and then she laughed. I almost went over the counter to strangle her, but all was well. I took the treasured passport, went to the check-in, and got checked in for the first leg of my international flight. Then I went to a restaurant to have some pho, an oriental soup bowl, to relish the taste and allow my heart to resume a more normal function. My original flight from Phoenix was delayed and arriving late, making the one-hour connection time much shorter. Mr. Joyce was on that flight and was unfamiliar with Southeast Asia or the people in our party whom he was to meet and travel with for the next two weeks. I went to the waiting lounge. They announced boarding the plane. I delayed and explained that a friend who was on the trip with me was coming from another flight, and finally, they said, "You either need to board or not." So using additional delay tactics, I finally did board, sat there, and waited. Fortunately, they did not close the doors to the plane, and at long last, Frank came through the door. We collapsed in our seats, looked at each other, and ordered our drinks. It was a great trip, from landing in Bangkok and then flying up to Chiang Rai to crossing over into Laos and traveling via a riverboat on the Mekong River for much of the trip. We were able to stop for several days at the provincial capital of Luang Prabang and also to see the Plain of Jars, two sites not available for visiting while we were in Laos from 1966 to 1968. Visiting the capital and taking a day to go out and revisit the university where we taught were highlights of the Vientiane area of Laos. We also were able to spend some days down at Pakse and further south to the falls that lead into Cambodia. All in all, it was a great trip that had a rocky start.

11. Judy's birthdays had become a big event when she had a milestone birthday in our retirement. Her sixtieth birthday is listed as a story in the previous chapter. Her sixty-fifth birthday was in 2009, and while this was not a surprise as the other ones have been, we did take a cruise around the islands of Tahiti, including Bora Bora, and then an extra day's stay at one of the bungalow huts out over the water. Our youngest son, Jon, had spent part of his honeymoon in Tahiti, so we were just catching up with some of the travel that they had already done. The weather and lifestyle were quite enjoyable; however, it's not inexpensive for those considering traveling there.

12. Big surprises are always best, and Judy's seventieth birthday ended up being a big surprise. I had just returned from Laos on her birthday, and so with that trip, she was not really expecting anything. Her surprise party was well planned before I ever left for the overseas trip. On January 22, I arranged a dinner party at Birt's Bistro, the restaurant on the Benevilla campus. Many of her golf friends and couples as well as other friends,

totaling over fifty, were invited to the dinner and cocktail hour as well as two special out-of-town guests. One was her best friend, Faye, from when we lived in the D.C. area from 1989 to 1992. Faye secretly flew down, and I had picked her up from the airport earlier that day. She made herself scarce until mid-afternoon. I had to go to a Benevilla board meeting that afternoon and so was not home. Arrangements were made to have Faye sitting out on our patio when Judy returned home from golf. Faye did not want to be out there by herself, so our brother-in-law, Ron, came over, and the two of them were visiting out on our patio when Judy returned home. She said she heard voices and couldn't figure out what was going on; she walked out to the patio, and there sat her good friend from Maryland, Faye. I understand she was flabbergasted. The plan then was for the two of them to come by and pick me up at Benevilla following my board meeting so that we could travel to a favorite Mexican restaurant up the road, Abuelo's. So Judy, driving with her friend, came by Benevilla a few minutes before six o'clock, when my meeting was to be over. I came out to the car, and we said we had a few minutes before our reservation at Abuelo's and I inquired if Faye would like to see a bit of the Benevilla campus, including the restaurant, where many people liked to eat. Faye, in on the surprise, said sure, so the three of us made our way to the restaurant. The unusual restaurant, with garage doors open at both ends, had sounds coming from it, and Judy said, "I think there is something going on in the restaurant tonight." I concurred but said we could just stick our heads in, and as we got closer, the small band with "love boat" trumpeter Dan Reed struck up "Happy Birthday" to Judy. The full crowd of fifty was already there and well into their happy hour as Judy was welcomed to the group. She nearly melted. After she was getting adjusted to the attention, another surprise came out of a side room, and her youngest son, Jon, said, "Hi, Mom. Happy birthday." She screamed his name, and they hugged each other, and to me, this was worth the price of the ticket. Suffice it to say she will never forget that evening of that weekend and was truly amazed that I could pull something off like that with so much planning while being gone the previous two weeks. You will need to go to the next chapter to find out what surprise was in store for her seventy-fifth birthday.

CHAPTER 15

Later Retirement Years, 2015–2021

The summation of these years could be that I am still enjoying life, have less energy to pursue leadership roles yet am very supportive of passing on the torch to others to assume those roles

,

and am recognizing the mortality of our lives by the increasing number of friends passing on. I am still traveling, still playing golf, still playing softball, and still enjoying the amenities of the area and friendships. However, I enjoy most of these with less intensity. My enjoyment seems to be less with my personal achievement and more with seeing the success of others.

While I was looking for new adventures and perhaps, as they say, completing my bucket list, this period also became a time to downsize

,

reconnect, to revisit places of personal historical importance, to get one's life in order, and to provide for the eventual transitions that are like the two most well-known certainties: taxes and death. It is also a time when there is a realization that your anticipated lifetime will not be impacted by policies and procedures to the extent that it will impact future generations. Time to move on; this is getting a bit too morbid.

What were the significant living changes during this time? The decision to leave homeownership of our fifteen-year-old home in Sun City Grand was something that we considered for the future, but it ended up happening a bit earlier than we had planned. We loved Sun City Grand— the activities, the friends, the convenience to host family, and the many fun memories that had been created. What was becoming increasingly less enjoyable were increasing price costs, additional upkeep and repairs, and all those things that go with homeownerships. At some point in time, a move would be necessary, but when would that time be? Colonnade, a senior living community of Sun Health Foundation, was on an adjoining property, and we had several friends who had moved there and loved the experience. We had checked this out in the early 2000s and thought it was not for us, and it was not at that time, but years had passed. The Colonnade had new construction beyond the *casitas*, individual home types, to villa living, four-story buildings similar to condos. Two of the four condos had been built and fully occupied, and the remaining two were being built. It was an opportunity to be the first residents of a new unit and make decisions on adding upgrades while they were being built.

It was time to seriously consider and push the pencil for pros and cons, including expenses. One positive critical factor was the arrangement between Sun City Grand and the Colonnade, where Colonnade residents would have full access to facilities at Sun City Grand. That would include golf, softball, cards, etc. This is what finally closed the deal, and on April 24, 2016, the move was made. As with the move to retirement and to Sun City Grand in 2001, this too became a life change. It was "turn the key, enter your apartment (we called them suites), lock the door, and leave the world behind." There were many activities, such as group travel on cruises and trips to neighboring states. Transportation was provided for local functions of interest, there were on-site celebrations of holiday parties, there were increasing recreational and dining facilities being built, and in short, life was good. Life was very good—until the pandemic hit in 2020.

Moving to the Colonnade provided the transition desired to have the flexibility to travel and not worry about the home property. This provided the opportunity to truly enjoy the later years in life and be more carefree. The social activities were truly outstanding, and with the soon-to-be-three-hundred residents, there was a definite feeling of family. Some of the places revisited during this time were family visits, including our fiftieth wedding anniversary celebration by taking the family on an Alaskan cruise and a land tour to Denali, Alaska. Another family trip was the fifty-five-year anniversary celebration that returned us to the San Juan Islands in the Pacific Northwest. Again, we took our family to celebrate with us, the full ten of us. Another family-related trip was with my brother and sister-in-law, along with two other couples who traveled with us on a South American cruise that traveled around the tip of South America to the end of the world. We were able to revisit Uruguay, where we had lived from 1973 to

---

Richard Stuckey

1975. This particular trip visited the southernmost city in the world, appropriately entitled "the end of the world." On this trip, we were also able to visit a number of places where we had been before, such as Rio de Janeiro, Iguaçu Falls, Buenos Aires, and Santiago, Chile. Several stories are detailed later in this chapter.

One positive impact of the move to the Colonnade in 2016 is that I felt a calling to assist others who are more in need than I was. There were people there who lost loved ones, who encountered health issues that happened after they moved there, others who became lonely, others who needed the simplest of support to move a box, to relocate an item of furniture, to play a game of cards, those who simply needed a visit. These are things I could do, I was happy to do. Several people commented to me, how could they ever repay me? I responded, "I am happy to serve and do not expect any payment! I am happy to help!" I just hope when I need something later in life, there will be someone there willing to do that for me. In my mind, this is a very positive approach to aging in life. We do what we can while we can, and we pass it forward.

Stories:

1. We had become accustomed to cruising for much of our international travel. On a cruise ship, it was so nice to get on the ship and unpack, and your room was your hotel for your entire trip. Land travel often means changing hotels every night or two, packing,

406

and unpacking and is a tiring exercise, but it is exercise nonetheless. So it was with a bit of hesitation that we booked a trip with three other couples for a wildlife safari in South Africa. We did not go entirely blind into it as it was strongly recommended by our son and daughter-in-law who experienced this safari trip at the conclusion of the World Cup soccer events in South Africa several years previous. To break up the trip, we decided to return to Amsterdam and spend several days there, especially since it was the first visit there for the other three couples. We were able to act as host, and by staying there for several days, we also revisited one of our favorite places, Alsmeer, which is a huge flower auction distribution center for the flowers from the Netherlands that are shipped all over the world. Of course, no visit to the Netherlands is complete without visiting several of the famous museums, taking a canal trip through the city, and visiting the Red Light District. What a great way to start our trip! From there, we went to Cape Town, South Africa. At a lovely sea resort town and for our booked trip, a family hosted us for a nice dinner in the wine country. Scenic views and travel through the vineyards were among highlights. We did not get to the island where Nelson Mandela was held because of overbooking, but we did try. After a quick stop through Johannesburg on the way to King's Camp, a private reserve next to Kruger National Park, we were awarded a satellite location about a quarter mile from the main campus of King's Camp where we had exclusive reign, the eight of us, of the site—great lodging, great views, a feeling that we were in the park, and required transportation provided to the main camp when needed. Morning and evening safaris for four days were most enjoyable. We did see the big five game animals, all within the first day or two. A driver and the armed guard were there for our protection in case we inadvertently aroused the animals with which we came in very close contact. Following our safari stay, two of the couples returned to the States, and we and the other couple, whom we frequently cruise with, scheduled a two-day extension to visit Victoria Falls. We were glad we did; the falls are beautiful, and we were with the couple on our plane ride to enjoy that site and the surrounding area. We saw beauty and also poverty, but once you are that close, you might as well spend the extra time and money, especially at our age, because a return is highly unlikely.

2. Another cruise occurred when, for our fiftieth wedding anniversary in 2016, we took our entire family on an Alaskan cruise that also had a land tour to Denali Park.

The ten of us embarked from Vancouver, Canada, for the cruise to Anchorage and the intended trip by train from Anchorage up to Denali Park. It was our third cruise to Alaska, the first being in 1986, thirty years earlier, with Judy's parents in celebration of their fiftieth wedding anniversary. We also went several years earlier than our fiftieth with the Duttons, a talented musical family who performs in Branson, Missouri, and also in Tempe, Arizona, during the winter months. It was during this trip that we helicoptered to the top of the glacier and actually were able to commandeer a dog sled with huskies, which became one of Judy's favorite outings. It was expensive to take this offshore trip, but we decided to do it, and because it has become a memory, we have no regrets spending the money to do so. The point is that when the opportunity presents itself, do it. Most times, it is worth taking advantage of that rather than regretting later that you did not. Now back to my story of our fiftieth wedding celebration with family. It was the first cruise for several in the family and also had new destinations for many in the family. We got along fine, and everybody was having a good trip, enjoying the food, the activities on the ship, and the shore excursions, exploring new ports. All of our grandkids enjoy learning and experiencing new adventures. Partly because of spatial considerations, three cabins were secured for sleeping and living quarters on the ship. In one cabin was the family from Washington with their two younger children. In another cabin was the Oregon family with their younger child, while the elder child stayed in our room. With two days left in the cruise, Judy became ill. She went to bed early that evening, having the chills and nausea. She made it through the night, but the next morning, I went down to the health clinic and made an appointment for her to see the doctor. She was so weak by this time that we had to get a wheelchair to put her in to wheel her down to the health clinic floor. It was there that we learned she had had contact with the flu. It was advised that all of our family members get the expensive flu protection medication. We did; fortunately, no one else in the family contracted the flu. As a precaution, the elder grandchild moved back in with his parents and brother for the last couple of nights on the cruise. Judy was quarantined to her room for the last day of the cruise, and when it came time to get off the cruise, she was not allowed to do so until after all others had disembarked. I stayed back with her, but this meant that we were going to miss the train and the ride from the port up to Denali Park. We would be able to take the trip by bus, which we did; we called it the sick bus as there were eight to ten total people on the bus who had plans to go to Denali Park but needed alternate transportation. The train ride was slow, and although we started several hours later and made a stop or two, we arrived prior to the train at our location. The time at Denali Park, three days, was wonderful and refreshing, and we were blessed with wonderful views of the mountain peak, which is often not seen. It was a wonderful trip, a memory that will be remembered forever by all in the family.

3. In keeping with big celebrations for major anniversaries and for Judy's birthdays, in 2019, Judy had her seventy-fifth birthday. Within a week of her birthday, our good friend and neighbor at the Colonnade was celebrating his eightieth birthday. Together, we planned an event for as many guests as we could accommodate at the Colonnade. Unfortunately, the large LaVita Room, which seats and serves meals for over two hundred, was not available because of renovation. Working with the activities director, we were able to utilize the large library space and surrounding halls, with food in an adjoining room, for our celebration. A part of the celebration is the surprise part, and this had no end to surprises for Judy. Judy's favorite pianist, Nicole Pesce, was the surprise performer this time. We had heavy hors d'oeuvres, over one hundred friends attending, and some special out-of-town friends. She did know that many from the Colonnade would be attending but little else. Among the out-of-town guests who attended were our good friends and cruisers from Paradise Valley in Arizona, our good friend who was actually known as our "Iowa daughter," which was a big surprise, and our two sons and their families, complete with all the grandkids. Each of these persons was kept in seclusion until the event and introduced as they came out from a back room into the main library to join Judy at a table or an adjoining table. She was overwhelmed, and the performance was great. It was the first time that many of our Colonnade friends had heard Nicole Pesce play the piano. They raved about her performance in the

event. The life enrichment programs we have at the Colonnade have sponsored her at least three times in the succeeding two years for additional performances. What a wonderful weekend it was, and again, while it did put some pressure on the checkbook, it was certainly well worth it. Now what do I do for her eightieth when it comes up?

4. After nearly a year of planning, we were ready to embark on another cruise, again with our good friends from Paradise Valley, my brother and his wife, and some mutual friends from Canada. This would be the first time cruising with my brother and his wife, and we were looking forward to it. Our destination was around the tip of South America to the end of the world. The cruise began in Buenos Aires, Argentina, and concluded in Santiago, Chile. The couple from Paradise Valley and we decided to take a pre-cruise package that spent some time in Rio de Janeiro for several days and then to Iguaçu Falls for several more days before a day in Buenos Aires and embarking on the ship. This pre-visit cruise was returning to locations that we had been to before, but it was a first for the couple from Paradise Valley. While we were looking forward with great anticipation to the cruise, it did not start out well. We were to fly from Phoenix to Miami and, from there, on to Rio de Janeiro. Because of a short connect time in Miami, the other couple and Judy were nervous and so wanted to take an earlier flight to Miami to allow for additional time to make the connection. You know me. I love the

tight connections and excitement (you would think that what I had experienced going to Southeast Asia five years earlier would've cured me of that); still, I did not put up a lot of resistance to changing the flight. It also meant that we were changing the return flight to come back in from Santiago to Phoenix through Dallas rather than Miami, which would shorten the trip. We arrived at the Phoenix airport at around eight o'clock in preparation for our 10:00 a.m. departure to Miami. The other couple were already there and got checked in. When we went to the kiosk to check in, it would not accept our reservation. So we went to the desk, and there, we learned that there was a mix-up, and for some reason, we did not get transferred to the earlier flight. We had confirmation and a phone call that morning reminding us of our flight. A call to the travel agent got passed around since they officially were not open yet and our agent was not yet in. We had our bags, and the clock was ticking. We had to have our bags checked forty-five minutes before our flight left; otherwise, they would not accept us on that flight. The short story is that we did, in fact, miss our flight because the time had elapsed beyond the deadline for checking our luggage. The other couple went on the flight, and we said we would see them in Miami and hopefully get down on the same flight to Rio. So we waited over five hours at the Phoenix airport for our next scheduled flight, and we did make that flight and the connection from Miami to Rio. That screw-up was just a sign of things to come. We arrived safely on our overnight flight to Rio, and after a short bus tour of the city and some sites, we got checked into our hotel. It was mid-February, and the Mardi Gras celebration had already begun. Having been at a Mardi Gras event in New Orleans meant that we definitely needed to see a Mardi Gras in Rio. There was to be a Mardi Gras celebration in the neighborhood of our hotel, about two miles away. The other couple agreed that we should take this in, so we boarded a courtesy bus to take and drop us off at the site of the celebration. It was wild. The divided highway was blocked off for four or five blocks, and they were lined along the beach; however, it was less crowded than the other side. We walked along, viewing the strange-looking people, strange dress apparel, many participants under the influence and most having a great time. I am sure we stuck out—four Caucasians, Western dress, trying to fit in but not succeeding. After an attempted heist by young kids trying to take the phone out of my wife's hand and tugging at my ring on my finger, they were shaken off, but foolishly, I suggested we go across the street so that we could see the parade going by more clearly. We did, and as we fought to go upstream, we felt we had seen enough and were going to try to go back to the street, where we could catch a ride back to the hotel. However, the crowd just kept coming, and so it was suggested that we turn around and go with the crowd, get back to the other side of the street, walk down several blocks, and then cross over where there was a lesser crowd. It was shoulder-to-shoulder jostling to maintain one's position and perfect for a heist. One did occur and not to my liking. A twenty-five-year-old guy came busting through between Judy and me, and I raised my arms to protect my space; he plowed through, ran up to a sidewalk vendor who had a drink hoisted, took a couple of sips of the drink, and was on his way. We walked on six or eight steps farther and commented about the rudeness and craziness going on. Someone said, "Everyone got his or her valuables?" I reached down for my phone in my front pocket, and it was gone. I reached in my other front pocket for my billfold; it was gone. I immediately became sick. Evidently, when I had raised my arms to protect my space, the accomplice behind him slipped a hand in my front pant pockets and pulled out the phone and the wallet. Fortunately, I had removed $150 from my wallet before going on this excursion, yet $250 remained in the wallet, along with the credit cards and a small amount of converted dollars to Brazilian reals. We walked up another three or four blocks and stopped at the corner where a dozen Brazilian police were gathered. I tried to use my best Spanish to the Portuguese-speaking Brazilians and had only moderate success. They said I could go to the police station about a mile up the beach to file a complaint. We were tired and just wanted to get back to the hotel, so we did go and caught a cab, and fortunately, they did accept dollars. Back at the hotel, we spoke to our Princess cruise staff and the hotel staff, made some calls, canceled the credit cards, and decided to have an early dinner. Instead of going down for five blocks to a popular international restaurant street, we ate at the site out by the pool. I then went down to the police station, against the advice of others, to file my complaint. It was an education. I had to wait in line for the next officer to take my report. Finally, I reached the head of the line and then received paperwork to fill out. Having done that, I went back up and had to wait again for my completed form to be taken back to their desks to transcribe it into the computer. All the while, there were three or four Brazilians retained for theft or other inappropriate behavior. Most were in handcuffs, leaning against the wall; several were waiting for family members to post their bail. Finally, after two hours at the police station, I had completed my report, and they told me they would be in touch. I guess that meant I had to come back to their facility to be in touch. After the airline fiasco for the Phoenix-to-Miami flight, this was a second big strike to this trip, which made me wonder if I had made the right decision to go on this cruise. What would I do without my phone and without my wallet and credit cards for the next three weeks? I had to keep in mind that while this was a major disappointment for me, I should not spoil this trip for the other seven in our party. After several more days of touring Rio and visiting Sugarloaf Mountain, the famous beaches of Rio, and other sites that we had visited in 1974, we flew to Iguaçu Falls to once again stay at the Das Cataratas hotel and experience the fantastic Iguaçu Falls. Oh, how I missed my phone and direct access to the Internet and living with the inconvenience of using the ship Internet! Then it was on to Buenos Aires to embark on the ship and meet our other four passengers. There were many sites, including the end of the world, and a fun time at a wine farm near Santiago, Chile. The cruise came to an end, and we disembarked on March 5, 2020, and flew back to Phoenix. The passengers who boarded our ship on March 5 to do the reverse cruise did not know that they were signing up for a cruise that would be extended more than the original cruise itself because of the COVID-19 pandemic, which came into full view in early March. Fortunately, we were not a part of the cruise/pandemic scenario. While many were hopeful that the pandemic would be a matter of a few weeks or months at the most, the year 2020 will likely not be forgotten by any who were of age living at that time. Little did we think the intended plans to travel to see our family in the Pacific Northwest at summer would be canceled and our trip to Cabo in November 2020 would be in question. After being in semi-lockdown for most of the year, we did go and meet my brother and his wife in Cabo for a couple of weeks, and this time, there was no additional drama in Cabo compared to several other previous visits that were part of the stories in earlier chapters.

5. In the early summer of 2020, plans were made for the celebration of our fifty-fifth wedding anniversary in 2021. Recall that in these retirement years, celebrating the birthdays that end in five or zero as well as anniversaries becomes a big event. For the fiftieth, see Story 1 in this chapter. For the fifty-fifth, after much

discussion, the plans were to spend a week together in the San Juan Islands, and after further research, Lopez Island was chosen for the third week in August 2021.

6. My ratings for major spectacular world waterfalls are as follows: (1) Iguaçu Falls; (2) Victoria Falls; and (3) Niagara Falls. Likewise, my ratings for flower gardens

are as follows: (1) the Keukenhof Gardens; (2) the Butchart Gardens, near Victoria; and (3) the Longwood Gardens, just outside Philadelphia. These ratings are shared with readers in the event that they have a chance in the future to visit a waterfall or a flower garden.

CHAPTER 16

Balancing Life and Recommendations

My hope is that you have enjoyed traveling with me through life and have gained a perspective on what it was like for me and for others my age. Many revolutions have taken place, from the industrial to the technological to the social and, yes, to the political. In some respects, perhaps we have been too spoiled all along the way, getting things too easily and expecting many benefits to come to us free of charge and free of our working for them.

We continue to have leaders and persons who are not satisfied with the status quo and work hard to make this life fair and more equitable to all. I encourage those who have read this book to be one of those. I also encourage people to become more civil to one another, more understanding of other viewpoints. How boring this world would be if everybody thought alike and became one solitary body of human thinking and action! Diversity in thought and action is our key to continuous growth and innovation.

Treat others with respect, value their thoughts, and try to put yourself in their shoes. Do you understand why they act and think as they do? You may still disagree with them, but perhaps you can do so with civility. Listen more and talk less. How often have you become friends with someone whom you thought you would never become friends with, perhaps because you did not understand or get to know them? Benevilla, the organization I volunteered a substantial amount of time and talents to, has a motto that the service we provide to other people should be made with the compassion and love that we would treat our own family members with—that is, every service or deed that is done or provided is done with the thought that they are one of our family members.

Life is a series of challenges and choices. Everyone wants to make the right choices all the time. That rarely happens.

There's nothing wrong with making a bad choice; it just doesn't get us to where we would like to be. What is important is that we learn from our bad choices. Oftentimes we can learn more from bad choices and challenges in life than we learn when things are going smoothly. Do not give up; get back up and in the ring for the next round. Surround yourself with friends who are generally interested in the betterment of our society. They may have different ways or ideas of accomplishing that. Violence is not the answer.

Sometimes the task ahead looks very daunting. I am just one individual; how can I make a difference? Everyone has a circle of influence. Some circles are larger, and some are at higher levels. What is your circle now, and what do you perceive your circle to be in the future?

Working for a goal and achieving the goal becomes more meaningful if it is earned than if it is given to you. There are needs for some people to be given things; however, encouraging them to reduce their dependence on receiving is important. People with some skin in the game will feel much better about themselves if they have contributed, even though it may be a small part.

In the world in which we live, it is important for us to have jobs that pay relatively well so that we can support ourselves and our families with the necessities of life and have some left over for discretionary spending. While this is important, do not become over-obsessed with money. It is convenient to have, but don't let it be the ruler of your life. Many of the happiest people whom I have met have very limited resources. Money can help make you happy, but money by itself will not make you happy.

Have you heard that there are three important legs of a triangle as one gets older in life? One is family and friends, another is health, and yet another is finances or resources. If you have all three, you are truly blessed. If you have two of the three, you can be quite happy. With just one, life becomes much less enjoyable. With none of the three, life will be very miserable. Do the exercise yourself and remove one of the legs. Which leg, if you had a choice, would you remove?

You can never have too many friends. Business friends and friendships can be very important in the working world. Family friends for most families are very enjoyable and become even more precious with time. Social friends are great friends to have because most people depend on social life to be truly happy. Good friends increase your knowledge tremendously and are a valuable resource for consulting, decision making, and assistance in those things that may not be your cup of tea.

If in reading this book, you gathered that I have had a happy and productive life, by my standards, that is true. There have been some disappointments, some sadness, some questioning times, but those have all been outweighed by the more happy times. Do not be depressed with sad times but strive to have more happy times than sad.

In conclusion, I hope you have picked up a thought or two as you journeyed with me through my life that will be beneficial and make your life worth living. It is healthy to recall memories and stories, as I have done. Now I provide a couple of pages for you to write your own memory or story. By doing so, you'll make this book unique and one of a kind, for no one else will have your story in his or her book.

End

APPENDIX A

Wildhare Editions

Dear Subscribers,

Yes, it has been a while and much as happened. The Wildhare has had some "swings" in softball after the past so many months, that thoughts crept into the mind, is it time to hang it up? Could I go out in style, rather than hang on to the end and be considered a so-so player? These and other questions seeped and infiltrated the leaky cranium of the WH. For those faithful subscribers, the WH softball career continues.

Now to the results. The tourney team Smith Electric is off to the best start ever - winning the last four tournaments they have entered. This is sure to elevate them from a AAA team to a major team. WH has played a role, but not as large as he once did. He played in all four tournaments, but has elected to sit out the tournament this weekend down in Tucson, where Smith Electric will go for an unprecedented 5th title in a row. (In-laws are in town this week, and Smith had 13 players going so thought I could take a pass).

On the local internal league team, stacked with talent, the Gear Up boys have found difficulty gearing up for the competition. Numerous 1 or 2 run loss games have the early league favorites tied for 3rd (in this four team league). Gear Up has lost games in almost every conceivable fashion, including blowing a 13-4 lead going into the 7th inning to lose 17-15. However, in the last week, Gear Up, has turned things around, although it is too little too late. WH has played a major role in this turn around.

I quote from the highly respected INDEPENDENT paper,

buried on page 10, "Overall excellent defensive play from Rick Clot, Dave Eberhart, and Dick Stuckey (WH) won the day for Gear Up. First baseman Mr. Stuckey fielded a ground ball, tagged out the runner going to second, stepped on first for the second out, and then threw out the runner going from from third for an inning-ending triple play." That was some quick thinking for a guy who has trouble walking and chewing gum at the same time. In the next game, playing right field, WH made a fabulous on the dead run catch in right field that ended the threat and save the game for Gear Up.

Then just off the press from yesterday's game, following a horrible round of golf, the steamed WH took it out on the softball. First at bat, before the in-law (out-law from CO) arrived, he smashed an opposite field wind aided ball over the right center field fence. His second at bat with the in-law in place in the stands, he lofted a high double down the left field line. His third at bat was a smash off the left center field wall, and to show he was human, his fourth at bat was a ground out to second base. Gear Up won 27-11 followed by the hitting barrage.

Softball is fun, but as the earlier doubt expressed, the WH realizes he needs a life beyond softball. One diversion recently was the guru on hole 8 for the closest to the pin women's golf member/guest tournament. As evidence, attached is a photo of one cute foursome that came through. Most of you will recognize a cactus bunny in the group.

Until the next edition, whenever that may be, good luck and keep your chin up.

432

WH The Record speaks April 21, 2007

With the next softball game nearly a month away, the
Wildhare, is resting up for the Prescott Tournament in mid
May. A busy travel schedule and a weary body telling the
Wildhare it is time to take a break from softball this summer,
so other than two tournaments (May and July), WH will be
engaged in other activities. The Mrs. hopes this will include
vacuuming, cleaning and cooking, but the Hare has other
ideas. Much of the free time is thought to be more in line
with catching up with fan mail and signing autographs.

Going on a hitting binge that had fellow colleagues asking
WH what he had for breakfast, WH smashed an opposite
field over the fence home run, another smash off the wall in
left center field and a high towering double down the left field
line in a recent game. Another 3 for 4 day followed that had
a smash to the shortstop whose hand is still smarting as the
only out. With this hitting prowess and dependable fielding,
WH helped his fast charging Gear Up buddies to three
consecutive wins, to at least shore up third place in the
league. Only one game remains in the league, and WH
feels he can leave the rest of the team to defend for
themselves as he journeys to Branson, MO this coming
week. Perhaps WH will find a new career in Branson.

The value of a WH on a team is further evidenced by the
recent tournament play by Smith Electric. Having won 4
consecutive tournaments, Smith Electric went for number 5
'Hareless'. The result was a second place finish. Losing 3
close games on Saturday, by scores of 20-19, 15-14, and
22-20, one could argue a boost by the WH could perhaps
made them 3-0 instead of 0-3. On Sunday and battling for
the tournament title, Smith Electric battled back winning 3

games and losing 2.   They lost the title game 21-18. You can be assured that WH will be going to their next tournament.

Until later, enjoy your respite from the Edition.

Wildhare, Senior Editor
WEE, Inc.

Subject: WH Rocks and Rolls Sept. 27, 2007

The city of Surprise is a buzz with talk of the hitting prowess of the Wildhare in a real clinic established yesterday at the Del Webb Memorial Stadium located in the confines of Sun City Grand. What happened remains a mystery although rumor has it, WH was just flexing his muscles for his trip to Las Vegas today to participate in the softball tournament with Smith Electric the next three days.

After a rather lackluster and ordinary performance for a couple of games with the Weekly Realtor team in the summer league at Grand, the Weekly group lost a couple of games. Then last Friday, the team broke lose with the assistance of the Wildhare and got back on the winning track. Yesterday, Sept. 26 may go down in history. It all started with an hour walk on the track to loosen up prior to the 9 AM game. A semi-intentional walk in his first at bat, the Wildhare came out swinging thereafter. The second at bat was a line shot double over the left fielders head that scored two runs. In the third at bat, an inside the park round tripper over the right fielders head with two on, was followed by a shot off the wall in left center field for another round tripper in his fourth and final at bat. Three more rbi's to run the total for the day to 8 along with scoring himself four times. Weekly after leading by a slim 8-5 margin won going away 18-5.

To cap off a stellar softball day, the WH decided to try his luck at the game of golf and shot what for him is a respectful 86. Yes, he did play all 18 holes.

What waits in store for the Smith Electric team in Vegas? Stay tuned for the next episode of the Wildhare

435

Edition. WH welcomes this opportunity to escape Surprise for a few days, as yesterday everywhere he went people were coming up to him to congratulate him on the near season performance. Well, anyway, you should be aware the WH does like to embellish his reports a bit - yet he remains one of the most humble persons the WH has ever met.

Wildhare, Senior Editor
WEE, Inc.

Wow, such a long time since the last Edition, the Wildhare has been besieged by requests for another edition. One would need to go to the blog site to see when the last edition was printed. Explanations later, let's get to the tape.

Today, moments ago, the Wildhare led team that recorded a 9-1 Saturday league record played their first double elim tournament game at SCG field. Picking up two super subs the opposition was laying in wait for the Saguaros. The game was nip and tuck most of the way with the Wildhare led Saguaros in the lead most of the way. The Wildhare managed this team and thus often batted himself down in the batting line up. Today, he registered himself in the # 8 position of the batting order. First time up, a screaming home run with two runners on, second time up, an inside the park homer with two men on base, and the third time up another towering fly ball that easily cleared the fence with two runners on. The fourth time up in the top of the seventh, runners on second and third, tie game at 15, the first two pitches were nowhere near the strike zone, so on the next pitch an intentional high inside pitch the Wildhare swung with a high chop and grounded to the shortstop who barely nipped the Wildhare at first base. The three batters below the Wildhare went a combined 1 for 12 in the game, thus the reason the Wildhare felt he needed to make contact. The Saguaros held the opposition scoreless in the bottom of the seventh to send the game to extra innings, however the bottom three batters for the Saguaros went one, two, three like they did all day and the opponents scored a lone run in the bottom of the 8th to win 16-15. Let the record show the Wildhare had 9 rbi's in the game.

The Wildhare was conflicted this weekend with Smith Electric playing three games over at Papago and the team WH managed playing a potential two games at SCG today. Since Smith Electric had an abundance of players, the WH thought it best he not desert his team. The Saturday league team managed by WH got off to a 9-0 start and lost the final game of the season last Saturday, now they face a win at all costs to remain in the tournament.

In the Thursday Red League with the top players from Grand, WH is on the Quizno Subs team. At the conclusion of 2007, the team was 6-6 before WH went surfing safari in Tahiti for two weeks. In the absence of WH, Quizno's lost 3 and tied one. Then upon return, the WH had a commitment on game day Thursday with Mrs. Hare over to Mesa, AZ so missed two more games which Quizno's promptly lost to move them into the cellar. Two days ago, WH returned and with a 3 for 3 plus a walk performance helped Quizno's to a victory to lift them 1/2 game out of the cellar. So impressed with WH, the manager moved him to pitch the second game and bat second. WH had solid hits including a spectacular catch of a WH hit ball beyond the wall to rob WH of a home run. Quizno's lost the game, yet remained 1/2 game from the lowest rung on the ladder. One week remains until second season starts.

I could bore you with stats of many other games, but suffice it to say, the WH is fine, he is back, does not plan to manage the second session of the Saturday league and promises to not wait as long for the next edition. May the new year be all pleasant and all happiness for WH subscribers.

Wildhare, Senior Editor
WEE, Inc.

438

Yes, indeed the Wildhare still lives and is in action. Such a long layoff in correspondence, I have no excuses.

Just to catch you up a bit, 3 games ago the Wildhare hit for the cycle that would be a Home Run over the fence, a triple, a double and a single. Then this past Monday, WH missed the cycle by going 3 for 4 and missing the home run. Today, in action before heading for the Midwest, WH again missed the cycle by not having a triple. He powered one over the fence; the only one of the game but it was not enough to help his 365 Storage Team to victory as they fell 14-9.

The coach is almost beside himself realizing the big WH stick will not be around for the next 3 games. Guess that is life.

365 Storage has a 2 – 4 record so hopes to improve later in the season that ends around the pop popping July 4 holiday – then we move into the second half of the summer schedule.

Yesterday was a sad day for the softball club; one of our members was run over and killed by a garbage truck. As President of the softball club, there has been nonstop phone calls and e-mails to make arrangements for a memorial service at the ball field this coming Friday following the third game. The player was a likeable guy, was a youthful 79 years young and played on the team I coached 2 summers ago. I will miss not being at the service, but believe as of 10 minutes ago, most everything is under control and assigned. The Arizona Republic called for an interview with me this morning – seemed almost like old times when I was back working, but with an interview like this one, it was not so important to be very careful and choose your words wisely. They plan to do a story on Friday and we have submitted a photo to the newspaper – in his softball uniform of course.

Will provide another edition upon return and re-engaging in softball games.

WH, Senior Editor
WEE, Inc.

Oldest Son's Birthday, June 20, 2008

News Flash – Tickets still available for tomorrow morning's 7 AM game. The Wildhare returning from a two-week vacation to the Midwest found his league softball team struggling at 3 wins and 4 losses. On Friday, the Wildhare contributed with 3 hits in a closely contested win to even the record at 4.

Lying off until Wednesday, the Wildhare strength program (getting the big middle to follow through on the swing), he contributed a 2 for 4 day but made his hits count. A bases loaded triple cleared the bases. On another at bat, trailing the game 11-7 and two guys on, the Wildhare powered one well beyond the left center field fence to close the gap to one. That brought the team, 365 Storage to within one and with the help of teammates and two more innings a 14-11 win was notched.

365 Storage plays tomorrow morning at 7 when they try to improve their 5-4 records.

Today, playing a double header out at Festival, WH had a banner day. The 300 foot fences were a bit too long to scale, but in 10 at bats, the Wildhare notched 5 triples, two doubles, and two singles before making an out in his last at bat. Sensing that he was a year older, what with having a son turning 37 on this very day, the old man felt it necessary to stake out a claim that old men are not dead yet. We will not mention one fly ball where WH had to move 1-2 steps, camped under it and promptly dropped the ball out of his glove. In the second game, the WH was called upon to pitch and after a 1-2 year absence was surprised that he did not yield his first walk until the fourth inning and then issued two more walks in the 7th when the game was out of reach. The Sun City Grand boys swept both ends of the double header by 10 runs each.

The Wildhare heads to his euchre club in about 5 minutes to see if his club still remembers him. More to come soon.

Wildhare, Senior Editor
WEE, Inc.

Subject: Wildhare Continues to Shine

Senior Softball in Sun City Grand at Surprise Arizona, the Wildhare continued to light up the scoreboard. Riding a four game winning streak, the Storage Shed team took on the League leading bankers from Northern Trust. In a closely contested game, the Storage boys came out on the short end of a 9-7 game. The Wildhare's 3 for 3 plus a sacrifice fly was not enough to pull the team over the top.

Bound and determined not to let that happen again, the Wildhare was up and at em early this morning. Thinking he had a 7 AM game he arrived at the ballpark at 6:35 only to discover, Storage 365 had the third game beginning at 9:30 AM. Seems he would have had enough time to properly dress. Thanks to the Mrs. Hare, she caught him about to leave with his game shorts on backwards. The Wildhare thanks the Mrs. for calling this to his attention to save further embarrassment at the field.

Evidently, the rest at the field had no detrimental effects as the Wildhare's bat was booming going 4 for 4 with two doubles and two singles and driving in 4 runs in a 9 – 1 victory. One game remains in the first half of the season with Storage 365 finding them ½ game out of second place in this 9-team league. After the game

445

on Wed. there will be a week off as new teams are formed and play resumes on July 14.

Meanwhile the Wildhare will bask in the sun, enjoy more pool time, and get a few more projects completed around the house. The Smith Electric tournament team travels to Pine Top to play in a softball tournament with 20 teams on July 11-13, so you can be assured the Wildhare will have another tale to spin. Until then, my good folks, have a good 4th of July and week following.

Wildhare, Senior Editor
WEE, Inc.

You may read about this in a future Wildhare Edition, just some added proof that the W.E. is not all B.S.

WH

From: PEGGY MOORE [mailto:DICKPEGMOORE@COX.NET]
Sent: Monday, July 21, 2008 12:56 PM
To: Rich Bolas; Independent; John Elfritz; Ketcham Bruce; Michael Melissa; Lyle Gordon
Cc: Mick Mckean; Don Hansen; Terry Braun; Malde Jim; Dick Moore; Bob LaBreche; Dick Stuckey; Wayne Siers; Dave Stark
Subject: SUN CITY GRAND SUMMER SOFTBALL 7/21/08

TREEDAH MAGEE REALTOR   18   PAUL TONE INSURANCE   14

The "REALTORS" broke out of their slump, picking up their first win behind the pitching of Tom Quamma. Dave Baer, Tony Cuda, Jim Palzer and Dick Stuckey all had 4 for 4 days at the plate with Dale Schroeder smashing a key two out double in the 6th inning to seal the victory.
    Pitcher John Linert, Art Molina, Pete Houghton

and Robert Blainey had 3 hits each for PAUL
TONE INSURANCE.

365 STORAGE   11   FUZZY'S   10

The "STORAGE GUYS" plated 3 in the top of the
5th inning to tie the game at 9 then scored 2 in the
top of the 7th for a two run lead. FUZZY'S loaded
the bases with one out, but couldn't get the job
done. Mike Heitman went 4 for 4, Marlin Campbell
3 for 4 with a double and sub Dale Busenbark
doubled and tripled for the winners as Joe
Carucci picked up the win.
    Brian Morgan went 3 for 4 with 2 doubles and 2
RBI, sub John Truttman added 3 hits and Jim
Malde doubled, homered, drove in 2 and scored 2
for FUZZY'S. Jim Bobo went 3 for 4 with a double
and an RBI while Phil Guido and Ron Remm
added 2 hits each with Remm hitting a double.
Every player had at least one hit as FUZZY'S
suffered their first loss.

GLEASON TAX ADVISORY 9   NATIVE
NEW YORKER   6

Some good hitting, pitching, and a solid defensive
gave the "TAX MEN" their first win of the new
season. Six players contributed two hits each with
pitcher Artie Stackpole, Bruce Spiegle and sub
Rick Lents among them.

one is for you Dad!!!!!!!!!

Aug. 9, 2008

The Wildhare went to the ball field this
morning, playing as a sub in the 9:30 AM
game. It was a mixed emotion day for the
Wildhare trying to shrug off the past 10 days
of missed softball due to the passing of his
father. As soon as he got to the field, WH
was reminded of how much his Dad loved
baseball, and of course, WH wanted to do
his father proud on this day. In a tight game
that saw WH's team down 9 – 3, the team
fought back with 5 runs in the top of the 6th
to tie the game at 10 runs
apiece. Unfortunately the Scorpions (other
team) came back to score five in the bottom
of the sixth. Up to this point WH had two
singles and a sac fly for his three times at
bat. In the top of the 7th with one on and one
out, WH got the pitch he wanted and drove

it well over the left center field wall for a round tripper. Dad that one was for you!!!! With two on and one out, a double play ended the game at 15-12. As Dad and others would say for every winner there has to be a loser, and so it was on this day.

During the absence of the WH, his team, Treedah McGee, won two games and lost one to keep a hold on their second place standing in the 8-team league. WH will play again on Monday and then be off for a couple of weeks, play one game, and be off for another week. Can the team hold it together in the absence of WH? Time will tell, but there are more important things in life than winning and losing ball games, and WH experienced those this last week.

Wildhare, Senior Editor
WEE, Inc.

Welcome to the new subscribers to the Wildhare Edition, you see the Wildhare has temporarily misplaced (LOST) his listserv for the edition, so just typed in a bunch of names. When his side kick (the little bunny) comes he is confident this mess can be sorted out. For the new subscribers, you will be notified when your subscription dues are due; the last invoices were sent out some four years ago. The Wildhare likes to promote his lack of prowess on the field by embellishing through the printed word. Although mostly truthful, self-credits must be taken with a grain of pepper.

Long time subscribers may recall that the manager of Treedah MaGee Realty due to his many travel absences unceremoniously stripped the Wildhare of his playing jersey in the month of August. When WH told his manager, Coach Stark that he would be missing a number of games and comparing the schedule WH was only going to make 3 of the remaining 11 games, Coach Stark wanted to take the jersey right off the back of the heralded WH. Guess Starksky felt one of his few bonafide blue chip players was leaving him high and dry. He was right because a Treedah MaGee battling for second place in the league with a decent record with WH plummeted to an under 500 season and a 5th or 6th place finish.

WH came back in September and having been placed on waivers was immediately picked up by Fuzzy's Sports Bar team, where he was once again placed into the cleanup spot in the batting order (also asked to clean up around the dugout) and handsomely produced for his new team mates. Some of you will recall Manny Ramirez impact after his trade from Boston

to LA. WH's first game started with a
sacrifice RBI fly plus a 3 for 3 performances,
the lack of a triple costing him not hitting for
the cycle. WH has concluded that a triple in at
his age is the hardest one to get due to the
excessive running – it is easier to hit it over
the fence and walk around the
bases. Second game, WH produced
another 3 for 3 performances, and likewise
in his third game. By this time, other teams
were clamoring for WH to be a sub, so he
did acknowledge one, but produced only a 1
for 4 outing in that game, and then the
season came to an abrupt end.

With the field shut down for a month for over
seeding for the fall and winter season, WH
had a chance heal his aging body in
preparation for the World Championships to
be held in Phoenix in October. That
accounting will be the topic of the next issue
of the Wildhare Edition. Stay tuned.......

Wildhare, Senior Editor
WEE, Inc.

March 5, 2009

After many, well some, ok one or two, calls
from subscribers concerned that their
subscription to the Wildhare Edition may have
lapsed, and simply concern for the health of the
extraordinaire Wildhare, the big W, has
relented and issued yet another edition.

Travel in the months of January and February,
the session between seasons, and some
voluntary conflicts have prevented the Wildhare
from playing as much softball as
necessary. Fans of the Wildhare have become
concerned about the absence of the Wildhare
at the ball field, but in his typical reassuring
fashion, their hero has committed to them that
he has not yet hung up his rubber spikes.

Playing on two teams this Spring, the Paul Tone
Tournament team (65's), and the league team

with In-Line Chiropractic. The Paul Tone team
played in a tournament out in Festival, at
Buckeye, Arizona in January and came in a
respectable second, losing to a major
team. More recently, like last week, and
immediately upon return from cold Ohio and
Chicago, the Wildhare warmed up fast by going
8 for 10 in the opening three games on
Wednesday. This was a seeding day and the
P.T.'s won two games and lost one. Dropping
way behind like 12-2 they did make a game of it
by losing only 17-14 to the Sidewinders. They
won 16-15 over the scorpions from Prescott,
and 18-15 over the Las Vegas Elks. Taking the
top four teams for the double elimination, P.T.
was seeded third for Thursday's action. P.T.
beat the Scorpions and had a very poor showing
against the Sidewinders losing 14-4, and
dropping them down to the losing bracket. On
Friday, P.T. beat the Elks vs. Scorpion winner
(Elks) and then had to face the Sidewinders
where they would need to win two games to
win the tournament. This they did is some tight
games early in the game and then broke it open

in the later innings. WH cooled off some during a couple of these games but finished the tournament with a very respectable 16 for 25, a .640 average, plus several intentional walk. Next week, P.T., travels to Laughlin, NV to compete in tournament play.

The In-Line Chiropractic team needs to get some adjustments; they are currently 1 – 5 holding up the cellar. WH has played in two games, one way back and losing 14-11 where WH went 3 for 4. Then just this last Tuesday after trailing 12 -3, In-Line came back and tied the game in the 7th at 14 a piece, but lost in extra innings 19-14. In the seventh, vying for his third hit of the day, a drive down the left field line that appeared to be dropping in for a double ended up being caught in a spectacular catch by the left fielder. If the catch is not made, no need for extra innings and In-Line has a victory.

The next game is today in 3 hours, fans from as far as Ohio have arrived for the match, so WH is hoping to be on top of his game. The is well known to embarrass WH whenever he can, as exemplified on a Cabo fishing trip where this individual place sardines on the hat of a resting WH, and took him to task in his own game of euchre. He has promised to be in the stands and bring a new definition to the term of heckling.

So, WH is off for another day and hopes the readers can get back on track with the edition after such a long lapse.

Wildhare, Senior Editor
WEE, Inc.

May 11, 2009

Another Wildhare Edition, appropriate for bedtime reading, the can, or some other insignificant time.

In reverse chronological order, the Wildhare has just returned last evening from a senior softball tournament in Prescott, Arizona. Eleven teams competed for three championships and Paul Tone (Wildhare's Team) went a perfect 4-0 to win the championship in their division. For some reason Paul Tone was placed in a lower division and found themselves outperforming the other teams in their division by double digit wins in each of the games excepting the championship game won by a score of 22-14.

Wildhare had an outstanding tournament, going 11 for 14, plus a sac fly, and two bases on balls. One of the outs, the umpire admitted he may have made a mistake in the call at first ruling WH out when he was clearly safe, thus it should have been 12 for 14. One game, WH had two doubles and a triple, plus the intentional walk. In the field, entering the game at first base in the 7th inning (as a joke to the all star first baseman), WH finished off the game when the bases were loaded with one out, and the batter hit a ball to first base, WH calmly stepped on the bag, and fired to home to get the runner from 3rd for a game ending double play. That was the good news for the Prescott tournament.

Now the other side... WH's took his significant other (his wife) to Prescott early Friday morning, and they went the back way to Prescott, stopping at Yarnell, AZ for breakfast. Found a terrific authentic local establishment where the Mrs. Got a huge 3 egg omelet and the WH loaded up on the Farmer's Special, biscuits and gravy, eggs and hash browns. Perhaps this was the key to his success at the tourney. WH and Mrs. Went with the team to the Prescott Brewery for dinner in the evening where his prime rib special was just so so, and the Mrs.'s Asian salad was a bit spicy for her taste. In the morning, both WH and the Mrs. Checked out of Forest Villas, having run WH's credit card Friday afternoon at check in. (Now I know subscribers are saying why all the detail – as Randy on American Idol says – "Hang on Y'all, Yo," we are getting there). The Mrs. Headed home to catch a Phoenix show Sat. afternoon, WH to the ball field to compete. Saturday evening back in Phoenix, WH went on a small grocery run, went to pay for his supplies, and whoops, no credit card. Where oh where is the Master Card??? Fortunately WH had cash in the billfold since he did not take in the gaming tables at Prescott, so paid in cash.

Was the credit card left at the hotel, at the restaurant or stolen???? Called the hotel, nope, no credit card there. Called the restaurant, and sure enough they had it in security. (I have a subscriber friend who keeps misplacing his credit card at restaurants, but I try to help him by picking it up for him). The restaurant would not mail it to me, nor allow a friend going to Prescott this weekend to pick it up for me – all because of the liability issues, so the only left ~~viable alternative~~ was to call the credit card company, have the card cancelled, order a new one and request the restaurant shred the old.

Let's see this is a softball article, where did we get off track??? The mind is the second thing to go and I forget what the first is.

Back to Spring Softball, the WH's team, In-Line Chiropractic, ended tied for fourth in a six team league with a just under 500 record. Sounds bad, and it is, but putting it into perspective the Arizona Diamondbacks would love to be "just under 500." WH had a decent season but nothing like the tourney in Prescott.

WH is now playing summer ball on the Smiles of Beauty team – yes it is a dentistry-sponsored team. Currently we are 2-2 in the league as it is just two weeks old. WH is sporting a 750-800 batting average, but he is relied upon heavily as one of only 3 top league players on the team.

Well, this 'short' noninformative communication is nearing the end and you are more or less caught up. I'll try to keep you posted a bit more frequently and stick to the facts as much as possible. When there are few facts, then one must improvise.

I heard there were frost warnings for the distant lands of Ohio and Michigan for this morning – well here in the desert we intend to top 100 degrees for the third straight day. On the average the frost warning and 100 degrees is just about right.

Have a good one and a tip for the Kentucky Derby, bet on that 50 – 1 shot, or have they already run the Derby. So long ya'all.

Wildhare, Senior Editor

Results of two games today and the write up by an independent source. FYI. After these two games, I managed to muster enough energy to go out and play 18 holes of golf.

WH

NORTHERN TRUST BANK 15   A.&J.'s LAWN CARE 6

    The BANKERS continue to set the pace with a convincing win over the second place LANDSCAPERS. Jim Malde led the offense, going 4 for 4 with a grand slam and an inside the park home run. Paul Kosokoff, Bruce Ketcham and sub Dick Stuckey added 3 for 4 efforts while John Schmidt picked up his third win pitching in front of a solid defensive team.
    A&J's had a chance to gain ground on first place Northern Trust today; but it was not to be, as Northern Trust routed them 16 to 5. Bob Aiken, Mike Hirsch, John Betholdy and Jim Witkowski led A&J's in hitting, each with 2 hits. Bob Aiken took the loss.

SMILES of BEAUTY 15   IN - LINE CHIROPRACTIC 3 (6 innings)

    The DENTISTS had on their best smiles as they scored 10 runs in the first 2 innings and ran away with a convincing 15-3 game in 6 innings. Dick Stuckey was a perfect 4 for 4, but it was the bottom of the order that carried the day. Lyle Gordon was 3 for 4 with a triple and

3 RBIs while Joey Rizzuto was 2 for 3 including a 2 run HR to the right center field wall. The supporting cast included 2 hits each from Phil Guido, Ray Smith, and Loren Hansen, Norb Lewendowski, and Charlie Schulwolf who also had a HR. Winning pitcher Artie Stackpole kept the Chiropractors bats silent.

Dave Baer had 3 hits and sub Tony Cuda had a home run for IN - LINE CHIROPRACTIC.

Once again, welcome all you subscribers. Here is another edition of the increasingly popular Wildhare Edition. The first half of the summer season at the resort area Sun City Grand has come to a close. Struggling on a mediocre team, that bounced under and just over the .500 mark; it was the strong performance and heroics of the Wildhare that allowed his team "Smiles of Beauty" to end the season with a smile and a 9 – 9 record, good for fourth place. Ironically, Smiles could beat the teams above them but lost several games to the cellar dwellers.

During the season, even the fans and misters and the 100 degree heat could not contain the Wildhare who had an impressive run of 10 consecutive hits over a three game span, then after a bit of a letdown, came on strong in the last game to go 5 for 5 in a thrilling 15-14 extra inning game. Believe it or not, the Wildhare was only the second player on his team in batting average, finishing with a .700 average. The Wildhare did lead the team in total hits, home runs, and extra base hits. In the unbiased view of the Wildhare, it seemed like the stands filled up when the Wildhare was playing, except possibly for the 7 AM games, too early for even the most sensible retired person. Could the Wildhare have the aura of a Manny Ramirez, A-Rod, or LeBron

James????

The softball field is shut down for infield renovation and a three-week respite from the heat. Play will begin again in late July for the second half of the summer season.   Until that time, my friends you will just need to do without the Edition. Despite requests to write editorials on politics, community affairs, golf, and retirement life, the Wildhare respectfully declines opting to write on subjects such as softball where his expertise resides.

Wildhare, Senior Editor
WEE, Inc.

6/28/09

Subject: Paul Tone Wins Another Tournament

Here is a Wildhare Edition Extra. The article and photo speak for themselves. This article was printed in the papers far and wide – perhaps you saw it in your local paper, or perhaps you did not.

Wildhare, Senior Editor
WEE, Inc.

"Paul Tone 65s Win Fourth Tournament" The local Sun City Grand softball team sponsored by Paul Tone Insurance won its fourth tournament out of 6 entered during the team's first season. Winning all four games including the championship game at the recent Prescott Tournament, the bats were blazing as 104 runs were scored. Leading the way were Lints, Steele and Sinclair with batting averages above .750 followed closely by Clot, Nagy and Stuckey with averages above .700"

Pictured in the photo are top row left to right: Gene Prosser, Dohrman Sinclair (sub), Rick Lints, Dick Stuckey, Harold Steele, and Fred Wilkinson (sub). Front row left to right: Jim Allison, Jules Nagy, John Richmond, Gary Francois, Rick Clot (sub), and Paul

Kosokoff. Other team members not pictured unable to make the Prescott Tournament is Ken Bedell, Moe Caba, John Hardy, Brian Morgan, and Sheldon Peters.

Subject: Wildhare Takes a Break Sept. 28, 2009

The Edition is back after several subscribers wondered if the Wildhare had taken a leave of absence. In essence, one could state that the Wildhare is always in a state of absence. The summer league ended this past Friday, and the Wildhare's team ended up 2nd in an 8-team league. The Wildhare pounded two out of the park in the last five games, finishing the season strong after a slow start. The final record was 14 – 7.

Play at Sun City Grand will not resume until Nov. 9 as the outfield will be shaved and reseeded with rye grass for the winter season. That does not mean the Wildhare will be sitting idly by. He has joined a Wednesday night double-header league that plays under the lights beginning this Wed. When the Wildhare asked the surgeon today whether he would be cleared to play this Wed. night, the surgeon said, "You want to what?" Thus the Wildhare will simply cheer his team on for the first evening. In addition to this league, the Paul Tone tournament team gets into action Oct. 10 and 11 in a senior softball tournament at Casa Grande, AZ and then competition in the World Championships Oct. 19-22 held in our own back yard in Phoenix.   Paul Tone goes into the tournament with high expectations. If we do well, you can be assured you will hear all about it.

Back to the surgeon. In an effort to become a better performer on the field, the Wildhare underwent cataract surgery on Sept. 2 in the right eye, then today he had macula puckering surgery of the retina in the right eye and is currently a one-eyed bandit. He will have his "pirate's patch" removed tomorrow afternoon, but will honor a morning committee meeting commitment going in disguise. After several weeks of healing, appointments will be made to do the same surgeries on the left eye. With all the softball games upcoming, the Wildhare could use some secretarial assistance to schedule his eye appointments and surgeries around the softball games. Some would question whether WH has his priorities straight.

WH apologies for the absence of his typical insightful play-by-play analysis of his recent games in this report. Maybe next time.

Wildhare, Senior Editor
WEE, Inc.

Fast Start disappointing   Oct. 25, 2009
Finish
Softball Champs

The long awaited World Championship Senior
Softball arrived in Phoenix this past
week. Internationally, nearly 350 teams
competed for the winner's crown. The Paul
Tone team was placed in the 65 year AA division
along with 12 other teams. Play began on
Monday. Two seeding games were played on
Monday and two more seeding games on
Tuesday. The Wildhare started hot out of the
gate, going 7 for 9 on the first day – a day that
saw P.T. winning handily over the Chicago Gray
Sox and a Texas team from Houston. Tuesday,
two more games, and again the Wildhare
contributed with 2 for 3 in each game, making
him 11 for 15 for the tournament. Paul Tone
won those games, beating a Chicago Classic
team and crushing an outmatched Texas El Paso
group.

Paul Tone was the only team that accomplished
a 4 – 0 record in seeding rounds, thus obtained
the #1 seed for the double elimination
tournament that began on
Wednesday. Comments being heard at the field

472

included, what is P.T. doing in our division, they are a superior team, and other superlatives that evidently went to the head of the players. Obviously P.T. was the odds on favorite to be crowned the winner on Thursday.

Wednesday, at 9:30 AM, Paul Tone played the winner of the 8 and 9 seed, which turned out to be the Chicago Classic. P.T. disposed of them in fine fashion winning 19 – 10, with WH going 2 for 4. Then the layoff waiting until 2 PM before playing the next game. What happened nobody knows, but the #4 seed, the Chicago Gray Sox were the opponent, a team P.T. won handily against on Monday? Well, this time it was not to be, the P.T. bats became toothpicks and the tournament seemed to unravel at the seams. The game was lost by a score of 15 -7 send P.T. to the loser's bracket where they would need to win 5 games without a loss to gain the coveted crown. All players realized it would be a challenge but we thought we were up for it. Wrong again. Thursday 8 AM who should we be facing but the Chicago Classic who

WEC, beaten twice and sent to the loser's bracket. In a tough fought game that found the Classic hitting impressively, P.T. went down 28-21, and went home with their tales between their legs.

What started as a great hitting performance ended in a good but not spectacular tournament? 15 for 26 would do me well in the majors, but is a bit short of what is expected from a top-notch senior softball player.

It was a successful year with Paul Tone winning 6 tournaments, had high hopes for the big one, but came up short. The new season starts next month with the first tournament Nov. 9 – 11 in Bullhead City. The addition of a couple of new players should help offset the one-year aging of the existing players.

The Wildhare would like to share better news with his readership, but being a fair and balanced reporter gives the good and the bad. The old familiar cry of "Wait until next year" for some reason seems to ring hollow at this time. Until the next report, stay warm, stay safe, and stay alert.

Wildhare, Senior Editor
WEE, Inc.

Fall Season
Great Hitting Demo

Nov 9, 2009

After a brief layoff, and the closing of the Sun City Grand softball field for over seeding the outfield, the field was opened for practice games for the upcoming season to begin Nov. 9. The Wildhare was a high draft pick and did not disappoint his manager and teammates in a scrimmage game this past Tuesday. In four at bats WH hit for the cycle, one over the fence, a triple, double and single. Despite the hitting heroics, the Camino del Sol (funeral home) team fell on the short end of a 21 – 20 score.

Then disaster struck, on Wednesday night, stretching to cut off a ball hit in the gap between left field and left center field, WH came up lame with a pulled groin muscle. This sidelined him for the evening.

Next morning, in the second scrimmage game, it was a no go for WH as he helplessly watched his team drop a second scrimmage game. Will he be ready for his home opener later this week, time will only tell?

476

In the interim, WH has committed to playing for the Paul Tone tournament team this week in Laughlin, NV. He leaves at 7:15 in the morning for 2 games on Monday, 2 more on Tuesday, and 2 on Wednesday. WH will take uniform but it is uncertain how much he will be able to play.

Claiming he felt like an 85 year old in a 65-year-old body, WH took the injury in stride, these things just sometimes happen. After an outing today on the golf course it is quite apparent, WH needs to stick to softball as long as he can – he is not ready for the big time in golf.

Look for a brief report on the week tournament and the first week of league of play in the next couple of weeks, prior to some much needed R and R in CABO starting on Nov. 20. Bio freeze, liniments, oils, and other additives to the lower mid torso have this house smelling like a jock locker room. To all the loyal subscribers, keep the faith, the Wildhare shall return.

Wildhare, Senior Editor

Bullhead City –
a bunch of Bull   Nov 12, 2009

Hot off the Wire.........

The ailing Wildhare after suffering a substantial groin injury that forced him from the game the past Wednesday, Nov. 4 meandered in support of his Paul Tone team to Laughlin, NV where they played in the appropriately named Bull Head City tournament just across the river. The P.T. team fought valiantly in a most bizarre tourney, one that leaves even the verbose Wildhare nearly speechless. Allow me to at least try.....

There were four divisions of six or seven teams in a division. P.T. was placed in the B division (second from the top), the younger 60 and 50s teams mostly comprised the A division. The tournament consisted of playing a round robin format – playing each team once and the team with the best record winning the tournament.

On Monday, P.T. played two games, the first won by an 11 – 2 ½ score. (More on the ½ run score later). Wildhare was really hurting and managed just one walk in three at bats. Anything hit in the infield was an automatic out for WH, as he could only do a slow jog to first base. The fans so appreciative of the fortitude and spirit of WH were rooting for him all the way.

The second game on Monday played against the Bombers saw both teams hitting directly into the sun and thus the low score. P.T. was leading 6-4 going into the 7th when the Bombers came to bat and notched 3 disputed runs in the top of the 7th. A tag out at third was ruled not an out when the third baseman retrieving the ball from the glove dropped the ball and the runner was ruled safe. P.T. scored one run in the bottom of the 7th, had runners on 1st and 2nd when the batter hit a line shot just foul down the third base line that would have scored the winning run. The foul ball was ruled an out and the game over. The tournament director did not want any extra inning games, so he ruled that in the case of a tie, the visiting team would be awarded ½ run. Thus the final, 7 ½ to 7. WH went one for three and with a guy on second in the bottom of the sixth, hit a deep ball to the warning track where the left fielder made a nice catch.

Realizing, the limitations on his running, WH suggested to the coach that he lower WH from 5 and 6 in the batting order to a lower position. (Even the coach listens to WH and he dropped him smack to the bottom.) WH also offered to sit out, but that was not acceptable to the coach.

Tuesday... the P.T. team bounced back with a thirteen to three game, WH driving in the winning run to create a 10 run cushion and shorten the game due to the mercy rule. Again, WH could only muster a one for three performances that left him with a measly 2 for 8 for the tournament thus far. The second game, WH got his bat working and went 3 for 3 and helped the team win their third game by a 12 to 7 score. Unfortunately, the Bombers won both their games to go 4 -0 compared to P.T. at 3-1.

Wednesday with only one game on the schedule, WH went 2 for 3, and thus ended with 7 for 14, a respectable .500 batting average (and really outstanding considering his black and blue swollen leg). The Bombers were playing their game when the P.T. team departed, but even if they lost, both teams would have been 4 – 1 and the Bombers would have won the tie breaker due to beating P.T. in the tie game they were given ½ run.

Obviously, the WH is still shaking his head over this new way of playing senior softball. Who can he take his appeal to??? The Better Business Bureau does not seem that interested. WH called his coach of the Sun City Grand league and told him to get a sub for WH today, as WH wanted to try and heal his aching body. WH was quoted talking to newspaper reporter as saying that he felt like a 60-year-old man trapped in an 85 year old body.

WH is looking forward to an R and R week in

CABO in another week. Even retirees need R and R now and then. Some have suggested WH give up softball, but those close to the game, emphatically state that for the good of the game, WH must remain in the game. This is exactly what this trooper plans to do.

The tournament may have left WH speechless, but certainly not writer less as those who have read thus far can testify. For the few who have subscribed without knowing they have done so, they may unsubscribe by writing a personal e-mail to..

Wildhare, Senior Editor
WEE, Inc.

WH   Ailing WH 4th in a Row
Dec 2, 2009

Associated Press

In this small bedroom community of old geezers
skirting the outskirts of Phoenix, the few
spectators watched history in the making. A
groin stressed Wildhare ambled to the softball
field of dreams, agreed to play catcher, swung a
less than normal effective stick, and had his ego
harmed by asking for a runner the few times he
reached first base safely. One could question
the value of the sports superstar to his team in
such a condition.

The setting was the week before Thanksgiving
and the WH gamely gave it a try on a Tuesday
game and although going only one for four and
playing catcher, helped his team to victory to
start the 3 game winning streaks. According to
an anonymous teammate who wishes not to
offend other players, just the mere presence of
WH in the lineup and seeing the grimacing star
put forth his best effort was enough to raise the
level of other teammates to a higher
standard. In a tough come from behind win,

the Paul Tone insurance guys notched a victory.

Thursday, one-week pre Turkey day was special for WH as amongst the 12% filled stands were supporters of WH from as far away as Denver, Colorado. Again, catcher was the position, runner for WH when he got on base, and a similar protocol to that of Tuesday. Cheered on by the three musketeers from Colorado, WH went 3 for 5. Two of the Coloradoans did not make it to the game until nearly mid game, due to the excessive traffic jam in this small community. A few details on the game, Paul Tone hung close but saw the game slipping away when trailing 13-11 going into the last of the 6th whereupon the opponents scored 4 additional runs to seemingly put the game out of reach 17-11 going into the 7th. The insurance boys came up and promptly plated 6 runs to tie the game had the bases loaded and the great WH coming to the plate. Licking his chops in a most unfortunate at bat, WH hit one up the middle where the extra fielder fielded the ball, stepped on 2nd and threw to first to beat the hobbled Wildhare. However, on the play the runner from 3rd scored the go ahead run. The next batter popped a lazy fly ball to the outfield leaving the runner stranded on 3rd. The bottom of the seventh, with the top of their line up at bat, the opposition was only able to get a single batter on base and lose the game. The headlines next morning should have read, "Wildhare sacrifices self by hitting into double play in order to score the winning run.

A week off did wonders for WH as he travel with family to Cabo and had a chance for the groin to heal some more. Returning to the field on Tuesday, he was promoted to play first base since the coach felt that he was ¾ healed. Once again, though a less than impressive bat, WH drove in the winning run for the second game in a row. First at bat he hit a smash that hit the 3rd base bag and bounced mostly straight up into a surprised third baseman's glove, who shell shocked looked at the ball and then decided to throw to second to get the force. Leading by a 6 -2 margin, Paul Tone had a big inning in the top of the sixth scoring 3 runs and then with the bases loaded again for WH, he delivered a shot to left center to score two runs increasing the score from 9-2 to 11-2. The opposition scored 5 in the bottom of the 6th to close the gap to 11-7 and P.T. was only able to score a single run in the top of the 7th. You guessed it, 3 runs were scored in the bottom of the 7th to make the final 12-9, making the 10th run scored the winning run.

Tomorrow, another day, another game. Can the Wildhare go for the Triple Crown? Only time will tell, but it will be an early bed check time tonight so that WH is well rested for this important game. Tomorrow he will need to share the news with his teammates that this will be his last game for a while as he was cleared earlier today to have retina surgery on Monday. If there is not a single game write up after the game tomorrow you will know WH did not succeed in his Triple Crown bid and that P.T. likely lost.

Whilst a few many think this edition is long and rambling, be assured WH went through it 4-5 times to edit and shorten it approximately 6 fold. And that's the way it was and is. Happy December to all.

Wildhare, Senior Editor
WEE, Inc.

WH   Stop Holding your breath
Dec. 4, 09

Knowing all subscribers were sucking in air
holding their breath on today's 4 in a row event
win and a triple crown winning run batted in,
the edition felt it deserved its avid supporters as
quick a report as possible. This is likely the last
report until well after the New Year. I do hope
you all can survive. Back to the game.

In a slow start the Camino del Sol funeral home
team (please note the errors in yesterday's
report where the league team was
inadvertently referred to as the Paul Tone
team). The Paul Tone team is the tournament
team that had to pull out of this week's
tournament due to team injuries. The Camino
del Sol team is the Sun City Grand league
team. The editor will get the lengthy report in
one way or another. If you wanted to skip
reading this second paragraph, feel free to do
so. It adds nothing to the game.

Falling behind rapidly and deeply the funeral
team was nearly buried from the start but came
back from a near death 12 run mercy rule when

488

they found themselves trailing 14-3 going into the bottom of the fourth. The sol boys put 3 markers on the board to make it 14-6 after four. The Wildhare moved from catcher to first base, a key move by manager Andy, the boss, Campbell. He was in the soup, but his brilliant move nearly pulled out a win. Holding the opposition scoreless in the top of the fifth, the good guys plated 5 runs in the bottom of the fifth to close the gap to 14-11. Another scoreless top of the sixth put the funeral boys in good position.

The bottom of the sixth saw one run scored and runners on 1st and 2nd with two outs and the Wildhare at bat – you get the picture, another opportunity for perhaps the winning run for WH if he can put one over the fence. The WH hit the ball hard a line shot that carried to the warning track, but unfortunately the fleet of foot left fielder was able to go over and snag the ball. Inning over.

Another scoreless top of the 7th and again the

Sol boys are positioned well, two runs to tie, and three to win. The first guy leads off with a double, but the next 3 batters meekly make outs to end the game at 14-12. Good effort but they came up short. For the game, WH had his hitting problems again hitting into a fielder's choice, a single and two hard hit balls to the left fielder.

Surgery on Monday will keep the WH out of action for a week for sure and possibly the two weeks leading up to the Christmas break. Hope you have enjoyed these tantalizing reports and that you almost feel like you were at the game. Thus it goes, this on the 3rd day of December in the year of 2009.

Wildhare, Senior Editor
WEE, Inc.

WH *A Fast Start* nov 9, 2010

The popular slugging Wildhare continued his impressive stats following the World Championships. The Fall League in the Northwest Valley's greatest ballpark commenced on Nov. 2. The Wildhare played two games that day, helping another team gain a 15-13 win by going 4 for 4 at the plate. For his own team, Treedah McGee, his 3 for 5 plate appearances were good enough to establish a 17-9 lead going into the bottom of the seventh whereupon the opposing team plated 9 runs to snatch an 18-17 victory.

On Nov. 4, battle resumed, and TM (Treedah McGee) with the help of WH's 3 for 4 gained an impressive 25 – 15 victory. The good news for Wildhare fans ends there, as the World Champion Paul Tone team headed for Bullhead City without WH for a tourney on Monday, Tuesday, and Wednesday of this week. Prior commitments for international travel to seek out other softball fields to display his prowess preventing him from joining the team. Then to make matters worse, just as his TM team was about to take the field on this Tuesday morning, Nov. 9, the WH is spotted leaving town in an unmarked car and headed for the airport. Rumor has it that he will return in a week, but that means 3 games missed, and then his first eligible game back on Nov. 18, another conflict has arisen such that he is reported to have silently asked a fellow teammate to cover for his missing umpiring assignment.

Yes, WH can do it all, play ball and umpire. Oh the legends WH is establishing for generations to come. Stayed tuned for the next Wildhare Edition that will not be forthcoming soon (since he won't be playing). You know WH does not like to see a lot of fluff in his edition, as he is unknown for sticking to just the facts.

Wildhare, Senior Editor
WEE, Inc.

June 11, 2012

Sorry Fans, to keep you on pins and needles over the weekend wondering how the Wildhare fared last week in his softball games. At ease, all is well, Wildhare assisted his team to two more wins as they recover from a lower half standing and move up to the 4th place in the 10 league standing. Wildhare backed off a bit and had for him a disappointing 4 for 5 followed by a 2 for 4 outing, meaning the week was still a pleasing 6 for 9 for Coach Young and his fellow teammates.

Games resume for the Wildhare on Tues and Friday of this week. Only 6 games remain on the first half summer schedule, so you fans out there dying to see WH in action need to get out here in the next 3 weeks. Stay tuned.

WH

Special Edition – Wildhare Returns from vacationing to applause of teammates and fans

A two-week vacation to South America is just what the doctor ordered for the aging Wildhare, but not so for his teammates. The days of summer are upon us in Arizona and the Wildhare left his teammates in mid May with a 2 -2 record having lost each of the two runs by a single run. Upon his return May 27, he found a desperate team reeling from tough losses and going 1 – 3 during his absence. Promptly inserted into the # 4 position in the batting order (batted # 3 before leaving), the Wildhare responded splendidly for his compatriots.

The Wildhare learned that two of his team's losses during his absence were giving up 7 and 9 runs in the 7th (last) inning of the game. The heads up leader on the team soon had it figured out, don't let the other team bat in the 7th so promptly WH and his teammates went out and took care of business blasting the opponents 13 – 1 in 5 innings for a "mercy" game ender. WH was

493

just warming up with the bat and went 3 for 4.

Next game was a thriller, falling behind 10 – 2 after three innings, it was not over. Nancy's Dream Team (that is the one WH plays on) took on the once undefeated Salt River Solar boys and kept sneaking up on them. Trailing 11 – 7 in the top of the 7th, Nancy's Boys plated 5 runs to take a 12 – 11 lead going into the bottom of the 7th, Solar came back with one to tie the game. Nancy scored 5 in the top half of the extra inning and held Solar scoreless in the bottom t0 take a not so convincing and improbable win 17 – 12. WH went 5 for 5 in the game and had 7 of the 17 Ribbies.

When questioned after the game by a reporter, the humble WH just said he did what he is not paid to do, and felt he owed the team for skipping out on them the previous two weeks.

Two more games coming up next week stay tune.

Wildhare, Senior Editor
WEE, Inc.
 P.S. To the casual observe you may see two new addresses on the e-mail list, they are Ken and Mary Hofstetter who traveled with us to South America. During the trip the ever-versatile Wildhare was engaged in sensitivity training for Ken, thus he is copied on the e-mail as a prime example of how WH demonstrates his humility in other aspects of his life. As Ken's wife, Mary has told me so often; they travel with us just so Ken can get his continuing educational credits in sensitivity.

494

VH, Senior Editor
WEE, Inc.

APPENDIX B

States and Countries Visited

All fifty states have been visited.
The following countries have been visited:

- Algeria
- Argentina
- Australia
- Austria
- Bahamas
- Belgium
- Bolivia
- Brazil
- Bulgaria
- Canada
- Chile
- Colombia
- Costa Rica
- Croatia
- Cyprus
- Czech Republic
- Denmark
- Ecuador

- Estonia
- Finland
- France
- Germany
- Greece
- Guatemala
- Greenland
- Honduras
- Hungary
- Iceland
- India
- Indonesia
- Iran
- Ireland
- Israel
- Italy
- Japan
- Laos
- Liechtenstein
- Luxembourg
- Malaysia
- Mexico
- Monaco
- Morocco
- Myanmar (formerly Burma)
- Netherlands
- New Zealand
- Nicaragua
- Norway
- Panama

- Paraguay
- Peru
- Philippines
- Poland
- Portugal
- Romania
- Russia
- Saint Kitts
- Saint Lucia
- Serbia
- Singapore
- Slovakia
- South Africa
- South Korea
- Spain
- Sweden
- Switzerland
- Thailand
- Tunisia
- Turkey
- United Kingdom
- United States of America
- Uruguay
- Venezuela
- Vietnam
- Zimbabwe

Appendix C

Cruises Taken (Year, Destination, Travel Partners)

1976: Weekend cruise to the Bahamas (Judy and Dick)

1986: Holland American Alaskan cruise with Judy's parents, Lou and Wilma Stealy, celebrating their fiftieth wedding anniversary, and also with Lorraine and Ron Birkey

2002: Crystal cruise, New England Colors, Northeast Seaboard (Judy and Dick)

2003: Princess cruise, Caribbean (Judy and Dick)

2005: Oceana cruise, Turkey, Greek Islands, Croatia, Athens (Tom and Judie Balcerzak)

2006: Crystal cruise, the Fjords of Norway, fortieth anniversary (Judy and Dick)

2007: Princess cruise, Tahiti (Lorraine and Ron Birkey)

2008: Oceania cruise, Western Mediterranean (Ken and Mary Hofstetter)

2009: Princess cruise, Mexican Riviera (Don and Suzie Wakefield, Jim and Mary McMurry)

2009: Celebrity cruise, Azamara, Panama Canal (Ken and Mary Hofstetter)

2010: Princess cruise, Australia and New Zealand (Ken and Mary Hofstetter)

2010: Princess cruise, Caribbean (Frank and Annette Joyce)

2010: Norwegian cruise, Baltic Sea (Frank and Annette Joyce)

2011: Princess cruise, Northern Coast of Africa (Ken and Mary Hofstetter)

2012: Princess cruise, Hawaii (Don and Suzie Wakefield, Jim and Mary McMurry, Frank and Annette Joyce)

2012: Avalon Waterways cruise, Galapagos Islands (Ken and Mary Hofstetter)

2013: Disney cruise, Caribbean, Judy's seventieth birthday (Jon, Jessica, Jacob, and Logan Stuckey)

2013: Viking River cruise, Eastern Europe, Budapest to Bucharest (Ken and Mary Hofstetter and their friends, Ron and Nancy Schrock)

2014: Holland American cruise, Alaska (Judy, Dick, and the Duttons)

2015: Royal Caribbean cruise, Caribbean (Ken and Mary Hofstetter, Gary and Jennifer Haarer)

2016: Princess cruise, Alaska, fiftieth anniversary (our entire family—JJ, Amanda, Casey, Emily, Jon, Jessica, Jacob, and Logan Stuckey)

2017: Princess cruise, Caribbean (Ted and Marietta Johns, Noel and Gretchen Estergren, Fred and Jody Grawey)

2018: Royal Caribbean cruise, Harmony of the Seas, Caribbean (Ken and Mary Hofstetter, Greg Smith, and Michele Matt)

2019: Celebrity cruise, Reflection, British Isles (Ken and Mary Hofstetter)

2019: Princess cruise, Baja of Mexico, Sea of Cortez (group from the Colonnade)

2020: Coral Princess cruise, Buenos Aires to Santiago (Larry and Rhonda Stuckey, Ken and Mary Hofstetter, John and Holly Woelfle)

APPENDIX D

List of Awards and Honors

- High school sophomore class vice president, 1959–1960
- FFA (high school chapter) sentinel, 1959–1960
- FFA (high school chapter) secretary, 1960–1961
- FFA (high school chapter) president, 1961–1962
- High school student council president, 1961–1962
- FFA judging team, 1960–1962
- FFA parliamentary procedure, gold medal winners, 1960–1962
- High school yearbook editor-in-chief, 1962
- FFA Ohio State farmer, 1962
- Star District FFA beef producer, 1962
- All Northwest Ohio Athletic League basketball team, second team, 1962
- Goshen College Maple Leafs Athletic Club, 1963–1966; president, 1965–1966
- Goshen College men's varsity basketball team, 1963–1966
- Goshen College men's varsity baseball team, 1963
- International Voluntary Services Inc. appointment to Laos, 1966–1968

- Department of Plant Pathology graduate student award scholarship winner, Michigan State University, 1968
- Master's degree, Michigan State University, 1970
- PhD, Michigan State University, 1973
- Selection as plant pathology advisor to the Uruguayan Ministry of Agriculture, located in Montevideo, Uruguay, with faculty appointment at Penn State, Michigan State, and Texas A&M, 1973–1975
- Little Eden Camp, Onekama, Michigan, camp director for youth, 1969
- Department of Plant Pathology, University of Kentucky, Lexington, assistant extension professor, 1975–1979
- Department of Plant Pathology, University of Kentucky, associate extension professor, 1980–1984
- Department of Plant Pathology, University of Kentucky, extension professor, 1984–1989
- Crestwood Christian Church, chair of associate pastor search, 1979
- Crestwood Christian Church, youth sponsor, 1978–1984
- Crestwood Christian Church, education committee chair, 1981–1983
- Crestwood Christian Church, board of directors, 1982–1988; board of directors president, 1985–1986
- Goshen College, alumni board vice president, 1981–1983
- Goshen College, alumni board president, 1983–1985
- American Phytopathological Society, numerous committees over the years
- *Fungicide and Nematicide Test Results*, business manager, 1980–1986

- American Phytopathological Society, public policy board, 2001–2007
- American Phytopathological Society, annual meeting keynote speaker, 1998
- American Phytopathological Society, new suite of publications, entitled Plant Management Network, committee chair, 2002–2008
- American Phytopathological Society, annual Volunteer of the Year award, 2007
- National Extension Council on Integrated Pest Management, team member, 1978–1988
- Purdue University, sponsored evaluation of IPM programs in Central and South America, May 4–31, 1980
- Purdue University, training program for international students in IPM education, team member, 1981–1985
- University of Kentucky Association of Extension Specialists, president, 1985–1986
- University of Kentucky, Extension Specialist of the Year award, 1984
- University of Kentucky, search committee for College of Agriculture, extension dean, 1988–1989
- Southern Soybean Disease Workers, steering committee, 1977–1986; secretary, 1981; president, 1983
- Selected as one of ten outstanding U.S. soybean researchers to travel to leading soybean research laboratories in the United States and England, 1981
- Subject of a New York City–based film crew with Ciba-Geigy to produce a wheat disease and management video, 1986

- Lead author and associate author of two chapters in the *National Wheat Integrated Pest Management* publication, 1989
- Author and co-author of well over a hundred refereed articles, symposia contributions, popular press, and extension advisories
- Invited presenter to the World Soybean Conference, Buenos Aires, Argentina, 1989
- Organized many state and regional symposia for educational purposes for colleagues and laypeople
- Invited speaker to many workshops held in Kentucky and adjoining states
- Invited to the USDA major conference on emerging technologies in the United States, Chicago, Illinois, 1980
- Invited speaker to Bayer Corporation, Monheim, Germany, 1987
- Invited speaker to Ciba-Geigy Corporation, Basel, Switzerland, 1987
- Testified before the U.S. House Agricultural Committee of Congress on the need for the Agricultural Research Initiative, Fall 1989
- Testified many times before the House and Senate Agricultural Committees of Congress, 1992–2001
- Invited reviewer of many USDA/ARS programs, 1988–2001
- Led tour of Europe in wheat production, research, and development for leaders of NAWG and WRIC, 1990

- Organizer of national grain groups—including wheat, corn, rice, sorghum, barley, and oats—to promote agricultural research funding, 1989–1991
- Represented the National Barley Growers on policy issues in Washington, D.C., 1990
- Invited guest of Pres. Bill Clinton and Vice Pres. Al Gore at Farm Bill symposium, Ames, Iowa, 1994
- Election and invitations to serve on many boards, i.e., Nature Conservatory, Iowa Chapter; Food, Land, and People; Foundation for Agronomic Research; Agricultural Research Institute; National Policy Association; and committees too numerous to list
- Invited speaker to the American Embassy in Vienna, Austria, to speak to Austrian professors and embassy personnel on GMO safety issues, 1996
- Presentation of special award from CAST to Nobel Peace Prize laureate Dr. Norman Borlaug, 1998
- Coordinator of CAST's twenty-fifth anniversary symposium, "Food Supply and Sufficiency: Domestic and International Dimensions," Chicago, Illinois, 1997
- Invited to throw out the first pitch at the major league spring baseball game in Surprise, Arizona, 2004
- Member of Truth in Love Committee, a church effort to create truth and transparency, Sun City Grand, Arizona, 2005–2007
- Softball Club, Sun City Grand, Arizona, president, 2003, 2004, 2006
- Rotary Club of Sun City West, president, 2014
- Benevilla, board chairman, 2011–2012
- Benevilla, capital campaign program, chair, 2010–2013

- Benevilla's highest award recipient, the Bill Wolfry Award, 2015
- Search committee member for senior pastor at Lord of Life Lutheran Church, 2015

ABOUT THE AUTHOR

Richard E. Stuckey was a leap year baby, born on February 29, 1944, on a small farm in Archbold, Ohio. The eldest of three boys, he spent his first year living with his parents and grandparents in the home of his grandparents. When he was two years old, his parents moved out of their parents' home to rent a home from an uncle. When he was four years old, his parents borrowed money to purchase their own land for farming. Thus began his adventure.

His love of agriculture and sharing moments with his cousins became an important part of his life. Richard's parents, married for sixty-five years, were conservative, hardworking, and respected members of their community. Their Mennonite heritage led them to reject smoking, drinking, dancing, and theater. It was this culture that led Richard to occasionally feel deprived yet appreciative of home values with abounding love. Both parents believed in and supported education. Richard's father took eighth grade twice, customary for rural America in those days, and his mother lacked a high school diploma yet took a few college Bible courses. Imagine the pride they had when their eldest son went to college, got a degree, and later pursued and achieved a PhD in plant pathology!

Through his high school years, Richard loved participating in Future Farmers of America (FFA) and playing sports. He was allowed to go out for basketball beginning in the seventh grade because there was less farm work in the winter. By his junior year, he was allowed to go out for baseball. Like most parents, his parents became enthusiastic spectators at his games, especially at the varsity level.

The college years gave rise to the realization that there was life beyond farming. Farming was hard work yet enjoyable. Richard's family were acquiring additional land, and he realized that there would not be room for three sons to take over his father's business. He decided on a life for himself outside of farming yet staying connected to agriculture and food production.

The college years were preparation for two life-changing decisions made in 1966. The first was falling in love with his life partner, Judy. They married on July 23, 1966, and have been blessed with fifty-five-plus years together. The second was a decision to join International Voluntary Services Inc. for two years in Southeast Asia. It was an opportunity to see the world. So much of that experience continued to impact his decisions for the following fifty years.

They welcomed their first son, Jeffrey James (JJ), on June 19, 1971. Five years of graduate school and achieving a PhD opened many doors for future employment. The first step along the way was another two-year international assignment to Uruguay, South America, with the objective of increasing the quality of fruits and vegetables for the export market as he was a consultant to the Uruguayan Ministry of Agriculture. It was in Uruguay that they welcomed their second son, Jon David, born on March 29, 1974.

Upon completion of the Uruguay assignment, Richard became employed as an assistant extension professor of plant pathology at the University of Kentucky. In less than ten years, he moved from assistant to associate to full professor. The love for international travel once again led his family to spend a yearlong sabbatical in the Netherlands. Richard and Judy wanted to give their two sons an international experience.

Returning to the University of Kentucky was the same and yet not the same, although honors and awards kept coming his way. Once again, the intrigue of a new career became appealing to him. Richard would describe this decision as one of the toughest decisions in his life, to give up tenure and job security at the university to venture into the unknown world of living and working in the political city of Washington, D.C. After declining the job offer of director of the National Association of Wheat Growers Foundation twice, he finally relented on the third offer and accepted the new job. The challenge was there to achieve a new summit. Having already achieved a wide range of influential colleagues, this circle became greatly expanded.

Over the next three years, many new programs were developed to the point that this success led to his dismissal. A book could be written about the cost and consequences of being too successful. While devastating at the time, the first rejection for Richard later became a blessing. Most disturbing to him was the unethical and dishonest manner in which this took place. Nonetheless, this event strengthened his values of honesty and treating all people with respect.

The job of executive vice president of the Council for Agricultural Science and Technology was Richard's last nine years (1992–2001) of full-time employment. A twenty-year-old organization was struggling at the time; however, Richard and his energy put new life into the organization. Twenty years after his retirement, the organization is still growing strong despite several bumps along the way. This position and organization gave Richard access to a new level of contacts, ranging from other nonprofit leaders to heads of regulatory agencies and the Office of the White House as well as house and senate representatives. He also became associated with CEOs and vice presidents of corporations, consumer advocates, and many leading scientists in their field.

Richard defines "retire" as retiring from a previous life's work to a new energetic and engaging life. His three chapters on retirement share the transition that occurred from a sixty-hour workweek to what became a new busy, satisfying norm.

The reader is encouraged to delve into the chapters that give further clarification to each of the above subjects and influencers of Richard's life.

Richard, along with his wife, Judy, currently resides in an independent division of a senior living community in Surprise, Arizona.